MW00738067

ABOUT THE AUTHOR

Gerry Madigan, a Dubliner, works as a management consultant and lectures part-time with the Dublin Institute of Technology. He has been presenting courses, seminars and workshops on various topics in the area of leadership development, communication, presentation and management skills for the past ten years. During his early years, he worked in the music industry as a musician, musical arranger and record producer, and eventually moved into artiste management and music publishing. Prior to establishing his own management company, he worked in the financial services sector as a financial consultant, specialising in portfolio appraisals. He is a member of the Irish Institute of Training and Development and the Marketing Institute of Ireland, and holds a teacher's licentiate in public speaking from the London Guildhall School of Music and Drama. Although he co-wrote a number one bestseller with his son, Julian — *The Agony of Ecstasy* — this is his first book as a solo writer. Gerry and his wife, Marina, a radiographer, have six children.

The
Five Plateaus
of Progress

Practical Lessons in Self-Development,
Personal Leadership and Positive Living

Gerry Madigan

Oak Tree Press
Dublin

Oak Tree Press
Merrion Building
Lower Merrion Street
Dublin 2, Ireland
http://www.oaktreepress.com

A catalogue record of this book is
available from the British Library.

ISBN 1 86076 145 3

Printed in the Republic of Ireland by Colour Books Ltd.

Contents

CHAPTER TWO

CHAPTER THREE

CHAPTER FOUR

CHAPTER FIVE

CHAPTER SIX

ACKNOWLEDGEMENTS

To my dear wife and eternal companion, Marina, for the strength of her unconditional love, patience, understanding, support and encouragement in making this book a reality. For the love and patience of all my children, which serves as a driving force to charge my batteries, and keeps me young at heart. To the memory of my dear mother, for her constant love and support in all of my endeavours, and for the great lessons she taught me in my childhood. My brothers and sister and Aunt Alice, for their concerned love and support.

I have worked with many great men and women in leadership positions over the years, from whose encouragement and example I have learned so much. Their names are too numerous to mention here individually, but suffice to say that I have stood on the shoulders of many giants during my journey through the Plateaus of Progress.

Thanks to David Givens at Oak Tree Press for having faith in me as a writer, and to the Oak Tree Press team, my editor Brian Langan for his diligence and patience, and Jenna Dowds and Janet Brown, for all their work in bringing this book to press.

Finally, I must express my gratitude to my Heavenly Father for the many blessings He has bestowed upon me, for the ability to develop my talents and skills, and for the capacity to formulate my knowledge in writing this book.

Preface

I have been conducting courses, seminars and workshops on Personal/Leadership Development since 1989. In 1994 I launched the Personal Leadership and Executive Excellence Programme — a management training course for the corporate sector. Drawing upon my own experiences, and in the light of the feedback received from participants on my various courses, seminars and workshops, I formulated the concept of "The Five Plateaus of Progress" as a fundamental requisite for the development and growth of the individual, the business, the corporation and the family. The corporate body is comprised of individuals, just as the family is a unit of individuals. The growth and development of the family or corporation depends entirely upon the growth and development of the individuals within that family or corporation. The huge emphasis on "Total Quality Management" in the corporate sector has many positive factors to its credit. But I believe the initial focus should be on "Total Quality Leadership" in order to develop the qualities and capabilities of the individuals who are engaged in trying to implement Total Quality Management. The commercial and industrial sectors of our communities are top-heavy with extremely efficient "techno-managers" who haven't learned the essential skills of leadership that could turn them into extremely effective "leader-managers". Many managers find it easy to deal with the technology, but difficult to deal with people. People are every organisation's most important asset. Neglect of the people within an organisation eventually leads to serious damage to the very fabric of the organisation. People are always more important than programmes or systems.

With my concept firmly in my mind, and in programme format, the next step was to translate the entire concept into book form. However, there are thousands of self-help books on the market, and bookshops are crammed with books on popular psychology — how to change your life, realise your potential, unleash the dormant power that lies deep within, etc. The thought of actually writing a book on the subject of The Five Plateaus of Progress initially seemed to be rather superfluous. But as I read many of these books, and absorbed their concepts, ideas and philosophies, I realised that there was indeed a very great need for a book which would describe this concept of The Five Plateaus of Progress in a structured format with concrete guidelines. There are some excellent books on the market which promote the power of positive thinking, the need for self-discipline, the necessity for creating a more vibrant spiritual dimension in our lives, etc., and all of these things are very good. The more intellectual stimulation we receive, and the larger the intake of positive affirmations, the greater the chance we have of eventually translating those positive thoughts and ideas into positive action.

But The Five Plateaus of Progress is an entire concept, a "life-management" programme for more effective living. It can be effectively applied to all areas, dimensions, situations, and circumstances in your life, whether it be sport, business, domestic, management, etc.

The purpose of this book is to explain clearly and precisely the concept of The Five Plateaus of Progress, and to encourage individuals to develop a fresh perspective on their position in life, break out of their comfort zones, become the people they are capable of becoming, and actualise their potential through the practical application of the principles contained in the book.

So many self-help books offer quick-fix solutions and guaranteed results if you follow the steps outlined in the book. Let me clarify what *this* book is all about. It is not a miracle recipe for success, it is not a quick-fix formula, and it does not come with a money-back guarantee. Most of the principles contained in The Five Plateaus of Progress will be familiar to you. All I have done is to place them in some kind of order and illustrated their practical application. Hopefully it will encourage you to look at your life from a fresh perspective, and embark on a lifelong journey of growth and progress along the many and varied Plateaus of Progress. But always remember — success is never final!

This book may be used in many different ways, and each use will have its own merits. You can read it from cover to cover, as an academic or intellectual exercise, and then go back to the beginning and try to implement the various principles by doing the assignments at the end of each chapter. It may be used as a reference book by people in training and development, or it could be built into an existing course on personal/leadership development. Whatever way you use it, don't just accept it — test it! If you apply the principles contained in this book they *will* change the way you think and the way you act, which will obviously change your life. You will find inner strengths that you never realised you possessed, and it will develop your talents and existing strengths of character to heights you never even dreamed existed.

Bear in mind that this is a concept based upon timeless principles, and these principles never change. They are the constants in our ever-changing society. The progress through the initial Five Plateaus is something that has to happen in every dimension of our lives if we wish to make real progress, and experience the stimulation of personal growth and development. Once we arrive at the Plateau of Commitment, we commence a new journey through more complex and varied plateaus. We begin to live by a higher law.

You will never taste the sweetness and joy of inner peace and harmony, contentment, achievement beyond your natural ability, and the sheer exhilaration experienced through the knowledge and understanding gained by raising your standards, your thinking and your life to a higher plane, *unless* you recognise and actually experience these fundamental Five Plateaus of Progress in your life. The First Plateau involves grasping the reality of exactly "where you're at" by becoming **Aware** of your mission in life and your contribution to society. The Second Plateau deals with capturing the **Vision** of what your future could be, and how you can become the architect of your own destiny. The Third Plateau is learning and understanding the need for **Discipline** and being "in control" of your thought processes and behaviour, through developing the art of self-mastery. The Fourth Plateau means having the courage to shed excess baggage, break out of comfort zones, and implement the principle of **Change** in attitude and behaviour. The Fifth Plateau necessitates rising to the challenge of **Commitment**, which is essential to maintaining the momentum required to firmly embed these principles and practices into your daily life.

As long as you live your life in the valley,
you can never experience the magnificence of the overview.

It is only by climbing the mountain that you will arrive at the top, and see things in their true perspective. This process of progressing through the various Plateaus is all about expanding your horizons, pushing your boundaries, and making your life more worthwhile, more meaningful, and ultimately more enjoyable. By developing leadership qualities and skills, through implementing the principles on each Plateau, you will greatly enhance the quality of your work, your performance, your relationships, your achievements, and your life.

In concluding this preface, I offer a word of warning to those who would envisage using this book as a management training tool, or as part of an existing course. Unless you are striving to live by these principles yourself, and have actually progressed through the initial Five Plateaus of Progress in some dimensions of your life, it will not be a very effective tool. People may not believe what you say, but they must believe what you do. Actions speak louder than words.

"If our words are not consistent with our actions,
they will never be heard above the thunder of our deeds."
— H. Burke Peterson

In order to teach these principles and this concept effectively, you must believe in them. That testimony will only come through practising and testing them, by *living* them in your daily life. When you "walk your talk", you are endowed with one of the greatest leadership qualities of all time: *example.* The greatest teacher in the history of the world, when His disciples asked what they should do to be more like Him, said, "Come follow me".

I hope you enjoy reading this book, and that it will enhance the quality of your life. Feedback is something I often request from participants on my courses and seminars, and I would be delighted to receive some feedback from my readers. Your comments would be most welcome. Details of The Five Plateaus of Progress seminars and workshops are available through the publishers of this book, Oak Tree Press, from the following address:

Oak Tree Press,
Merrion Building,
Lower Merrion Street,
Dublin 2,
Ireland.

Introduction

*"There is no progress from ease to ease. We must
experience all depths before all heights."*
— B.H. Roberts

During my University studies in philosophy in the mid-1960s, I became fascinated with two aspects of the curriculum, which had quite a profound effect upon my life in later years. One was the area of psychology, the workings of the human brain and the immense capacity of the human mind. The other was the mystical area of Eastern Philosophy, and in particular the concepts of personal progression and the necessity for balance in life. As I left the world of academia and started my working life, I began to accumulate a wealth of experience in interpersonal relationships on just about every social and professional level of society. But in the back of my mind, I had so many questions that had their origins in my initial academic grounding. The sort of questions that many people still ask: "Why are people like that?"; "How could anyone act like that?"; "What is my purpose in life, in fact what is the purpose of this life?"; "Where did I come from, why am I here, where am I going?"

In recent years, my focus has been upon the corporate sector in conducting leadership development courses, and I never cease to be amazed at how naïve people in management positions seem to be when it comes to dealing with ordinary people. But it's not just the corporate sector; it's throughout our society. I believe one of the reasons is the very rapid pace of technological advances, and the contrasting slower growth and maturity of the individual. The amount of stress, frustration, disillusionment, worry, bewilderment — and in some cases despair — seems to be growing rather than diminishing. We are inundated with courses and seminars on "Stress Management", "Time Management", "Dealing With Change", "Corporate Re-engineering", etc. People want to take a break, to go away and find themselves. There don't seem to be any anchors to hang on to; the goalposts are constantly changing. However, in observing the various problems and discussing the techniques being used to alleviate the situations (the palliative approach), there is one glaring imbalance that jumps out at me, and that is the lack of constants upon which to base judgements, decisions, perceptions and behaviours.

As we strive to live our lives to the best of our ability, we need some constants, and these constants are called principles. A principle is eternal, timeless and unchanging. The practice or application may change, but the principle never changes, it is a constant. So let's start our journey by looking at constants.

CONSTANTS AND VARIABLES

"There is nothing constant in the world but inconstancy."
— Dean Swift

Our society is ever-changing, markets are fluctuating, trends are shifting, and nothing seems to be the same for any length of time. This is true, because we live in a finite world, and time *is* change.

However, if we have all variables and no constants, we will all end up going around in circles before too long.

When a ship sets sail for a destination, it has to chart a course, and it does this with the aid of a compass. There may be storms, changing winds and any manner of other variations on the voyage. But the compass is constant. It acts like an anchor, a base and a yardstick by which the ship's captain can measure the ship's progress. This does not mean that the captain is not at liberty to change course or direction at any time. He may have to change direction temporarily to avoid destruction, but he can always get back on track with the aid of his compass.

Life can be tough sometimes, it isn't always sunshine, and occasionally we encounter stormy weather. If a ship was to turn back every time it hit a storm, it would never make progress, but it learns how to weather the storms. We too have to learn how to weather the storms of life by learning how to use our own compasses. But we first have to establish firmly in our minds the shape, size and definition of this compass, through the acquisition of essential life skills! In an overly permissive society, we tend to move further and further away from the constants. We erode the guidelines, ignore the dangers, convince ourselves that everything is okay, justify our behaviours and ultimately find that we are drifting from one variable to another in a futile effort to find some constant upon which to anchor.

Our compass must be built upon truths and principles. What are these truths and principles? As we progress in each dimension, we will create our compass, our moral compass, rooted firmly in the depths of our spiritual dimension. This compass will guide and direct us through the storms and waves of turmoil as we experience growth and development in every dimension of our lives.

There is a tremendous lack of principles, ideals and values among the youth of today, and in society in general. Principles set firm parameters for us, and encourage us to live our lives in the knowledge that there is a line over which we will not cross.

The concept of "Plateaus of Progress" is based upon the use of various principles at different stages in our lives. By exercising these principles, we enhance the quality of our relationships, the quality of our lives, and the quality of joy experienced through accelerated progress.

DIRECTION

Direction is more important than speed. If you don't change your direction, you'll arrive at where you're headed.

Just as the captain of the ship sets his course and direction with the aid of his compass, we can set our course and direction with the aid of our principles. When the ship's captain plots his course along the map, the lines that he draws do not actually appear on the ocean. The lines are invisible, intangible guidelines that represent the shipping lane in which his ship will travel. The same principle applies to pilots when flying planes. Their flight paths are invisible, but because they have been written on the map, with the aid of the compass the pilot can maintain her flight within that flight path.

However, the pilot and the ship's captain both spent many years studying and learning how to use a compass effectively. Without study and practical experience, the compass would be of no use to either of them. Direction *is* more important than speed. This is where I believe that technological advances are too rapid, and the growth and maturity of individuals is too slow by comparison. That imbalance must be corrected. We become too frantic in our attempts to keep up with the advances, and lose sight of the constants that will actually keep us on track, or on course. So we have to look hard at where we're going, and also examine how we've plotted our course, and understand why we've set sail in the first place. As a ship's captain or airplane pilot constantly check their bearings, we also must constantly check that we're going in the right direction.

One of the greatest problems people face in life is the lack of direction, whether it be in their career path, spiritual search, or emotional growth. The feeling of being stuck in a rut can be one of the most depressing, enervating and soul-destroying conditions imaginable. The world seems to be passing by as you sit there watching it. But the way to get on track is to find firm direction in your life, and this involves effort and work.

THE STATUS QUO

*In both personal and corporate dimensions there is no
"status quo"; you either progress, or regress.*

I believe that there is no "status quo" in life; we are either progressing or regressing; nothing remains the same. We're finite beings living in a finite world where everything is changing, just as the seasons change, and time waits for no man — time *is* change. Recognising the need for change is one of the problems with which we are faced, and the other problem is being willing to actually change. The concept of "Plateaus of Progress" is based upon the need for the individual to adapt and change, to adjust their bearings from time to time, to alter course if necessary, and to have the courage to go forward and upward. We in the Western hemisphere have been slower than our Oriental counterparts in realising the need for balance in our lives, and the continuous progress required for self-fulfilment.

Financial independence comes from budgeting and saving. If you find that you haven't saved any money at the end of a year, then you have to look seriously at how you spend your money. This invariably requires the introduction of balance, self-sacrifice, planning and change into your lifestyle. Time rolls on, and the cost of living increases, and unless you keep abreast of growth and progress in every dimension of your life, you could get left behind. There is no status quo.

THE SEVEN CHAKRAS

Just as with the gateways of enlightenment in the seven chakras, when we break out of comfort zones and arrive at our next plateau of progress, it opens up a whole new dimension of challenges which will help us to grow and develop. It increases our understanding, enlightens and makes us more aware, clarifies our knowledge, and gives us self-fulfilment.

In the practice of Yoga in India, there is a belief that an energy force travels upwards from the base of the spine to the top of the skull, and as it travels upwards it passes through seven gateways of enlightenment — *Chakras*. The positive pole is situated in the skull, and the negative pole is located in the lowest vertebra of the spine. When the negative pole is released from its normal position, and travels upwards towards the skull, it can reach and unite with the positive pole. This condition represents the highest fulfilment in consciousness, and is referred to as the *unio mystica*, the mystic marriage.

The negative pole is called *Kundalini,* and is only released when a certain level of consciousness has been reached. It is then attracted by the positive pole, which is the residence of the God Vishnu, or the spirit. The level of consciousness required can be achieved by mental concentration, and by exercises and postures in Hatha Yoga (the control of the body). Then the Kundalini travels upwards in the channel located in the marrow of the backbone, called *Sushumna Nadi.*

However, in order to progress from one Chakra to the next, it is necessary to exert more effort, increase the level of consciousness, gain greater control of the body, and develop greater concentration of the mind. This can take many years, and in many cases becomes a lifetime's dedication for the serious Yogi. The same principle of effort and reward corresponds with "Plateaus of Progress", because it takes extra effort to break out of comfort zones and make progress to the next Plateau. I mention the practice of Yoga to highlight the similarity in thinking — that there must be progress in order to achieve the ultimate rewards or enlightenment. Progress doesn't just happen, you need to *make* it happen by making the effort to exercise the principles in your life.

T'AI CHI AND ACUPUNCTURE

"When a person pursues knowledge, and seeks to learn something, there is an accumulation of facts and knowledge. But when one practises the Tao, gradually there is a process of cutting away and a simplifying of life."
— Lao-tse, from the *Tao Te Ching*

My first encounter with T'ai Chi came through my involvement with the oriental martial arts, when I practised a Japanese style of karate called *Wado Ryu*. In reading about martial arts in general, I discovered this remarkable slow-motion exercise called *T'ai Chi Chuan*, or in English "The Supreme Art of Boxing". When I searched diligently for a teacher, and eventually found one in my own country, I was amazed at the effect it had upon my whole person with only about 15 minutes practice a day. The principle of T'ai Chi corresponds precisely with the principle of acupuncture, a highly scientific and effective form of alternative medicine. The acupuncturist works on the correct principle that there are 12 meridians in the human body, which carry the life-force through-out the body, and any imbalance of this life-force results in sick-ness. The highly scientific art of inserting acupuncture needles in strategic places in the body to regulate and balance the energy flow corresponds precisely with T'ai Chi. In T'ai Chi, the "Chi" or life-force is carried throughout the body, and the slow-motion ex-ercises help to regulate and maintain a balanced flow, thus pre-venting illness and keeping the body healthy and supple.

In order to diagnose a patient's illness, the acupuncturist takes the pulses in each wrist. However, this is rather different from the Western method, where the pulse usually just relates to the heart-beat. In acupuncture, there are six pulses in each wrist, each pulse representing one of the 12 meridians. When the life-force is flow-ing freely through the meridians, the pulse will indicate perfect balance. When an individual has practised T'ai Chi for about 15 minutes, and then checks their pulse, it will register perfect bal-ance for about an hour after the completion of the exercise.

Connected with these two amazing practices is the yin/yang symbol (see Figure 1), with which I became familiar when I lived on macrobiotic food for a year. No meat or dairy produce, all or-ganic food, and even cooking utensils were made of cast iron. Everything was either yin or yang, or a mixture of both, and the balance of yin and yang intake made for a healthy body. The terms yin and yang could be best described as referring to the male/female, or positive/negative properties of things, but I will not go into any great depth at this stage in elaborating upon the complexity of the principle. The oneness, wholeness and completeness of life is also represented by the balance of duality that must exist, that there must also be opposites. The yin/yang symbol and principle is indicative of the world of opposites, and also represents harmony and balance.

FIGURE 1: YIN/YANG

THE I CHING

"Everything flows on and on like this river,
without pause, day and night."
— Confucius

In studying the Eastern philosophies and art forms, I became acutely aware of their innate reverence for the five elements — Earth, Metal, Fire, Water and Wood — and how they figured largely in their understanding of life. The *I Ching*, or *Book of Changes*, as it is called, is a famous Chinese book of wisdom which deals with change, the theory of ideas, and judgements. Confucius and Lao-tse read and used the *I Ching*, and some of their most profound aphorisms originated from this book.

Chinese thinking at that time was never aimed at trying to understand things for their own sake, but always as part of the whole — the holistic approach. Gaining an overview was the important issue, placing all the details against the background of the interplay of yin and yang. Even in macrobiotic cooking, it was important not to use such alloys as aluminium or Teflon; it had to be cast iron. All of this emphasises the need for a holistic approach. Every department of life is interconnected, every dimension of our being is related, just as every part of the body is connected.

Every organ in the body has a separate function,
but they cannot function separately.

Mother Earth and the Native American

"When all the trees have been cut down
And all the rivers have been poisoned
And the last fish has been caught
Then, and only then, will man realise
That money cannot be eaten."
— Old Indian saying

As a child I was always fascinated with the cowboy and Indian movies and stories. But my fascination grew into wonder, amazement and a profound respect for the noble Native American races as I discovered more about them and their origins. What impresses me greatly is their reverence and respect for nature, for Mother Earth. Their traditional and instinctive civic pride in their stewardship of this earth is something we have been trying to teach to our young people in schools and colleges for centuries.

The Native American Ten Commandments

1. Treat the Earth and all that dwell thereon with respect.

2. Remain close to the Great Spirit.

3. Show great respect for your fellow beings.

4. Work together for the benefit of all mankind.

5. Give assistance and kindness wherever needed.

6. Do what you know to be right.

7. Look after the well-being of mind and body.

8. Dedicate a share of your efforts to the greater good.

9. Be truthful and honest at all times.

10. Take full responsibility for your actions.

They live in close harmony with nature, observing the changing seasons and the law of the harvest, sowing and reaping, and performing their ancient rituals at the appropriate times of the year. The idea of buying and selling land is absolutely anathema to the Native American races, because they believe that we all have the use of this beautiful Earth, but it is only as stewards, not as owners — Mother Earth is not for sale!

SELF-FULFILMENT AND SELF-ESTEEM

Everything in nature grows and unfolds from within.
But man, the most intelligent of all the species,
is always trying to grow from without.

The Law of Growth (see Figure 2) states that whenever we fail, we should adjust and try again. But this little word "adjust" is what gets so many people. They either forget to adjust, and keep on failing, or they cannot bring themselves to break out of a "comfort zone" to adjust and try again.

Doing something worthwhile, engaging in active service for others, and honest hard work are all excellent pursuits of self-fulfilment. By doing the right things, we feel good about ourselves, and our self-esteem rises.

FIGURE 2: THE LAW OF GROWTH

Try ⟶ Fail ⟶ ADJUST ⟶ Try Again!

The lack of self-esteem can sometimes be attributed to repetitive failure, or perhaps to some external negative conditioning influence. The lack of self-fulfilment comes from the lack of accomplishments and achievements, which can often be attributed to the lack of self-esteem. Is this sounding like the chicken and egg eternal round? Well it's not quite as futile as that, and there is a solution to the problem.

Whatever the reason for our low self-esteem, we have the ability to change it because it is only a perception, and perceptions, like attitudes, can be changed. The greatest confidence-builder in the world is *achievement*. This does not mean gigantic world-class achievements; it's the little day-to-day achievements that slowly but surely build the self-confidence, which in turn builds the self-esteem.

Self-fulfilment is also experienced through achievement, but this type of achievement is a step-by-step progress along designated guidelines, and involves considerable effort. But the sense of self-fulfilment, of inner peace and harmony, of joy and satisfaction, brings such a fresh dimension to your existence that you wonder how you ever lived without it. You didn't: you only existed!

Principles and Natural Laws

Freedom is not procured by a full enjoyment of what is desired, but by controlling the desire.
— Epictetus

The greatest freedom that we can enjoy in this life is through obedience! How's that for a paradox? Think of how hard the poor millers used to work in grinding flour before the advent of the millwheel. But imagine the freedom they had when they obeyed the laws of hydraulics! They were able to harness the mighty power of the river, and make it turn the enormous millwheel, through compliance with the natural power in observing the law of hydraulics.

How does the aeroplane take off and fly? It is by using nature and obeying the laws of aerodynamics that the designers construct the aeroplane, and the pilot can make it fly. The greatest designers and builders in the world cannot construct a machine that can fly, unless they obey the natural laws of aerodynamics. The natural laws, civil laws, moral laws, the laws of physics, etc., are all constants in this world. They must be obeyed if we want to enjoy real freedom. Can you imagine the absolute chaos that would ensue if people decided to ignore the traffic laws and rules of the road?

In the concept of the "Plateaus of Progress", I talk about the principles upon which each thought or action is based, and these are the natural laws with which we must comply if we expect to make progress. You may not agree with, or even believe in a prin-

ciple, but the principle exists regardless of your opinion. It's very
much like the principle of truth.

> *Truth may touch you, bore you, or it may make you feel*
> *uncomfortable. But that is just your reaction to the truth.*
> *It doesn't alter the reality of truth.*

Can you imagine saying that you don't believe in the law of gravity? That's fine, but if you jump out the window of a 50-storey
building, whether you believe in the law or not, you're going to
experience that law in action as you hurtle to the ground!

THE FOUR DIMENSIONS AND BALANCE

> *"A man cannot do good in one department of life, while*
> *attempting to do evil in another department of life,*
> *because all departments are linked together."*
> — Mahatma Gandhi

The divisions of our human make-up are generally illustrated by
the four dimensions — Mental, Emotional, Physical and Spiritual
(see Figure 3). Our growth can be measured in each of these dimensions, but our overall well-being and happiness depends to a
great extent upon how mature we are in each dimension. Maturity
is the art of making decisions in the light of experience, but it's a
lot more besides. It not only relates to the ageing process, but to
attaining a certain level of knowledge and understanding that enables us to assess and respond to situations and circumstances in a
responsible manner. When a flower is planted, it will not bloom
unless it is fed, nurtured and watered to stimulate its growth. This
is also true with human beings, that complex species that needs
constant mental, physical, emotional and spiritual stimulation in

order to grow. It is the lack, or imbalance, in stimulation that creates the problems.

FIGURE 3: THE FOUR DIMENSIONS

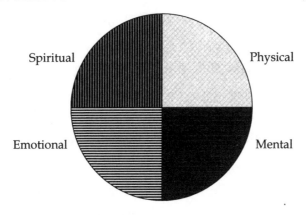

Spiritual

Physical

Emotional

Mental

It is the ability to work, love, rest and play in balanced measure that demonstrates the individual's adaptability in life. This adaptability is developed through the balanced stimulation of all four dimensions, and that stimulation comes from expanding horizons, pushing boundaries and breaking out of comfort zones in the pursuit of happiness and excellence.

INNER PEACE AND HARMONY

When your words and deeds correspond to your principles
and values, then your behaviour will speak peace to your soul.
And only then will you achieve that inner peace and
harmony which will allow you to expand and grow,
unhindered by internal conflict.

When we talk about normal adaptability, there is one great constant by which we can measure this condition and that is the level of inner peace and harmony that exists within the individual. It is only when one is at peace with oneself, when inner harmony exists, that one can adequately direct one's energies towards successfully adapting to the environment, to the outside world, and to external influences.

However, this condition is initially quite elusive, and in many instances it may seem to be completely beyond our grasp, even beyond our comprehension. But it is by living the principles contained in the Five Plateaus of Progress that we eventually arrive at a state of inner peace and harmony. By living the principles, we are aligning our behaviour with the natural laws — living in harmony with nature.

Music is a great medium to use for comparisons or illustrations. I believe we can compare being in harmony with nature to the composition of music. A basic harmony in music consists of two or more notes sung or played simultaneously, with each note sung or played at a specific pitch. For example, in a scale we have eight notes, and the first, third and fifth notes represent a major chord; i.e. when all three are played simultaneously, they are in perfect harmony, they sound beautiful, and it is pleasing to the ear.

It's interesting to note that a musical chord represents the most perfect example of synergy, when "the whole is greater than the sum of its individual parts". The overtones created by the musical harmony of three notes sounded together is pure synergy. No single individual can possibly sing a chord by himself or herself; they can't sing all three notes together.

However, if any of the notes in the chord are slightly above or below the specific pitch, they become a discord. The ensuing discordant sound is grating, and sounds horrible to the ear. That is why a singer who sings out of tune will still sound absolutely awful, no matter how brilliantly the band or orchestra are performing. Why? Because the singer is not in harmony with the music.

WHY SHOULD I BOTHER?

In the darkest hour before the dawn, a question in your mind.
Why should I bother to rise today, will it benefit mankind?
As a member of this human race, and a player in the field,
I must arise and take my place, not to temptation yield.

When you don't feel appreciated at work, when you feel that you aren't achieving anything worthwhile, when the same problems seem to be presenting themselves again and again, when you know in your heart and soul that you are capable of so much more than this mundane existence that you've been living, don't you sometimes ask yourself, "Can all of this change?" or "Why should I bother?" Don't get disheartened, there are peaks and valleys in life all the time, just as there are highs and lows in business. But if we all gave up as soon as the lows came along, we would never be around to enjoy the highs. The highs are generally the result of our persistence and diligence during the lows. The result of "hanging in there".

The beauty of the concept of The Five Plateaus of Progress lies in the fact that all the principles are eternal, and they have been tried and tested in every culture, in every society, in every conceivable situation and condition, and they work! The most difficult part is absorbing and assimilating them in order to apply them. They have to be internalised, they have to be fully understood, they have to become part of your very makeup. But you will never gain a strong testimony of their effectiveness unless you test them, try them, use them, work them, live them!

If your situation is as mundane as you think it is, and if you really feel totally unimportant, neglected, unappreciated, lacking in self-esteem, unadventurous, and not realising any of your hidden potential (you'll never find it at this rate), then you have two choices. The *first choice* is to remain the same and get regressively worse until eventually you are swallowed up in the ever-decreasing circle which you are creating for yourself. The *second choice* is that you change the situation, don't accept things as they are, do something about it, start living and begin to create that real self that is waiting inside you. You do this by embarking upon a voyage of discovery through the Five Plateaus of Progress. During this voyage you will shed excess baggage, stimulate your emotional, physical, mental and spiritual dimensions, break out of comfort zones, and develop and grow at such an accelerated rate that your head will spin!

Chinese Proverb

If there is righteousness in the heart,
There will be beauty in the character.
If there is beauty in the character,
There will be harmony in the home.
If there is harmony in the home,
There will be order in the nation.
If there is order in the nation,
There will be peace in the world.

ABRAHAM MASLOW'S HIERARCHY OF NEEDS

Abraham Maslow's Hierarchy of Needs has a lot of merits, and indeed a lot of it is basic common sense. We must respond to the primary drives in our nature, i.e. the need for food, water, sleep etc. But when we progress through each level of need, as we strive towards self-actualisation, the one dimension that is not really catered for in this theory is the spiritual dimension (see Figure 4). The term "self-actualisation" represents a state of self-fulfilment where the individual has realised their highest potential. Maslow's Hierarchy of Needs certainly does highlight the complexity of human needs, and does explain a darker side of human nature where we have seen examples of looting, plundering, robbing for food, etc., during wars and conflicts.

FIGURE 4: ABRAHAM MASLOW'S HIERARCHY OF NEEDS

However, the contradiction arises when we read about the concerned individual, the one who has risen above base human nature, the one who is "in control" of the urges for self-gratification at the expense of others. The one who has developed the qualities of compassion, love, tolerance, patience. The one who can see further than the immediate problem, and can see deeper than the physical dimension. People like Primo Levi, Victor Frankl, Mahatma Gandhi, Mother Teresa and many more wonderful human beings whose actions touch us deeply and make us grateful to be part of such a special and unique human race.

Everyone needs to be needed,
Everyone wants to wanted,
Everyone loves to be loved.

The Potomac River Story

I was very touched by the account in the newspapers about the rescue operation that took place when an aeroplane crashed into the Potomac River in the middle of winter. I'm sure you remember the account of Air Florida Flight 90, which crashed into the 54th Street Bridge in Washington DC in the winter of 1982.

The plane came to rest in the icy water of the Potomac River, underneath the bridge. A helicopter kept ferrying passengers from the wreckage to safe ground, and each time they arrived back at the wrecked aeroplane, the same man was helping yet another survivor to safety. Every time they lowered the harness to him, he strapped one of the survivors firmly into it, and sent it back up to the helicopter. Finally the pilot of the helicopter shouted down to the man "You're next". But when they returned to pick him up he had slipped from the safety of the wreckage, and drowned. He had exerted all of his efforts in helping the other survivors to safety and, when it came to his turn, the cold and fatigue were too much for him and he slipped into the icy river.

We can become too preoccupied with the need to constantly quantify and analyse the level of input or output. But how do you measure empathy, concern, vision and values, or the totally uncharacteristic actions of individuals whose souls have been touched, hearts softened, and whose minds have been inspired by the actions or words of another human being? These are the intangible and unquantifiable principles that are evident in these people's lives. It is living by a higher law, and not by the laws of social acceptance, that separates the great people from those who are self-centred, materialistic, and constantly searching for that elusive inner harmony and peace which can never come, because it has to come from within, not from the outside world.

The way to true self-actualisation, to recognising and actualising your true potential, is by taking stock of your situation, and through the steps outlined in the next five chapters of this book, capturing the vision of exactly what you want to become, expanding your horizons, living by the principles, and becoming that person.

"Worry not that nobody knows you; seek to be worth knowing."
— Confucius

SINGULARITY OF PURPOSE

You cannot be all things to all men. If you spread yourself
too thinly, the impact of your efforts will be diluted.
First things first, one thing at a time.

During the 1992 Olympic Games, I watched Linford Christie win the 100 metres, and I listened to the replays and commentaries, the praises, the excitement, the jubilation of winning, etc. But the thing that struck a chord with me was his talk about "tunnel vision". This is not the negative type of tunnel vision that we come across at times when people become intransigent and cannot see the other person's point of view. The "tunnel vision" that Linford talks about is the technique he uses to concentrate completely and absolutely upon winning the race, on crossing that finishing line *first*! He blocks out all external influences, listens to his inner self, conditions his mind to think "win", conditions his body to respond positively to his mental messages, and focuses upon just one thing — WINNING!

This type of singularity of purpose is one of the most powerful techniques in achieving goals. Whatever you *really want to be* must take precedence over all other thoughts and actions. It must become the dominating thought that occupies your mind, and it must translate into actions that reflect that thought. You have to give up dabbling at too many things, and stop spreading yourself too thinly.

You must take an idea or a thought, expand that thought, make it into a dream, visualise it, live it, and make it your life. Let the mind, the muscles, the nerves and every part of your being be full to capacity with this dream, and don't allow yourself to be distracted by any other less important ideas. This is how the great spiritual giants of this world have been created. They concentrate their efforts upon one single issue at a time with singularity of purpose. You've heard the expression "I'm in two minds about that project", but this is the complete opposite to that. This is being absolutely single-minded, focused, and concentrated.

> *"A double-minded man is unstable in all his ways."*
> — James 1:8

So much knowledge in this world has been gained by this process, the concentration of the human mind. But the power that this process generates will lift you from heights to greater heights, from one Plateau to the next in a constant upward progression to actualising your full potential. The greater the concentration, the greater the power.

"To everything there is a season,
and a time to every purpose under the heavens.
A time to be born, and a time to die;
a time to plant, and a time to pluck up that which is planted
. . . a time to weep, and a time to laugh;
a time to mourn, and a time to dance."
— Ecclesiastes 3:1–4

There is a time and a place for everything, and this brings me back to the point that I made earlier with my explorations of the various theories and philosophies of the East. There must be balance in our lives. The secret is being able to identify values and priorities, and to take things one step at a time as we seek to make real progress.

"Man is the master of thought, the moulder of character,
and the maker and shaper of condition, environment
and destiny. In the armoury of thought man forges
the weapons by which he destroys, but he also fashions
the tools with which he can build for himself great joy
and strength and peace. Between these two extremes are all
grades of character, and man is their maker and master."
— James Allen

THE PLATEAUS OF PROGRESS

"The heights of great men, reached and kept,
Were not attained by sudden flight.
But they, while their companions slept,
Were toiling upward in the night."
— Henry Longfellow

Bearing in mind all of the above-mentioned points, I believe that we have a duty to find the "inner self" that lies within each of us — waiting to be created! We will never know what talents we have unless we try them. We must strive to become "inner directed" rather than "outer directed", and intrinsically motivated rather than extrinsically motivated. But this will only come when we have discovered what Plateau we're on, and how we can get to the next Plateau.

I remember many years ago when I was training for a marathon road race. In the course of my training I found myself falling into a comfort zone. I was on a Plateau. Unless I increased my training schedule, I would not rise above that Plateau, and that would mean that I would not be fit enough to run the marathon. In many other areas of our lives (besides the physical), we can find ourselves on Plateaus. The secret of success lies in recognising the fact that we're actually on a Plateau, and then getting off it to move up to the next Plateau. This inevitably requires some sort of inspiration and effort, and in many cases change in attitude, approach, strategy, and level of commitment.

The Five Plateaus of Progress deals with the five initial and fundamental Plateaus necessary for self-fulfilment in every dimension. Each Plateau deals with various aspects associated with that particular Plateau. As you work on each Plateau, you will learn and apply certain principles pertaining to growth and development at that level. Don't move on to Plateau Two until you have fully completed the assignments for Plateau One, and so on up to Plateau Five.

By way of illustration, let me take a very broad example of progress along the Five Plateaus of Progress in the physical dimension. On Plateau One, Awareness, you take cognisance of exactly where you're at, what physical shape you're in and the condition of your physical health. Check your weight, height, blood pressure, fitness level, etc.

On Plateau Two, Vision, you would examine the physical state or condition that you would like to be in — what weight you would like to be, how fit, what shape, etc.

On Plateau Three, Discipline, you would need to introduce a certain level of discipline into your behaviour in preparation for the inevitable changes necessary to bring your vision to fruition.

On Plateau Four, Change, you would implement the changes already contemplated and prepared for on previous plateaus.

On Plateau Five, Commitment, you should have reached a stage where you are in control and have the capacity to maintain the discipline, change your behaviour permanently and become the person you are capable of becoming.

When you have completed the Five Plateaus of Progress, you can then apply the same principles to any situation in any dimension, simply by repeating the procedures. You will obviously have arrived at a higher Plateau upon completion of the Five Plateaus, but this is just the beginning, and should give you the taste for actualising your potential and reaching for greater heights.

We often hear the phrase "He was a victim of circumstance", but circumstance does not make the man, it reveals him to himself. Times of crisis can be very revealing! YOU can become the architect of your own destiny; the future hasn't happened yet, and you can fashion it to suit yourself.

Whatever your past has been, your future is always spotless.

A radical alteration of thought can result in a dramatic change of action, which transposes to a major transformation of material circumstances. It's up to you to go forward and upwards without allowing any obstacles to stand in your way, or excess baggage from the past to hinder your progress. This will involve strength of mind, character, and multiple sacrifice, because it is through self-denial that we gain the strength to overcome addictions and indulgences that enslave, hinder and control us. Someone once said, "The coward never starts, the weak die on the way. Only the strong come through."

We all have the strength within us to lead productive and self-fulfilling lives. But we also have the freedom to choose whether or not we wish to use this inner strength. I urge you to use this strength, choose wisely, commence your journey along the Five Plateaus of Progress, and become the person you're capable of becoming. But remember — decision is only the gate, *performance* is the way, and success is never final.

1

Plateau One:
AWARENESS

"The wise leader does not try to protect people from themselves.
The light of awareness shines equally on what is pleasant
and on what is unpleasant."
— John Heider, *The Tao of Leadership*

Isn't it amazing how unaware we can become of our thoughts, actions and behaviour, how stubbornly we follow the same route and how perplexed we feel when we don't seem to be achieving or progressing? If we remain on the same road, keep doing the same things and don't endeavour to introduce change into our lives, how can we expect things to change for us? There is always the frantic search for the "quick fix" in an effort to change overnight what has taken a lifetime to create — *our behaviour!*

The current emphasis on developing a Positive Mental Attitude is very laudable, but unfortunately it takes a little more than just a shift in attitude to undo the damage that we have allowed to creep into our lifestyle through our behaviour. We need to change our behaviour before we can expect things to change for us in any radical manner. Wouldn't it be great if we could just "think" ourselves out of situations? We have to "behave" ourselves out of these situations, by unlearning some of the bad behaviours and habits we have developed. It's really a reconditioning process, because most of our habits and comfort zones are the results of conditioning in one form or another.

If your car breaks down because it needs a good service, a puncture repair, or even a complete reconditioning of the engine, do you throw away the car? No, you fix the puncture, or get it serviced, or even reconditioned. Do you ever feel that you are only running on two cylinders instead of four or six? All you need is a good reconditioning. This starts on Plateau One by becoming AWARE of how you think, how you see things, how you behave, react, respond and contribute. Take the time to examine your belief system, the reality of your situation, and recognise exactly "where you're at".

If you attempt to live your life oblivious to all external factors, never recognising your predicament, constantly accepting every situation as just another fact of life, and being totally unaware of your attitude and behaviour towards others, you will never make progress in any dimension of your life. Do you spend your life worrying over the mistakes of the past, or blaming your predicament on some experience in your past life? Maybe you spend your life in anxious apprehension of the future — how will you cope, what will happen, where will it all end?

> *It is possible to gain a positive result from every experience in our lives, if we take the time to use it as a learning experience.*

This converts the negative effect of the experience into a positive effect, and we can use it to prevent us from making mistakes in the future. But always remember that your reality is in the present, today, where you're living. Don't live your life in the past, and don't try to live your life as if the future had already happened. Reality is NOW, not in the past or in the future.

> *You learn from the past, live in the present,*
> *and plan for the future.*

Excess baggage is one of the greatest obstacles to progress. Whether the excess baggage comes from bringing bad experiences with us from the past, or worrying about impending situations in the future, it is still "excess baggage" and must be discarded. I have come across too many people who have allowed unsavoury experiences from their childhood to taint their joy and success in life and in relationships. If you missed a dinner last week, no matter how hard you try, you can't eat that dinner now! That dinner is gone and you can never create the situation where that dinner will be available to you in the precise circumstances it was last week. However, you can make sure that you don't miss next week's dinner! So forget about what you missed last week, learn from the experience, and try to avoid the same mistake next week.

There are three types of people in the world:

1. People who *make* things happen

2. People who *watch* things happen

3. People who say, *"what happened?"*

Obviously you will want to be in the first category. But the transformation does not happen instantly; it takes time, patience, and endurance. We are all too familiar with how unsuccessful "crash diets" can be. These epitomise the "quick fix" solution mentality.

The longest journey begins with the first step, but there is no excess baggage allowed on this journey!

The story about the Chinese bamboo illustrates the rewards gained by persistence and endurance in our efforts. The Chinese bamboo is an amazing plant. It is watered and fertilised constantly for the first year, but nothing happens. The second year it is also watered and fertilised, and again nothing happens. The third year the same procedure, with no visible result, and in the fourth year the same thing happens. However, in the fifth year the plant is watered and fertilised as before, but this time the bamboo grows to a height of 90 feet in a period of only five or six weeks! Did the bamboo grow 90 feet in five or six weeks, or in five years? Of course the answer is five years, because the constant feeding and nourishing was essential for its eventual growth. Your progress works the same way, and it's only by systematically working through each Plateau, learning and living the principles, that you reap the rewards.

During this first Plateau, you have to do a type of "personal analysis" on yourself in order to heighten your awareness of where you stand in relation to progress in all four dimensions of your life — physical, mental, emotional, and spiritual. Ask yourself this question: "What is the purpose of life?" By the time you have finished reading and absorbing this book, and started applying the principles in your own life, you will have a very clear picture of the purpose of life, and most importantly, of *your* purpose in life! I believe that besides the need to be happy and contented, and to achieve inner peace and harmony, the purpose of life should also be to *matter*, to have made a difference that you lived on this Earth. Do you feel that you matter?

We are all born with different talents, and we all have various strengths and weaknesses. However, there are times when we can feel that we are quite useless, and even attempt to ignore our talents and strengths. Most of our talents are hidden until we go looking for them. How could we know that we're talented at music unless we explore the possibilities in that area? If we never lift a musical instrument, how will we know whether or not we have the talent to be an accomplished instrumentalist? It's very often through service to others that we discover certain qualities in our character. But we must recognise that we do have talents, and that we are special. Do we believe in our own self-worth? It is only by realising our individual self-worth and striving to develop our talents and qualities of character, that we will develop the confidence needed to progress at a faster rate.

When you die, what would you like people to say about you? Will you have touched the hearts of many people, or will all of your relationships have been lukewarm? Will you have built up so many barriers around your personality that it is almost impossible for anyone to make real contact with you? Remember that nobody knows the deepest thoughts within your mind, and nobody knows the real motives behind your actions or words, except yourself. You know what you feel, what you think, how you act or react, and it's by digging deep into your own mind and heart that you will become aware of exactly what sort of person you really are. This Plateau of Awareness is all about getting to know yourself better, and knowing "where you're at".

Once you have identified "where you're at", you can then set about correcting what needs to be corrected, changing what needs to be changed, and set sail on a beautiful, exciting journey as you take the necessary steps along The Five Plateaus of Progress. But don't let the contents of this book become a mere contribution to your harbour of knowledge. Make the experience a *voyage of discovery* in your pursuit of excellence, self-fulfilment and happiness.

Awareness falls into two basic categories: external and internal. External awareness is being observant and sensitive to situations, conditions, environment and the attitudes and approaches of other people. The internal awareness is the self-awareness, the awareness of your feelings, thoughts, actions, behaviours, attitudes and responses or reactions to the external influences. The identity crisis that most young people experience in their lives is the process of becoming aware of the self, realising that within this mortal frame there lies a spiritual and emotional dimension that is intangible but immensely powerful. Increased self-awareness *automatically* heightens your awareness of the external factors.

Awareness is an essential Plateau to investigate thoroughly. This is an identification Plateau. But once you have sufficiently ascertained and assessed the situation, once you are AWARE, then you must do something about it, and move on. You cannot afford to remain on this Plateau, because that would negate the whole principle of Plateaus of Progress.

> *"To reach the port of heaven, we must sail sometimes with*
> *the wind and sometimes against it — but we must sail,*
> *and not drift, nor lie at anchor."*
> — Oliver Wendell Holmes

The topics discussed in this chapter are aimed at helping you to increase your self-awareness, but they will have no effect unless you study them, absorb them, and put them into practice in order to fully understand the principles involved. This involves asking yourself many questions about your feelings, attitude and behaviour.

The following is a type of self-check questionnaire which should help you gauge your position at this stage, on this first Plateau.

Some Self-Check Questions

- How do you speak to your spouse, your partner, your friends, and is it similar to the way you address your employer?

- How do you ask for things, or do you constantly demand things?

- Do you bear grudges, are you ungracious in accepting service, and have you the capacity to apologise?

- Are you over-sensitive to people's opinions and criticisms?

- Do you react, rather than respond, to situations?

- Do you waste time thinking too much about past incidents, and worrying too much about future consequences?

- How would you describe your general attitude?

- Are you very moody, or have you learned to "grin and bear it"?

THE CHASM OF UNHAPPINESS

*Between the "actual" and the "ideal" lies a chasm of
unhappiness. The depth and width of this chasm is determined
by ourselves, and is directly proportionate to whether or not
our conduct is at variance with what we know to be right.*

Many years ago I attended a presentation on leadership by Don S. Gull, and he spoke about this great Chasm of Unhappiness that we create for ourselves (see Figure 5). Imagine this great chasm of unhappiness with a stream of misery running along the bottom. This chasm represents the distance between the "actual" (where you are) and the "ideal" (where you would like to be). It can be as deep and as wide as you want to make it. The chasm is created in the first place by your conduct. When your conduct is at variance with what you know is right, you're unhappy! No doubt you've experienced the feeling of doing something, even though you really know deep down in your heart that it's not the right thing to do.

So how do you bridge this chasm? You bridge the chasm with little blocks of achievement, and those achievement blocks are found in your behaviour. It's the aligning of your behaviour with your positive thoughts, your correct thoughts, that makes you feel good about yourself. However, the change is not exclusively directed at behaviour, it must be a complete change of heart and mind to be effective in bridging the chasm.

FIGURE 5: THE CHASM OF UNHAPPINESS

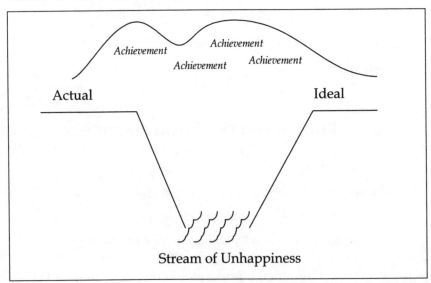

Let me illustrate this concept with a poignant example.

The Beginnings of the Chasm

Imagine that you're driving along the road on your way home from a busy day at work. It's late, you're hungry, tired, and you haven't really had such a great day. You spot a young woman at the side of the road with a baby in her arms, and she's trying to hitch a lift from the passing cars. Your initial reaction is to maybe stop and ask her where she wants to go, but then the overriding feelings of hunger, tiredness, lateness, etc., make you drive on, hoping that perhaps some other motorist will have the time to stop.

So eventually you arrive home. You relax, have a shower, and enjoy your well-earned dinner by the fireside as you watch the latest episode of your favourite soap opera on television. The thought of that young woman is still just below the surface of your conscious mind, and now that you are more relaxed, at your point of destination, and comfortably nourished, you think for a brief moment that perhaps it wouldn't have been too much of an inconvenience to stop for that young woman. You don't feel too badly about it, but you certainly don't feel too good about it either.

This is an example of the beginning of the chasm of unhappiness, and perhaps it could stay as a tiny chasm with a tiny stream of misery at the bottom, not too wide and not very deep.

However, on the breakfast news the following morning, you hear the harrowing news of the poor woman's misfortune.

It appears that her car had broken down, and she was frantic to get her sick baby to a hospital urgently. She had tried to hitch a lift from the passing cars, but nobody would stop to give her a lift, and her baby died in her arms!

How's that chasm now?

We're not going to deal with anything so heartrending or disturbing on Plateau One, but we must address the fact that *we create* this chasm by allowing our conduct to be at variance with what we know to be right. We have to bridge that chasm, and in order to bridge it we have to become aware of what we're doing, what we're thinking, and what we believe. Facing reality can sometimes be the hardest thing to do, because the fantasy world can often be too appealing to let go! So start building those achievement blocks to bridge the chasm, and bring the *actual* closer to the *ideal*.

> *The authentic person is strong,*
> *because he is what he seems to be.*

So often the chasm of unhappiness is created by our reluctance to face the truth, or to do the right thing in awkward circumstances. For example, the boss of an organisation who is afraid to promote an individual on merit, because of fears about what the other members of the organisation might say. The individual who is afraid to come forward in defence of a wrongly accused colleague, because of the fear of being ostracised or losing promotional prospects. The executive who promotes a close friend to a senior position, instead of a more deserving member of their staff. Nepotism, deception, fraudulence, duplicity, and all other forms of corruption are major contributing factors to the chasm of unhappiness. The way to bridge that chasm is by taking a stand, choosing the right path, regardless of the consequences, and becoming authentic by matching our beliefs with our actions.

In order to make continual progress at an even pace, we must be intrinsically motivated and driven. We have to feel good about ourselves, because when we feel good about ourselves we're automatically in positive mode, ready to take on the world. There is nothing like honest achievement to make us feel good about ourselves. Success by manipulation, fraud, deception, or at the expense of someone else, is a very hollow victory.

The achievements I'm talking about are not necessarily the enormous tasks that we undertake, but rather the little blocks of daily achievement. As we take each step in the right direction, we build our self-esteem, our courage increases, and we begin to develop that elusive inner peace and harmony that comes from bridging the "chasm of unhappiness".

Some Self-Check Questions

- Do you recognise any Chasms of Unhappiness in your life?

- How do you propose to bridge them?

- Are you guilty of manipulation, nepotism, fraud or deception?

- Are you proud of the manner in which you have achieved your success to date?

- What do you need to change in your behaviour, in order to start bridging the Chasm of Unhappiness?

THE REALITY FACTOR

Reality can never be clearly viewed through the spectacle of unreality, fantasy, or wishful thinking. It is factual, without frills or fanfare, and must be seen as it is, for what it is, without any preconceived notions of what we would like it to be.

I heard a recent radio interview with Dr William Glasser, author of the book, *What Are You Doing?*, which deals with Reality Therapy. It was fascinating to hear about the amount of unreality that exists, where people almost daily try to convince themselves that they're "Not really doing this!"

I call this the "HITS — Head in the Sand — Syndrome". This type of unreality is particularly prevalent among alcoholics who have not yet faced up to the truth of their situation. They live in a state of denial, not wishing to admit that they could have such disorder in their lives. You cannot possibly make any progress when you're in denial.

Facing reality is absolutely mandatory in trying to complete Plateau One successfully. You must take your head out of the sand in order to see where you are. In relation to rehabilitation, it is the first step on the road to recovery. This can often be a painful experience and sometimes it's not very nice to realise that certain aspects of your character leave a lot to be desired. But face them you must, because ultimately your performance *is* your reality.

The use of drugs is particularly popular with people who wish to engage in escapism, and sometimes they will excuse their abominable behaviour because they were under the influence of these drugs! Abominable behaviour is inexcusable, and to try to justify behaviour because of another indulgence is just totally unacceptable. But do we accept it, condone it, excuse it, tolerate it, and in some instances endure it? We become part of the problem if we allow this type of conduct to be perpetuated in our homes, schools, families, workplace and in society generally. We must take a firm stance and say, "Stop!" The alcoholic's best friend is the one who refuses to tolerate him when he is under the influence of alcohol, refuses to serve him more alcohol, and refuses to be in his company as long as he is in that state of inebriation.

Character flaws, just like flaws in any product or system, can only be rectified once they have been identified. Can you imagine going to the doctor with some chronic disease, but *refusing* to give the doctor all the details of your ailment, because of the fear you have of receiving the bad news? Under these circumstances, the doctor couldn't possibly diagnose you accurately. And how can you hope to be cured unless the disease is identified and diagnosed? To become a person of integrity, which means a "whole" person, you need to look at yourself in your entirety without hiding any skeletons in the cupboard. If you try to build on a foundation of unreality or denial, you will surely fail. You must build on reality. I know some people who are addicted to watching soap operas on television for the sheer escapism that it offers them. Because of this behaviour, their own domestic situations are in absolute chaos. They live in the fantasy world, and the real world is seen through the keyhole of unreality.

This Plateau of Awareness is the basis for building qualities, skills and character as you progress through the other Plateaus. But it has to be based upon reality, and not on what you *imagine*. You need to develop the ability to see things as they are, and for what they are. How many times have we walked into the same emotional or psychological hole? How often do people allow the same situations occur time and time again, even though they know at the outset what the result is going to be? It reminds me of the story about the rattlesnake.

The Rattlesnake Story

It was an old tradition in the development from childhood to manhood among a certain Indian tribe, for a young man to spend many days out in the wilderness on his own. This exercise culminated in spending his last night at the top of a high mountain, before his return to the tribe as a fully fledged man. However, this young Indian heard a noise in the grass when he was at the top of the mountain, about to make his descent. Upon investigation, it turned out to be a rattlesnake.

"Please, will you take me down from this cold mountain with you?" asked the rattlesnake.

"I can't. You're a rattlesnake and you'll bite me," replied the young Indian.

"No, I won't bite you. I will be so grateful to you for saving my life. If I stay up here I will freeze to death," said the rattlesnake.

"No, you're a rattlesnake, and it would be too dangerous to bring you down with me . . . you'd surely bite me," said the young man.

"I will not bite you, I promise. I beg you to have mercy on me and save my life by just allowing me to come down the mountain with you," pleaded the rattlesnake.

Eventually, the young man decided that he should have compassion on the poor little rattlesnake, so he took him at his word, wrapped him inside his warm coat and brought him with him down the mountain.

As they arrived at the bottom of the mountain, the young Indian let the rattlesnake loose, but immediately the rattlesnake spun around, hissed and bit him.

"Why did you do that? You promised that you wouldn't bite me," said the astonished young Indian as he lay on the ground in agony.

"You knew what I was when you picked me up," replied the rattlesnake as he slithered off into the grass.

Take a hard look at your actual behaviour, your thought patterns, attitudes, conduct and treatment of others, in stark reality, *not* as you would like or imagine it to be.

Is it possible to be fully aware of everything, and yet live your life in the realms of unreality? Reality is essential to bring everything back down to earth. You must become aware of your trips into unreal behaviour, and then employ the principle of reality to overcome these inclinations.

The subject of *assertiveness* warrants a mention at this point, because people who are lacking in self-confidence and assertiveness are very often living their lives in a semi-unreal way. The inability to say "no" to a request can put enormous pressure on an individual, and this can sometimes develop into an extremely stressful condition. By developing a stronger faith in yourself, your capabilities, your talents, and most of all, your self-worth, you can change your attitude and behaviour, and develop the confidence to face the reality of situations. Assertiveness fits somewhere between aggressive and submissive. It's the happy medium, and generally the most effective method of getting results. I won't go into this subject in any great depth, because there are plenty of assertiveness courses on the market, but let me just elaborate on a few pointers and keys to achieving successful assertiveness.

Assertiveness is positive, not domineering, not abusive, not threatening, and not a "put-down". To move from the position of being submissive or passive, we need to reprogramme our thinking. We need to do the following things:

- **Decide** precisely what we want and where we want to go.

- **Ask** clearly and concisely without fear.

- **Express** our opinions and feelings about situations and people.

- **Fear Not** — Don't allow fear to stifle our communication.

- **Be Calm** — Don't let the situation upset us or annoy us into panic or anger.

- **Give and Take Compliments** — Be self-assured and secure enough to accept graciously, and to give compliments without feeling awkward or fearful.

- **Persistence** — Don't give up too easily, and be prepared to fight your corner.

- **Use the DAN Principle** — Discuss/Argue/Negotiate.

Always remember that your physical demeanour and appearance represents an important part of communication — Body Language. Your style should reflect your mood, so go through a self-conditioning process:

- Think successful

- Feel successful

- Act successful

- Look successful

- Be successful

Six Keys to Achieving Assertiveness

1. **Stop Playing Safe**. Break out of your comfort zones, take risks, reach out, expand. By staying within your protective shell, you are perpetuating the condition of fear.

2. **Identify**. What's stopping you? Prioritise your motives and actions, and overcome the obstacles that are preventing you from expressing yourself confidently.

3. **Virtue Taken to the Extreme**. Stop being over-tolerant of other people and their behaviours. Enough is enough!

4. **Know Your Rights**. You must respect other people's rights, but you must know your own entitlements. You're entitled to have an opinion, to speak, to make your own decisions, to choose, to change, and to your privacy.

5. **Prepare for Situations**. Don't keep falling into that great big black hole. Visualise the consequences, and imagine the catastrophe scenario before it happens. Then you will never be stuck for words.

6. **Recognise "Put-Downs"**. Don't accept the old, "If I were you I wouldn't have done that", from your peers. Expose the real message. They're NOT you! Respond, and don't allow the veiled threats or comments to go unchallenged. Speak up and expose the underminer!

You must always tell yourself, "Yes, this is happening to me right now, this is reality!" Through heightened awareness, and the steady progress through The Five Plateaus of Progress, you will develop the ability to see things as they really are, to accept yourself as you really are, and to create your own reality within that environment. The past has already happened, and there is nothing that you can do in this world that can have any bearing on the past. The secret is to use your experience of the past to make yourself more prepared for the future. Your awareness of your own self-worth should give you the confidence to be assertive. You are a human being, you have rights, and your opinion does matter.

Some Self-Check Questions

- Are you in denial about certain habits or situations in your life?

- Does your behaviour reflect a positive self-image, wholesome character, good attitude, and clear frame of mind?

- Is the HITS syndrome evident in your life?

- Have you developed the ability to be assertive in your opinions and contributions?

- Do you fully realise your own self-worth?

OPEN-MINDEDNESS

"Some people love to learn, but hate to be taught."
— Sir Winston Churchill

Imagine going to the cinema and keeping your eyes closed throughout the film! Well the same thing happens when people read books, and attend courses and seminars with a "closed mind". The doors to the mind are closed, so nothing gets in. We cannot possibly even begin to develop any sort of concepts until we first open our minds to receive the idea. If the managing director of a company listens to his or her employees with a closed mind, they will soon create a highly militant organisation. The employees will quickly recognise the MD's refusal to accept and learn from their feedback, and will find an alternative method of convincing him or her of their grievances. If you attend a meeting with a closed mind, how can you possibly give an accurate appraisal of the points discussed at the meeting?

In the learning process, I believe we should always endeavour to absorb, assimilate and apply — the 3A Principle (see Figure 6).

FIGURE 6: THE 3A PRINCIPLE

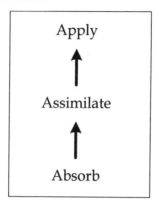

But how can we possibly assimilate or apply if the information is cut off at the initial stage of absorption? The mind will absorb nothing until it's "open for information".

Take a look at our digestive system (see Figure 7); we ingest, then digest, then absorb and finally assimilate. Apply this principle to the reception of knowledge, and you can see how essential it is to look at things with an open mind, not with preconceived notions. The process of absorbing and assimilating will determine whether or not you need to apply it in your own particular circumstances.

We listen to learn, but we must learn to listen.

In order to expand horizons and push boundaries, it is essential to obtain knowledge, and the first step in obtaining knowledge is to open the mind and let it in. If you read this book with a closed mind, you cannot possibly come to know or understand the principles or the concept, and therefore you cannot judge its value. In order to understand, ascertain the value, or accurately appraise anything, we must first ingest it. And the point of entry is the open mind.

FIGURE 7: THE DIGESTIVE SYSTEM

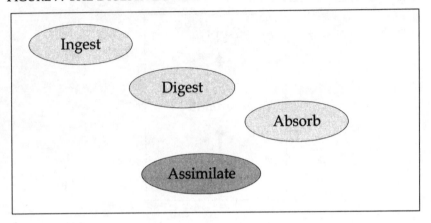

In the course of running seminars, courses and workshops, I invariably come across people who have been sent on the course by their company. From the beginning of the course, I can see the blank expression on their faces when the mind is closed. When I gather assignments from participants, it becomes so obvious that these individuals have approached the course with closed minds. The concepts have gone over their heads, the understanding of the principles is minimal, the application is non-existent, and the chance of gaining any slight piece of knowledge or stimulation from the course is absolutely impossible. This condition creates a powerful barrier to developing the qualities and skills of real leadership, because it contradicts a fundamental element of learning and leadership development, the ability to be taught, to *be teachable*. Are you aware of how well you really listen and *hear* what's being said? An essential element of communication involves listening.

Some people are under the misapprehension that they are obliged to *use* every piece of information that they acquire, and this false notion prevents them from having the desire to even enquire. *You* decide whether or not the information needs to be applied, but until such time as you have full knowledge of the information, you cannot make that decision. In order to give yourself the advantage of having that choice, you should first equip yourself with the knowledge. Being aware of a situation is the first stage, but it's impossible to discern or accurately appraise it unless you view it realistically with an open mind.

Some Self-Check Questions

- Do you genuinely listen and *hear* what's being said to you, or do you merely placate the person with the appropriate body language?

- Are most situations approached with preconceived notions and false assumptions, or with an open mind?

- Are you open to suggestions, or do you have a closed mind?

- Do you apply the principle of *Absorb, Assimilate, Apply*?

KNOWLEDGE

It is better to ask a question and be a fool for a moment,
than to ask none and be a fool forever.

Let me first clarify a fallacious notion, which exists among the pseudo-intellectuals and cognoscenti of the world, that "knowledge is education". Knowledge is the accumulation of information in various categories, on multiple subjects and in diverse disciplines. However, the education in life comes with the *understanding* of this knowledge, and then the practical implementation of that knowledge. *Knowledge and understanding are two different things.* I have come across many intelligent people in my life who are puffed up with the pride of their academic knowledge, but still remain extremely ignorant individuals. The more I come to know in life, the more I realise how little I know and how much more there is to learn. Take it as fact — "NOBODY KNOWS EVERYTHING!" We are all ignorant, but in different areas and on different subjects.

Intelligence is the creative use of knowledge.

To acquire knowledge of something is to know about something, and we should always seek to know, to find out, and to understand how things work and how systems operate. We cannot plead ignorance of the law, and that presupposes the existence of a certain level of maturity that would make us want to know our rights, and to have a desire to live within the law. Have you ever noticed how anxious children are to learn, to know everything about anything that they come across? Somehow, we seem to lose this desire as we get older, and after a while it turns into apathy unless we shake ourselves and get back into the learning mode. The child is constantly asking "why", and *we* should also ask "why" more often, to increase our knowledge and understanding.

Knowledge precedes action, but we must examine how we gain our knowledge, and on what it is based. Do we base our knowledge upon a belief or upon experience? Is it academic knowledge or practical knowledge? On this Plateau of Awareness, you must ask yourself those questions, and in examining the strength or truth of the knowledge that you already have, you must see how it has contributed to your perceptions.

I heard John McCarthy say in a television interview that he regretted not having gained enough knowledge in his life prior to his kidnapping and incarceration in Beirut. It was interesting to hear that statement from a man who had just spent about five years locked up in small rooms with his friend, Brian Keenan, not knowing when he might have been killed. In such a condition of confinement, one would have plenty of time to think about what's important in life, and no doubt one's sense of values becomes extremely acute and accurate. With the enormous wealth of knowledge available to us through the various media, it's amazing that we do not spend more time engaged in its acquisition. Do you read enough, study enough, explore, enquire and find out how things and systems work?

To gain knowledge effectively, we should endeavour to become involved as much as possible. The old Chinese adage applies as much to the acquiring of knowledge as to the imparting of it:

> *Tell me, I forget.*
> *Show me, I remember*
> Involve me, *I understand.*

I believe there are four different types of knowledge — *Academic, Practical, Experiential* and *Spiritual* — each one relating to a particular dimension. We deal with the fourth category in greater detail when we come to discuss the spiritual dimension, but the following brief description will help to clarify the categories:

- *Academic* knowledge (mental dimension) is gained from books, lectures, media educational programmes and general intellectual pursuits.

- *Practical* knowledge (physical dimension) is gained by hands-on experience and practical involvement in the subject.

- *Experiential* knowledge (emotional dimension) is gained through prolonged use of academic and practical knowledge, through experiencing its practical application in many and varied forms.

- *Spiritual* knowledge (spiritual dimension) is pure knowledge or truth, timeless principles, and understanding that can only be gained through the development and stimulation of the spiritual dimension.

There is quite a difference between academic and practical knowledge. For example, you know that a television transmits pictures of current events which may be happening at the other side of the continent. You know that all you have to do is press a button or flick a switch to have a vast variety of channels available for your viewing pleasure. But do you understand the precise technology used in transmitting those signals, what form they take, how they are decoded, how the lines or dots on a screen actually come together to create the picture? This practical knowledge comes from hands-on involvement. We often tend to accept things at face value without ever delving into their origins or trying to gain an understanding. We often just accept the academic knowledge.

You could read all the books ever written about the art of swimming. Talk to every coach who ever coached a champion swimmer. Watch all the world champion swimmers perform in Olympic pools. But none of this will make you a swimmer. You have to get into the water and then put the principles and techniques into practice. Then you will really learn *how* to swim. You will fully understand what swimming is all about, because you are now a swimmer.

You must become aware of how you have acquired knowledge in the past and develop a greater desire for understanding as you acquire knowledge in the future. Finding out how things work, knowing your civil and legal rights, your entitlements, and your obligations, are all essential life-skills that can help make life so much easier and worthwhile.

> *"The man who can read books, but does not,*
> *has no advantage over the illiterate man."*
> — Mark Twain

We must never cease in our quest for knowledge, and we should make every day a new learning experience. In every organisation, there is a strong emphasis on keeping in step with the latest technology, and the whole area of information technology represents a major part of every organisation's development. Every person at every level in any organisation should be constantly learning, acquiring an increase of knowledge and understanding, and heightening their awareness. But beware of becoming a workaholic. The balance between domestic work and leisure time must be maintained. And each dimension must be stimulated. If this learning process stops at any level in the corporation, it will weaken the entire organisation, because a chain is only as strong as its weakest link.

> *"The most successful corporation of the 1990s will be*
> *something called a learning organisation."*
> — *Fortune* magazine

Some Self-Check Questions

- By what means have you gained the most worthwhile knowledge in your life?

- Is most of your knowledge academic or practical?

- How much of your acquired knowledge has been transposed into understanding?

- Does your quest for knowledge also include a desire to understand?

FORCES

As we are constantly exposed to various forces, we must resist,
deflect or annihilate the negative forces, use the positive forces
to our advantage and go with the flow, and never succumb
to the coercive forces that weaken, impede or side-track us
from our objectives and goals.

Regardless of our profession or occupation, our domestic situations, our class structure, our social standing, or our leisure pursuits, we will always be subjected to various forces which will pull or push us in forward or backward directions. Have you ever observed some high-profile individuals who seem to have an insatiable appetite for work, and seem to overcome any obstacle that is placed in their path? Do you ever ask the question, "What drives that person to perform at such a level?" In relation to Abraham Maslow's Hierarchy of Needs (see page 18), I mentioned the primary drives for the basic physiological needs, and then there are the secondary drives, etc. But when we eventually become aware of the source that keeps us "hanging in there", and striving towards a better life, then we begin to identify what really makes us tick.

Market fluctuations, peer pressure, systems and procedures are all examples of external forces that can have a positive or negative effect upon our lives. If we allow these forces to direct our lives, we become "outer directed" as opposed to "inner directed". Our aim should be to become more inner directed, to be driven by a basic sense of values and of what is right for us, and to develop this *driving force* within ourselves. This we can do if we strive to critically examine the things we think, say and do, and become aware of our talents as well as our weaknesses. Without going too deeply into an elaboration's of Kurt Lewin's Theory of Force Field Analysis, suffice it to say that it breaks down into two basic forces — *driving* forces and *restraining* forces. A restraining force is anything that stops you from making progress in any dimension, and a driving force is anything that helps you to press forward and achieve.

Michael E. Porter, in his book, *The Competitive Advantage of Nations*, talks about the five competitive forces in the structural analysis of industries, and these forces determine industry profitability in global industrial competition. It is essential for firms to be aware of these forces, and to be able to ascertain their position in relation to them, if they are earnestly seeking to gain any sort of competitive advantage in the marketplace.

In order to recognise the source and the effect of these forces, we must first ascertain our direction, so that we will know whether we are being forced towards, or away from, our point of destination. *Direction is more important than speed.* When Alice met the Cheshire cat in *Alice in Wonderland*, she asked him which road should she take. He asked her where she wanted to go, but she said, "I don't really know". And the cat replied, "Then it doesn't matter which road you take".

We can break down the various driving forces in our lives into emotional drives, physical drives, mental drives and spiritual drives. This highlights the choices that have to be made sometimes between affairs of the heart and the mental control that is required to override an emotional drive. However, we must have sufficient enthusiasm about something in order to build it into a driving force. When we come to talk about the spiritual dimension, we will see how it can become the guiding and driving force in our lives, if we adequately stimulate that dimension.

Without a driving force in our lives, we can become most un-interesting people, quite apathetic, and eventually we will seek out synthetic methods of stimulation. A person with no interests, hobbies or sports will eventually have no friends, because the level of social interaction will diminish from lack of fuel. Some people make the mistake of being driven by the desire for the accumula-tion of vast wealth — they become *money-driven*. The monetary reward is a *by-product* of success. The financial rewards of success can be achieved with great effort and dedication, but the money is not the end in itself. Being innovation-driven, value-driven, prin-ciple-driven, or achievement-driven would be more appropriate driving forces. Money is only a *means* to an end, but it is not an end in itself. When you have earned the money, it gives you the freedom to go on holidays, to buy a house, to enjoy your leisure time, etc., but of itself it is not an end. Find the driving force in your life that will help to accelerate your progress!

When we come to discuss Vision, Values, Goals, and Commit-ment, you will be in a better position to identify the most powerful positive driving forces in your life that you want to stimulate. But on this Plateau it is important for you to identify the various forces that affect your life at present.

Some Self-Check Questions

- Are you driven by selfish motives and desires?

- Is money or power a major driving force in your life?

- Have you identified any negative emotional forces?

- Are you generally "inner" or "outer" directed?

MENTAL BLOCKS

Our progress can be severely impeded when we allow our thoughts and imagination to create a distorted perception of what we think the consequences of our actions might be. These mental blocks can become as real, almost tangible, and as formidable as a brick wall.

Some of the little problems and puzzles that Edward de Bono uses to demonstrate his principle of "lateral thinking" are quite effective in highlighting how simply and unconsciously we allow mental blocks to prevent us from taking action in certain situations. For example, connect the nine dots in Figure 8 by using four straight lines, without lifting your pen from the paper. Initially, it seems almost impossible, but that is because we have already imposed unnecessary limitations on ourselves with *false assumptions*. Before you read any further, just do this simple exercise.

FIGURE 8: DE BONO'S JOIN THE DOTS

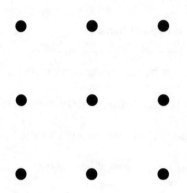

(Turn to the end of this chapter for the solution)

False assumptions and preconceived notions can be the greatest barriers to expanding horizons, pushing boundaries, and making progress. The concept of the self-fulfilling prophecy — "expect the best, and you get the best; expect the worst, and you get the worst" — should be used to our positive advantage. People will rise to the challenge of the expectations of others, and you should expect the best of yourself at all times.

The amount of self-imposed limitations we put on ourselves can sometimes be the sole cause of failure. I often refer to the "Lawnmower Syndrome" when I come across people with an extremely negative attitude.

The Lawnmower Syndrome

The story of the "Lawnmower Syndrome" goes like this. Jack looked out at his lawn one afternoon, and decided that it definitely needed to be mown. So he decides to ask his neighbour, Mike, if he could borrow his lawnmower. Just as he was about to walk over to Mike's back yard, he stopped and thought about the last time he borrowed Mike's lawnmower.

"Gosh, that's right, I forgot to leave it back to him, and he had to call in to me about three weeks later to get it back. Not only that, but I forgot to replenish it with fuel, and the height gauge got stuck in the lowest position on the mower."

This stopped Jack in his tracks, and the more he thought about it, the more annoyed he got with himself for his negligence. But the more annoyed he got with himself, the more annoyed he became with his neighbour for causing him the embarrassment. Suddenly, from the other side of the garden fence, his neighbour Mike shouted a hearty greeting, "Hi there, Jack, lovely day we're having!"

Jack shouted back, with great annoyance, "I wouldn't borrow your rotten old lawnmower if it was the last one on earth!"

These assumptions are blocks to learning, and we must examine them to see on what they are based. Are they based on knowledge, belief, or actual experience? Are they genuine assumptions, or false assumptions? Until we become aware of these limitations, and identify them for what they really are (blocks to learning and progressing), we cannot even begin to make solid progress.

I often make reference to Evelynn Glennie, who, at the age of twelve, was profoundly deaf. When asked by her guidance counsellor what she wished to be in life, she replied, "I want to be a musician". The guidance counsellor gently, and then firmly, explained to her that because of her hearing disability, that would be impossible — "Deaf people don't become musicians!"

But what Evelynn said next astounded me. She said, "You're not me. I know what I can do, and I want to become a musician."

Today, Evelynn Glennie is one of the most accomplished and famous percussionists in the world. The guidance counsellor, and society in general, could have been considered to be restraining or pulling forces in her life, but she was most definitely "inner directed". The driving, compelling force that was her will to make her dream a reality was so strong that she eliminated the restraining forces from her mind and concentrated upon what she knew she could do.

In theory, a bumblebee cannot fly because his body is far too big and heavy for the strength of his wings . . . but nobody told the bumblebee, and he flies! Chuck Yeager was told that it was impossible to travel faster than the speed of sound, but he thought that he could, and he did! Everybody said that it was impossible for a human being to run a mile in under four minutes. But a young man from Oxford in England, Roger Bannister, thought differently. On 6 May 1954, Roger Bannister ran a mile in under four minutes. Did we ever think that we'd see men landing on the moon? The world is full of people with strong character and determination, who will not accept restraining forces in their lives; they just ignore them and follow their inner feelings and driving force. They don't allow negative attitudes or false assumptions into the equation.

Ideally, it is always easier and more effective to remove the restraining forces, which gives the driving force the freedom to carry on. But whether they are physical or mental forces, you must eliminate them or they will hinder your progress. In most cases the blocks are only mental, but unfortunately the power of the imagination can build these mental blocks so big that they become very real and more difficult to destroy than the physical blocks.

We must examine how and why these mental blocks have been allowed to develop, and then we must find a way to eliminate them. The mental block is a typical example of the closed mind syndrome. We must flush out these negative mental blocks, and replace them with fresh, positive, open-minded attitudes and approaches to situations.

Some Self-Check Questions

- Do you have any mental blocks that impede your growth and development in various dimensions?

- Are there certain preconceived notions or false assumptions that prevent you from approaching people or situations?

- Do these feelings dissuade you from attempting new things?

THE PHYSICAL DIMENSION

Our emotional and mental capacities can be seriously depleted if we do not have good physical health. The lack of physical fitness creates an imbalance that impedes progress.

The commonly accepted broad divisions of the human makeup are Physical, Emotional, Mental and Spiritual (see Figure 3, page 15), and only by dealing with *all four* elements can we accomplish the result of effective personal development. Coming back to my comments on Eastern philosophy, the yin/yang principle, the principle of balance in acupuncture and T'ai Chi, etc. (see Introduction), I firmly believe that all frustrations are caused from a lack of stimulation or an imbalance in stimulation in these four areas. I cannot emphasise strongly enough the importance of maintaining regular stimulation in *every* area, because if there is an imbalance it will surely manifest itself in some outward frustration before long. I will deal with the other dimensions later, but let us look at the physical dimension in this chapter.

You never get a second chance to make a first impression.

The very first impression most people get is of our physical shape, size and demeanour. Within reason, you can be almost whatever shape and weight you want to be. Body sculpture, body building, weight loss programmes, keep fit programmes, aerobics, etc. are being shoved in our faces every day. Fortunately, or unfortunately, our physical demeanour usually says a lot about us. Whenever you hear about a dynamic and energetic salesperson, you immediately conjure up a mental picture of someone who looks fit and healthy. You don't expect to find an overweight alcoholic, badly groomed, sloppily dressed, fitting into that picture!

In the mid-1980s, when I worked as a financial consultant, a colleague of mine was anxious for me to join his team of consultants in a major international company. I agreed to have lunch with him, during which he extolled the virtues and professionalism of his marvellous company. After lunch he persuaded me to come and meet his boss. When I met his boss I was convinced that my initial response, to pass on the offer, was absolutely correct. His boss was loud-mouthed, with an enormous beer-belly, aggressive in manner, and used coarse language. I just couldn't imagine taking orders or suggestions from such an obnoxious individual.

I believe that, based on the premise that example is a most effective leadership principle, people in positions of authority must be able to "walk their talk". Having been closely involved with the whole area of drug addiction and drug addicts, this fact was confirmed to me when I read a passage in a book called *Go Ask Alice*. The story, which is comprised of her diary entries, is an extremely sad account of a young addict's life, and the many attempts she made to kick the habit. However, after one of her many counselling sessions with a doctor, she observed the following:

> *"Today I went to the headshrinker's, a fat ugly little man who doesn't even have the enough balls to lose weight."*
> — Anonymous, *Go Ask Alice*

How could she possibly have any faith in a so-called professional individual who couldn't control his own over-eating disorder, which was quite a minor problem in contrast to her chronic drug addiction. "Don't do as I do, just do as I tell you" is not the way to get results from anyone. People need to be able to look up to their leaders, they need to see that they can, and do, "walk their talk".

On this plateau of Awareness, I would like to deal initially with the *physical dimension*, and unfortunately it is very often the one that many people ignore. After all, what has the physical got to do with my mental development or emotional progress? It has *everything* to do with your progress in *every* dimension, because *all four dimensions are inextricably linked*. Just as every organ in the body has separate functions, but they cannot function separately. Remember the old adage: "A healthy body is a healthy mind". ASICS, the sports gear manufacturers, use the slogan *Anima Sana In Corpore Sano*.

In the Seven Chakras, it is essential to be "in control" of the body before you can move upwards through the other gateways of enlightenment. I think it is important to understand at this stage, on Plateau One, that the physical dimension plays a *major* role in our development and growth. Are you aware of the amount of stimulation you are giving your physical dimension?

I have already used the analogy of a marathon runner training for a big race to illustrate the concept of Plateaus. But let me just elaborate a little more on this aspect because it is very much based in the physical, and works well as an example of how we need to become "fit for life". Athletes have to train regularly and consistently increase their amount of training to increase their level of fitness, in order to run in a race. Try to take a holistic approach to the whole area of personal development, and you will begin to realise that the balance created by stimulating each dimension, actually *increases* our performance in every dimension.

Society in general has taken a very palliative approach to sickness; if you overeat or drink too much, you can always have a couple of pills the next day to alleviate the discomfort. But we must look seriously at our eating habits as part of our healthy lifestyle. Eating too much, drinking too much, sleeping too much, working too hard — in fact, any of these physical activities taken to extremes — can damage or deplete the stimulation of our physical dimension.

On this first Plateau, you have to take cognisance of your personal level of physical fitness as part of your self-analysis, because you have to know your starting point — "where you're at right now" — in relation to physical fitness.

This all relates to whole-brain thinking, but let me mention the famous endorphins at this stage. "Endorphins?" I hear you exclaim! The endorphins are neurotransmitters released by the glandular system after some kind of stimulation, and they excite the brain and help you to be more alert, creative, enthusiastic and mentally active. These are also the body's natural painkillers.

I like to run every morning. The running releases the endorphins and I feel ready to face the day, to work, to write and to play with a tremendous freshness and lack of any sluggishness in my system. You should engage on a daily basis in whatever type of exercise you enjoy, as a preparation for just living life to its fullest, and to benefit more from your daily life. Don't discount this aspect of this Plateau, and don't ignore the benefits that can be derived from it, but approach it with an open mind and test it. Just do it! Get fit for life, fit for leadership. The physical fitness is only the beginning, but an essential foundation for building emotional, mental and spiritual fitness.

"The road to hell is paved with good intentions." You may have the greatest ideas, concepts, plans and innovations, but unless you have the physical capacity, the raw physical energy required to do the job, you will never bring it to fruition.

Some Self-Check Questions

- Do you get sufficient daily exercise?
- Are you physically exhausted after even a small amount of physical exertion?
- Are you fit for life, or is your physical condition a liability instead of an asset?
- Do you ever use the physical activity of any sport as a refreshing form of stimulation and relaxation after a heavy day's work?

DEPENDENCE

The chains of dependence enslave and bind us, and prevent
us from standing on our own two feet. It is only when we
learn how to break these chains, and overcome the dependence,
that we can look forward to a life of freedom, joy,
self-satisfaction and achievement.

We read a lot about people striving for financial independence in
this world of ours, and in the business sector we hear a lot of talk
about developing the principle of interdependence. But neither of
the latter two can ever be achieved unless the first stage of "dependence" is left behind. When we talk about obstacles in our
paths we generally refer to either physical or mental. But dependence on people, situations or substances is more than just an obstacle or stumbling block; it is more like a heavy anchor that stops us
from moving. We can't even begin to make progress because it
will not even allow us get started.

The dependence can be physical, emotional, psychological or
mental, but whatever form it takes you must immediately try to
recognise it for what it is — DEPENDENCE. By way of example,
let's take the person addicted to nicotine because of a habit called
smoking, or the alcoholic addicted to alcohol because of a habit
called drinking. Without going deeper into the area of substance
abuse, all of these are conditions of dependence which have a
strong physical and psychological effect upon the individuals concerned. At this point, let me state loudly and clearly: *Addictions are*
fed by indulgence! And it's only by gaining control of our indulgences that we eventually curb the addiction, and then eliminate
it. This is far more easily said than done, and I don't mean to de-
mean the individual who experiences the agony of addiction. It is

a state of horrible pain, and can have devastating affects upon themselves, their families and their friends. However, the addiction had to have its beginning somewhere in the past where the individual decided to indulge in the substance. The continuous use, or perhaps over-indulgence, led to dependence, which eventually became addiction.

I have great empathy for the parents of any young person who has fallen into this dreadful situation, because I have recently been involved with my son's rehabilitation from a four-year drug habit. I understand the agony, the frustration, the lack of understanding, the lack of communication, the fury and the anguish. As part of the rehabilitation process, we co-wrote a book, *The Agony of Ecstasy*, which gave a dual perspective on the entire nightmare. It became an instant number-one bestseller, and the subsequent enormous response prompted us to produce our "Ray of Hope" drugs awareness seminars. Over the next 18 months, we presented these seminars to over 250,000 students and parents in schools and colleges in Ireland and the UK. Although it was a gruelling schedule, it was one of the most worthwhile projects in which I have ever been involved. Through our direct communication with addicts, former addicts, addicts in rehabilitation, and parents and students of all categories, we gained a tremendous education on the horrors of drug abuse, dependence, and addiction.

I will not go into the area of co-dependency to any great length at this stage, but it warrants a mention in so far as it is one of the most stagnating conditions that can afflict individuals. Unfortunately, because there is more than one person involved, and both are addicted, the problem may dwell in the world of unreality for many years before being exposed by a third party or by some extenuating circumstance. A classic example of co-dependency is the son who cannot let go of his mother's apron strings, and the mother who cannot let go of her son. The result is psychological chaos when the son decides to enter a marriage relationship.

We will deal with *habits* in greater detail at a later stage, but for the purpose of our awareness on this Plateau, we have to look at dependence in the broad light of our everyday behaviour, and that means observing our habits. We have the full spectrum of disorders from the mild habit of biting nails occasionally, to the chronic condition of Obsessive Compulsive Disorder (OCD). At one end of the spectrum, the problem is acute and can be dangerous, but it had to have its beginnings at the harmless end of the spectrum when it was considered to be just a nasty little bad habit. Dependence, which is developed through habitual indulgence, blocks progress! So become aware of, and clearly identify, any area of dependence on this Plateau, and start the elimination process.

You could be dependent on people, pills, drinks after work, talking on the phone, even attending meetings! There are so many types of dependence — emotional, psychological, physical, social, mental. But the bottom line is, do we allow ourselves to become slaves to our emotions, or are we "in control" of our appetites, desires and passions? To make real progress, we must become independent, and that means taking control of these desires. We have the mental, physical, emotional and spiritual capacity to be "in control" of our appetites, desires and passions. We are not animals, we are human beings with independent will. We don't need to follow instincts, we don't need to succumb to the pleasures of the flesh. It's generally the over-indulgence in any of these that creates the problem. Extremes are bad news. Even virtue, if taken to extremes, becomes a vice.

Having spoken to people in such organisations as Alcoholics Anonymous, Narcotics Anonymous, Gamblers Anonymous, etc., not one of these poor unfortunate people started out with the intention of becoming addicted. Their aim or goal in life was not to become an alcoholic, a junkie, or a gambler. It all started with the initial indulgence, which led to a gradual dependence, and eventually they were completely addicted.

Some Self-Check Questions

- Are you an emotional cripple, totally dependent upon regular *ego-massage* from friends and relations?

- Do you need synthetic stimulation to enjoy yourself?

- Are any of your habits addictive?

- Are you "in control" of your appetites, desires and passions?

- Do you make independent choices and decisions, or are you dependent on multiple sources of counsel first?

FAITH

The world's greatest leaders have all been propelled into their
positions of leadership, driven by the force of their absolute
faith in themselves, their vision and their capacity to achieve.

I listened to the famous racing driver, Jackie Stewart, being interviewed recently, and was quite surprised to hear him say that he left school at 14 as a failure. He went on to explain that he was dyslexic as a child, and in those early years that condition was not recognised or accepted as well as it is today, so he was considered to be a dunce, stupid, couldn't even read properly! However, he never thought of himself as stupid, and he worked his way up from lube-bay attendant, to assistant mechanic, then main mechanic, and suddenly he discovered his talent for racing cars. What a talent it turned out to be! Would you consider Jackie Stewart to be a failure?

It reminded me of the story of Evelynn Glennie, and I realised that these two people had one thing in common: they both had great faith in themselves. But what is this "faith" that we read and hear about? Faith is things hoped for and not yet seen. If we were given concrete proof of everything that we wished to believe in, there wouldn't be any need for faith. If Primo Levi, Victor Frankl, Jackie Stewart, Evelynn Glennie, Mahatma Gandhi, waited until they were shown the finished product before they embarked upon their noble and selfless pursuits, nothing would have been accomplished. But they all saw what could *possibly* be accomplished, or what they wished to accomplish, and they went forward in *faith*. They believed in themselves and in humanity.

I love the story about Harry Blondin, the French tightrope walker, who walked on a tightrope from the American to the Canadian side of Niagara Falls. At a convention I heard Dr Tony Campolo tell the story in his own inimitable style.

Walking the Tightrope

As Harry Blondin approached the Canadian side of the falls, the crowd was ecstatic as they cheered and shouted for this great feat of human endeavour – A man walking across Niagara Falls on a tightrope!

He shouted to the crowd as he landed on the Canadian side, "I am Harry Blondin, I have just walked across Niagara Falls on a tightrope from the American side to the Canadian side. Do you believe in me?"

There came an almighty roar from the crowd as they raised their voices in unison and said, "Yes, we believe in you!"

Then Blondin addressed his enthusiastic admirers again, and said, "I now propose to walk back from the Canadian side to the American side. Do you believe that I can do this?"

Once again the almost hysterical roar of the thousands of people assembled rose up with, "Yes, yes, we believe in you!"

With the crowd at fever pitch, Blondin once more addressed them, saying, "This time I will do it with somebody sitting on my shoulders. Do you believe that I can do this thing?"

With hands in the air, on the verge of hysterical collapse, waving their handkerchiefs, and with tears of excitement and elation streaming down their faces, the crowd in one enormous voice screamed, "Yes, Yes, Yes, we believe in you, we believe in you . . . Blondin, Blondin!"

At this exhilarating moment, Blondin looked into the crowd with searching eyes, and said, "Which one of you will be the volunteer?"

Absolute silence! Not a word, not a cheer, not a whimper, not even a smile. But the thoughts were probably going through their minds, something along these lines: "Is this guy serious, I mean is he for real, I mean, does he really expect me to trust him, and sit on his shoulders while he walks back along that tightrope . . . no way!"

The moral of the story is blatantly obvious. Thousands cheered and said "we believe", but when their *faith* was put to the test, they didn't really believe, because they couldn't put their faith in him. Just to put the record straight, one man did come forward, and he sat on Blondin's shoulders as he walked back across the tightrope. This man was his agent and he had absolute faith in his employer, Blondin. Thousands said they believed; only *one* man really believed. So think when next you say, "I believe". Do you only THINK you believe, or do you have real faith?

Faith without works is useless.

Put the faith to work with action. If you keep your faith to your-self, do nothing with it, and never translate it into action, then it will never be a source of inspiration or motivation in helping you to make progress. You must examine the basis of your faith, and be sure it is based upon some sort of truth and reality.

Is it based upon knowledge, experience or understanding? Sometimes the beliefs that we have are totally erroneous. As we already mentioned in the section on mental blocks, there are many times when we believe that we can't do something because of some fear based upon no foundation. We must subscribe to some belief system, to some code of practice, but the first exercise of our faith should be with ourselves. We must believe in ourselves. If you don't develop faith in yourself, you will never actualise your potential. You will be prevented from discovering the means of actualising that potential, because of your lack of faith.

A "high trust culture" is what many organisations continually strive to develop, and this high trust culture can only be achieved by exercising the principles we will discuss throughout this book. The political arena is overflowing with hidden agendas, which epitomises the low-trust culture synonymous with political argu-ment. However, trust will only come from faith, the faith we have in ourselves and in other human beings. How can we expect others to believe in us when we don't believe in ourselves? How can we expect others to trust us when we don't trust them? However, if you want trust, then you must be trustworthy. You must live by the principles and develop the qualities you expect to find in others. Faith can move mountains, so with faith you can easily remove many of the real and imaginary obstacles that stand in the way of your progress. We must build and develop our faith.

As we've seen in so many instances with successful people throughout history, their solid and unwavering faith in themselves became the powerful driving force that made them succeed. It's the strength of the faith you have in yourself and your ability that makes the dream become reality.

Some Self-Check Questions

- Do you believe in yourself, your talents and capabilities?

- Are you lacking in the faith you have in other people or organisations?

- On what is your faith based?

- At present are you buying into a high-trust or low-trust culture in your career?

CONDITIONING

Conditioning is the effect we allow external forces, situations and suggestions to have upon us, whether consciously or unconsciously, in shaping and developing our thoughts, actions, habits, character and attitudes.

The principle of proactivity, which we will discuss in greater detail during Plateau Two, is epitomised in the adage, "To act, and not be acted upon". But for the purpose of awareness on this plateau, we will focus upon the second part of that statement, being "acted upon". We often talk about good or bad conditions, and how children can be conditioned by certain types of environment or situations. But in today's world, we are constantly being subjected to conditioning, either consciously or subliminally. Whenever we turn on the television, we are bombarded with advertisements telling us what we should buy, where we should go, what we should do, what's good for us, what's bad for us. All of this can be accepted or rejected, according to the degree of control we have over ourselves, and how susceptible we are to suggestion.

Ivan Pavlov, the famous Russian physiologist, developed the theory of "Classical Conditioning", through his stimulus and response experiments with dogs. Pavlov would sound a tuning fork and then he would present the dog with some food. Initially the dog would salivate only when it saw the food. But, after repeated procedures, the dog began to salivate as soon as it heard the sound of the tuning fork. Eventually, Pavlov just sounded the tuning fork, but gave no food to the dog, but the dog still salivated. The dog was "classically conditioned" to salivate upon hearing the sound of the tuning fork.

If we look once again at the physical dimension, we can easily illustrate the principle of conditioning by observing the body builder who conditions his body with regular scientifically formulated exercise routines. But conditioning occurs on the physical, mental and emotional dimensions, and very often things like market fluctuations can have a severe effect upon our condition.

Anthony Robbins uses a technique called Neuro Associative Conditioning Syndrome (NACS), which is a method of eliminating the desire for something by thinking of all the negative and distasteful things associated with that desire. The system is apparently very successful in many cases, and would seem to be particularly applicable to addictions such as smoking or bulimia. But essentially it is a process of conditioning the mind to follow a certain behavioural pattern.

> *"Seek not to control; seek to be in control"*
> — Taoist Proverb

As human beings with intelligence, we need to be "in control" of ourselves and select the conditioning in our lives. We must avoid negative conditioning and develop a system of positive conditioning. In other words, use the principle of conditioning to our advantage. We have to exercise principles and practices in our lives that will enable us to be "in control" of our lives, and not be distracted or pushed off the track. In living by these principles, we start to *recondition* and mould ourselves into the types of people we want to become. It's a question of learning how to *respond* to situations.

The following very sad story which I heard will help to illustrate the need to go through this process of repetition, in order to develop an "Automatic Conditioned Response".

Automatic Conditioned Response

In the airforce they have a simulated training exercise which conditions the pilots in how to respond to emergency situations in the air. This conditioning exercise takes place twice weekly and lasts for an entire afternoon. But one of the trainee pilots was also on the airforce basketball team. He convinced the sergeant in charge to excuse him from this particular exercise, because of his need to practise basketball for the forthcoming championship match. He also explained that he had already done this exercise about ten times, so he believed that he was sufficiently familiar with it. The sergeant agreed, and the pilot was excused from the exercise.

Unfortunately, some time later, in the course of an air mission, this pilot's plane was hit. In the few minutes that followed the hit, he went into shock and panic. He was frantically calling out for instructions on what he should do, but in this situation it was seconds that counted!

Because he was unable to remember the precise instructions he had received in the simulated training, his plane crashed, and he was killed. In the moment of combat, and having been hit, he was not in a normal frame of mind, he was not able to think calmly and rationally. He could only rely upon whatever "Automatic Conditioned Response" he had developed. There was no time to think, ponder or evaluate; his response had to be Automatic, Conditioned, and Immediate!

We must develop automatic conditioned responses through the repetitive exercise of correct principles.

In martial arts training, music practice and many other art forms, the principle of repetition to develop a technique is widely used. To benefit from this Plateau, you must identify the areas in your life where you are conditioned negatively, and concentrate upon actively reconditioning yourself positively in order to respond automatically to situations. This is a process of refinement, just like tempered steel in a steel refinery. We must learn to be in good physical, spiritual, mental and emotional condition.

If you are living daily by correct principles and following a code of ethical conduct, then you will not be easily tempted to do something that you would regret. This element of conditioning is a character-building exercise. It creates people of integrity who can rise above the mundane and live by a higher law. This type of person doesn't wake up every morning having to make decisions about their conduct. The decisions have already been made through living correct principles.

For example, if you were propositioned by a colleague to engage in an extra-marital affair, you shouldn't have to think about what decision to make! You should never have to think, "Gosh, will I have an affair?" or "Should I cheat that man out of his money?" or "Will I neglect my family duties, and go off drinking for the rest of the day?" You don't wake up every morning, and think, "I wonder will I kill, rob, or maim anybody today?" But it's only by reinforcing these tiny decisions that you make each day that the conditioning takes place, and you develop an Automatic Conditioned Response. A few lines from Dorothy Law Nolte's beautiful poem illustrate the point:

> *"If a child lives with criticism, he will learn to condemn . . .*
> *If a child lives with fear, he learns to be apprehensive . . .*
> *If a child lives with encouragement, he learns to be confident . . .*
> *If a child lives with acceptance, he learns to love . . ."*
> — Dorothy Law Nolte

Consider for a moment how we create an environment for our children, and how our conduct within that environment is a major part of that conditioning process. Are we aware of how our behaviour affects others, and how we are part of their conditioning? The poem by Dorothy Law Nolte highlights the conditions we should strive to create, and also those we should try to avoid, if we wish our children to be conditioned in a positive way that will help them to grow and develop.

This not only applies to children, but to every member of our family, our workmates, and everyone with whom we interact socially. How we treat other people can have a lasting effect upon them and can be a major conditioning factor in their lives. We must learn to accept responsibility for our actions and behaviours, and therefore we should behave responsibly.

Some Self-Check Questions

- Are you aware of the various conditioning factors in your workplace, during leisure pursuits, among your family?

- Have you developed any Automatic Conditioned Response in your life through living by correct principles?

- Do you consider yourself to be a factor in the conditioning process that your work associates and family are experiencing through exposure to your behaviour and example?

- Do you base your decisions upon principles or on other people's opinions?

- Are you "in control" of some or many areas of your life?

VALUES

A monetary tag on our values does not adequately reflect their true value, which is determined by the amount of integrity, peace of mind and joy that they bring to our lives. Our true values are what matter most in our lives and should be the major determinants in how we prioritise our time.

We're coming now to the very core and foundation on which we are going to build in the future — our values! It's futile to even consider an approach to Plateau Two until you have firmly identified your values. So what is a value and what do you value?

A value is really something of great worth, something that gives meaning to your life, something that gives you a sense of direction, that can make you prioritise, something that drives you to rise to greater heights. Not to be confused with principles, because two people can have the same values, but adhere to different codes of practice and principles.

Let's take the scenario of a widowed mother of five children.

Principles are not Values

This good woman has two teenage sons who absolutely idolise her and value her as a mother, a guardian, a comforter and protector, and they both have a tremendous love for their mother. They are conscious of the need to provide for her basic comforts in life, but unfortunately there is a grave shortage of money to provide for these comforts. One son goes out at dawn to work hard for an honest day's pay — exercising the principle of work, honesty, diligence and awareness of his mother's needs. The other son doesn't subscribe to these principles, but with the same values in his mind he goes off to rob a bank in order to provide for his mother's welfare.

They both had the same values, but opposite sets of principles. Can't you see how important it is to adopt a proper code of conduct, based upon correct principles, in order to conform responsibly to your values? *The end does not justify the means!*

Your future vision (which will be discussed on Plateau Two) is based on your values, which act as anchors in turbulent waters. When the storms of life come, and the tempests rage, our values anchor us firmly and keep us on track. Values become like a compass, a moral compass to direct and guide us through these troubled waters.

In the corporate sector, we hear a lot about vision/values and mission statements, but our values are something we have to live, not just state! Our values become an integral part of our existence; they *are* the core of our existence.

For example, do you put a high value on the relationship you have with your spouse, your partner or your friends? If you do value these relationships highly, are you constantly protecting them or do you allow them to stagnate or to be exposed to precarious situations that could jeopardise them? Your true values should be reflected in your daily behaviour and the decisions that you make. But if you don't identify your values, you will be neglecting to secure a firm foundation on which to build.

When we lose something, we often refer to it as having "sentimental value", which means that, although we miss the item dreadfully, we don't miss the monetary value of the thing. We have family values, social values, community values, and we must become aware of exactly what we value in our lives. Unfortunately, in many corporate mission statements, the priorities do not reflect the true values that should be at the core of the corporation.

Once you start to identify and live by your values, you begin to provide a protective boundary for yourself, which will dictate your behaviour and also provide a line beyond which you will not go. Conversely, it allows you to have your own space, because *you* decide who or what can infringe upon your territory, or come within your boundaries. The richness and quality of our lives is determined more by what we value than by what we have.

Some Self-Check Questions

- What do you value?

- Do you value money, job, friendship, loyalty, relationships, talents, qualities?

- Do you value your time, your employees, your special relationships?

ATTITUDES

The ability to change and adapt one's attitude to situations,
people, problems and circumstances is a clear sign of great
emotional and mental maturity. Conversely, the inability to
change and adapt one's attitude denotes stubbornness,
blinkered vision, laziness and immaturity.

Someone once wrote that attitudes are more important than facts, and when you consider the role of attitudes in your personal development, you can understand what he was saying. Man is the only known creature who can reshape and remould himself by altering his attitude.

"Attitudes are nothing more than habits of thought
— and habits can be acquired."
— John C. Maxwell

We can approach situations in life with a positive or negative attitude, or worse still with an indifferent attitude. How we approach it will be a major factor in determining what we get out of the situation. Remember the closed mind attitude I talked about? It becomes increasingly difficult to develop accurate perspectives if we constantly look on situations with a jaundiced attitude. How can we develop fresh perspectives, or gain any sort of edification, if we're coming from a totally negative attitude? Our perception and understanding of situations can be severely distorted if we adopt the wrong attitude in our approach.

When we interview someone for a job, we endeavour to ascertain that person's attitude, because their attitude will be a major determining factor of their suitability for the job in question. We try to gauge their level of aggression, apathy, moodiness, whether they have a positive or negative approach, are they reactionary or responsive, etc. Their attitude can be the determining factor to convince us that they would fit in with the company ethos.

A simple example of attitude is the optimist and the pessimist. The optimist considers the glass to be half full of water, while the pessimist considers the glass to be half empty. The optimist looks out through the window and admires the beautiful sunrise, while the pessimist sees the stains on the window. J.D. Salinger's book, *There Must Be A Pony*, is a delightful and humorous story about the difference between an optimist and a pessimist. Are you aware of your attitude?

You are where you are and what you are
because of the dominating thoughts that occupy your mind.

We should make great efforts to develop the famous PMA (Positive Mental Attitude), and this we can do by adapting our behaviour to correspond with our values.

I remember when I worked in the music industry, the most common cause for dismissing personnel from bands was bad attitudes. You can imagine when 12 people are travelling together, working in such close proximity, staying overnight, eating, travelling, working and sleeping together, the amount of tolerance for someone's poor attitude would become very minimal.

During my time as a financial consultant, I remember having a top producing consultant on one of my teams. However, because of his atrocious attitude to the rest of the team, it became necessary to dismiss the individual, even though his production record was superb. The rest of the team found that he was affecting their peace of mind and the general atmosphere in the team.

We must maintain a very healthy vigilance on our attitudes, because the weeds, or diseases of attitude, can easily creep in to destroy our positive mental attitude. Sometimes it can only take a few words from an inconsiderate colleague to change our attitudes. We mustn't allow this to happen. Constantly endeavour to develop a strong, enthusiastic, positive and open attitude to life.

Some Self-check Questions

- Do you have a good attitude?

- Are you capable of adapting your attitude?

- How do others view your attitude?

- What do you do to develop a positive mental attitude?

LEADERSHIP

"Leadership is the ability to get a man to do what you want him to do, when you want it done, in a way that you want it done, because he wants to do it."
— Dwight D. Eisenhower

I could write a book on this topic alone, and in fact this book is all about the development of that great quality — *leadership*. People become leaders by *leading*, taking the initiative, sticking their necks out and going for it! The question is often asked: "Are leaders born or made?" I believe many people are born with natural leadership abilities, which they can decide to develop or ignore. But, just as people can also be born with great musical talent, swimming talent, artistic talent, it doesn't stop other people learning and developing those same skills. They may never develop them to the same high level of being an artist, but in the process of learning the skill, their lives will be greatly stimulated and improved.

Leadership is not a word on which I like to put too rigid a definition, because I consider it to be an amalgam of many qualities, exercised in a responsible and compassionate manner. You could have the potential to become the greatest leader of all time, but unless you do something to create a catalyst to actualise that potential, it will remain just that — potential.

> *"One of our most important success needs is*
> *for someone to make us do what we can."*
> — Ralph Waldo Emerson

There are many great leaders in the world, and I often refer to the famous Genghis Khan and the Mongol hordes. Initially, the impression most people have of this man, and his great armies, is of wild, ferocious, savage human beings who, with blood-curdling screams, attacked and plundered village after village! But these warriors had the remarkable qualities of being *swift, silent* and *skilful*. Genghis Khan recognised that among his people, who were downtrodden at that time, there existed tremendous talents. But they were a divided nation, and they were neither inspired nor motivated by anyone. To change things for the better, and subsequently have such a profound affect upon the world at that time, he *judged* their talents, he *united* them, and he *inspired* them. He was a man of *vision*, as all great leaders are men and women of vision.

But the vision has to come from values and a critical awareness of situations as they now stand.

- Do you accurately and fairly *judge the talents* of your workforce?

- Do you endeavour to *unite them* to create greater synergy in your team?

- Do you *inspire them* by your example, your encouragement and your vision?

It is *leaders* who stick their necks out, who accept responsibility, who take the risks, who inspire confidence in their workforces, who encourage and show the way, and who are ultimately *accountable*.

Developing leadership involves acquiring the means with which to best deal with people, circumstances, situations and future events in our lives. The future is something we can try to ignore, predict and even control in some instances. But ultimately, we must learn the leadership skill of *responding* to it as it comes. Leadership is the *human dimension* of every organisation; it is concerned with *people*. However, it's impossible to lift someone up unless you're already up there yourself. There's an old Chinese proverb which says,

> *"What is above knows what is below,*
> *but what is below cannot know what is above."*

You cannot know what it's like at the top of the mountain until you have gone through the gruelling experience of actually climbing the mountain. Nobody just lands on top of a mountain, they have to climb there.

In the light of everything you have read during this chapter, it should be obvious to you that the road to happiness, self-fulfilment and excellence demands the inculcating of leadership qualities into your attitude, thinking, behaviour and approach to every situation.

Good leadership is all about offering opinions, contributing to the solution of the problem, effective delegation and making decisions. Every leader should employ the five key elements of effective leadership — *Faith, Focus, Decision, Example, Commitment*. The boss says, "Do this!" The leader says, "Let's do it this way." The leader takes the initiative, encourages and offers praise for a job well done, and shows faith in others by delegating. While people sit around and criticise, the leader will do something about the situation.

Good leadership in action is a joy to behold, but there are also innumerable examples of poor leadership. These are the people who should never have been placed in positions of leadership. Poor leadership is recognised by its secretive administration, and protective territorial procedures. Poor leaders want to do everything themselves, partly because they want to receive all the glory, and partly because they are afraid to delegate. They manifest their lack of faith in their staff, never offer encouragement or praise, they are over-critical, make unfair judgements, and cannot make decisions. This is how the low-trust culture and the "them-versus-us" syndrome develop. A leader should exude confidence, but the bad qualities of poor leadership are all examples of insecurity and fear, which stifle growth and development.

A beautiful quote from an unknown author puts it very concisely and succinctly:

> *"Leaders need to submit themselves to a stricter discipline*
> *than is expected of others. Those who are first in place*
> *must be first in merit."*

Contrary to many of the false notions that exist among many people in senior management positions, it is a leader's responsibility to encourage and train subordinates to be in a competent position to take over their position. The old-fashioned practice of "protecting my patch" does not make for a high-trust culture, and certainly doesn't encourage leadership development.

> *"The real qualities of leadership are found in those who are*
> *willing to sacrifice for the sake of objectives great enough*
> *to demand their whole-hearted allegiance. Simply holding*
> *a position of leadership does not make a man a leader ...*
> *if you would be a real leader you must endure loneliness ...*
> *if you would be a real leader you must endure weariness.*
> *Leadership requires vision."*
> — Clarence Scharer

The quality of management depends to a very large degree upon the qualities of leadership within the management. So often, we hear tremendous affirmations being expounded in management seminars, but affirmation without discipline and application is a sure recipe for delusion. The Total Quality Management movement must, by its very nature, seek to incorporate leadership qualities and skills, otherwise the organisations become top heavy with efficiency at the expense of effectiveness, which eventually leads to dissatisfaction among the workforce.

The following chart indicates some of the more obvious things a leader should and shouldn't do.

Good Leaders . . .

Do:	Don't:
Encourage	Discourage
Praise	Ridicule
Support	Humiliate
Accept	Reject
Build up	Put down
Sustain	Frustrate
Empathise	Dismiss
Inspire	
Unite	
Lead by example	

Some Self-Check Questions

- Do you take the initiative, and lead?

- Do you offer encouragement and praise to your staff?

- Are you receptive to opinions and contributions from your subordinates?

- Can you delegate effectively?

- Have you developed the skill of making decisions?

- Do you inspire your subordinates?

- Do you lead by example?

ASSIGNMENTS FOR PLATEAU ONE

The purpose of these five sample assignments is to heighten your self-awareness and help you to more fully understand the principles discussed in this chapter by becoming involved through the practical application of those principles.

1. Identify one mental block of which you are aware, and evaluate how it is stopping you from making progress. Consider methods of eliminating this mental block or false assumption from your mind through heightened awareness of its presence, and by consciously altering your attitude, thought patterns or behaviour.

2. At this early stage in your progression, take time to identify your real values in life, and list your top five values as you see them at this present time.

3. Choose one physical activity suitable to your lifestyle that would enhance your physical fitness, and start doing it daily. Don't be vague or disorganised about this exercise, but draw up a schedule for the daily accomplishment of this task and to monitor your progress.

4. Start keeping a daily journal, and record your feelings as you implement the principles discussed in this book. This journal will be an invaluable resource as you endeavour to monitor your physical, mental, emotional and spiritual development. As an exercise in heightening your self-awareness and increasing your rate of progress, record in your daily journal any occasion that helped to increase the chasm of unhappiness in your life, or any conscious effort you made to bridge the chasm.

5. With regard to attitudes, faith, conditioning and open-mindedness, identify areas in your life that need a shift of focus or change of behaviour to enable you to develop the leadership qualities necessary for real progress. Don't just think about these situations; write them down, evaluate them, and then examine ways in which you can alter the situations.

In order to derive the maximum benefit from this chapter, you should be actively engaged in doing these assignments for a minimum of one week before proceeding to Plateau Two.

Answer to Figure 8

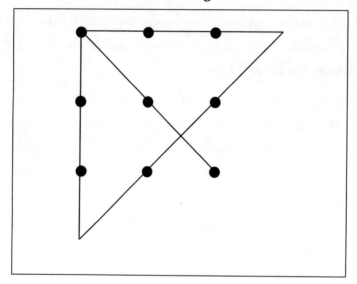

2

Plateau Two
VISION

"Some people see things as they are and say why?
I dream things that never were, and say why not."
— George Bernard Shaw

In Chapter One we talked about leadership qualities and how leaders are people with vision. Leaders are those who have a vision of how things could be and strive towards making that vision a reality. When people have no vision, it is similar to the "closed mind" syndrome. It's the lack of imagination, visualisation, and being able to paint the picture, which leaves that person without a picture of their preferred future.

If you only look at what is, you might never attain what could be.

Vision is "where you would like to be", and it follows on from Plateau One, where you found out "where you were at". Having ascertained your starting point on the map, it is now time to haul in the anchor and set sail on the voyage. How can you possibly encourage people to follow you and buy into your ideas, unless you have a vision of where you want to go?

Some years ago, a young woman attended one of my courses, and I asked her what she wanted to be in life. She replied that this was the reason why she was on the course, because she didn't know what she wanted to be. Unfortunately, she was looking for someone to tell her what she should be, but she was not prepared to search her own mind to find out what she would like to be. Hers was very much a passive participation on the course.

Vision is a mandatory leadership quality. The leader should be in the position of leadership because of his or her ability to capture the vision of how things could be and to convince the others to join in helping to make that vision a reality. Having the vision is one thing, but the ability to share that vision demands leadership skills. If the chief executive of a corporation has a vision of where that corporation will be in the future, he or she must develop the ability to make that vision a "shared vision". They have to drive that vision right down the line to the ground floor of the corporation. It's only when the rest of the corporation captures this vision that the vision starts becoming a reality.

We will be covering quite a few topics in this chapter relating to vision, but the purpose of this chapter is to illustrate how important it is to be able to capture the vision of how things can be for you in the future, to strive towards that vision, and to use it as a guiding light as you try to stay on the path of progress.

But you need to *use* every talent and skill that you've got. One of the most important things to use on this Plateau is your *imagination* and the power to *create a vision* of *where* you want to be, *what* you want to be, and what you want to *have* in the future.

The right side of our brain is called the intuitive or creative side. We must try to activate that side of our brain to paint pictures, and to create a picture of how our future could look. The expectations we have of ourselves have a lot to do with this. Remember the theory of the "self-fulfilling prophecy"? We need to rise to the occasion of our own great expectations of ourselves. We need to tell ourselves that we *can* do it! Don't ever underestimate the power of your dreams. You have the capacity to turn your dreams into reality, provided you never lose sight of that vision.

"Where there is no vision, the people perish."
— Proverbs 29:18

Some Self-Check Questions

- Are you content with where you are at the present time?

- Do you feel you have actualised your potential yet?

- Have you achieved everything that you set out to achieve in your career?

- Are you at the top of the ladder in your career, or have you arrived at your point of satisfaction?

- Have you got everything you ever wanted out of life, or is there more that you would like to have?

THE HUMAN MIND

The amount of success we have in achieving and accomplishing our goals and aspirations is in direct proportion to the level of development in our mental capacity to overcome, to press forward and to be "in control" of our thought processes.

There are so many theories and hypotheses about the mind, that at times it becomes an absolute maze of confusion. In spite of all the knowledge and studies about the mind, we still know relatively little about its workings. However, we do know some important things about the mind which can have a serious effect upon how we survive in this world. We know that it is a powerful force, that within it we find the personality of the individual, the willpower and the ability to overcome many physical aspects of life — "mind over matter". You can do anything, if you've a mind to!

Sigmund Freud's theory of the three divisions of the mind is interesting, but only insofar as it gives a possible insight into identification of aspects of the mind. We are really more interested in how we can increase the mind power, and use it more effectively for making progress. Freud divides it thus:

- *The Id* — The basic raw pleasure principle.

- *The Ego* — The reality principle of control, decisions, etc.

- *The Super Ego* — A type of moral conscience which balances the other two.

It's nice to have a knowledge of these theories and hypotheses, but in relation to this Plateau of Vision, the primary consideration is in trying to create a mental picture of where you want to be, and to use your mental powers to solidify this concept. The vision is first created in the mind. Everything begins with the thought, and the thought lies in the mind. The thought is father to the deed. How well you control your thoughts will determine how successful you are in making your vision a reality. The growth of an oak tree begins with a tiny acorn. If you consider your thoughts as the acorn, and capture the vision of how great the oak tree can become, then you can make that acorn grow into a mighty oak tree.

On Plateau One, we dealt primarily with the conscious mind, the initial awareness. But the subconscious mind can sometimes hide a tremendous amount of information that we don't really want to face. The mental dimension plays a major part in our development and growth, and in relation to the mind it is important to realise that besides the conscious and subconscious sections, there is also the creative subconscious mind. This area relates to the Super Ego that Freud talks about, and I believe that this is the connecting link between the mind and the heart. This is the channel through which the spiritual dimension exercises its potential.

A similar division of the mind could be as follows:

Conscious – Subconscious – Creative Subconscious

Perhaps a mention of the "subliminal learning" system might be worth a mention at this stage. Subliminal acquisition of knowledge or information is where the information bypasses the conscious mind and goes directly to the subconscious mind.

In our conscious state, we are aware of so much more than the things upon which we are directly focused. For example, while we are engaged in conversation with an individual during a social function, we are also aware of the fact that there are many other conversations going on all around us. Food and drink are being served by waiters and waitresses. There is music playing in the background, and people are entering and leaving the function all the time. The temperature in the room is warm, the decor is quite ornate, the pictures hanging on the wall are all of a particular style, the carpet underfoot is of fine quality, etc.

We automatically absorb so much more information than we realise. The recognition of this fact has prompted the creation of audiocassette tapes, which are produced through a process of multi-layered recording of positive affirmations and directions. It is claimed that you can use these tapes to learn while you sleep, or even just have them playing in the office during work hours. They are based upon the principle that the sounds will penetrate to the subconscious mind, without the need for the conscious mind to actually listen to or study the information. But when this process is structured into subliminal learning tapes it becomes an active attempt to bypass the conscious mind and go directly to the subconscious mind. This does not conform to the law of the harvest — "you reap what you sow" — but rather it falls into the area of "quick-fix solutions". You want to learn, but you don't want to go through the effort of working for the information. This is really a mild type of "brain-washing". The principle of "effort and reward" is crucial to making real progress in every dimension of our being.

I believe that the more we exercise our minds through intellectual stimulation, the greater the increase in our mental capacity. So much of today's learning procedures and so-called educational games are directed at the more passive side of our learning abilities. There is a vast difference between reading a good book and watching the film version of the same book. They are different types of stimuli. The process of reading is intellectually stimulating through active visualisation, the bringing to life of the characters, trying to understand them, giving them form and structure, etc. In order to bring the characters to life, we have to use our imaginations. But watching television is very often a more passive form of stimulation, where much of the intellectual work has already been done for us. Which activity do you imagine would be the most beneficial to the growth and development of your mental capacity?

Some Self-Check Questions

- Are you continuously striving to develop your imagination?

- Does the subconscious mind take over at times and cause you to indulge in daydreaming?

- How do you stimulate your mind?

POTENCY AND ACT

Some of our greatest talents, qualities and skills may never be realised until we expand, explore and stretch ourselves in every dimension, to find the catalyst that will ignite the dormant potential that lies waiting to be actualised.

We're constantly being told to "actualise our potential". But what does it really mean? Let's look at the word potential. It comes from the Latin word *potens*, which means power, and that's exactly what it is — the dormant power within ourselves. Potential means that there is an ability or capability for power. But until such time as you discover the catalyst that will release that power, it will lie dormant. The word act means to move, to effect, to take action. In the theory of potency and act, the potency cannot be utilised without action.

Take the example of a washing machine. A washing machine has the potential to wash clothes. But in order to actualise that potential, two things have to happen. The washing machine has to be plugged into the power socket, and then it has to be switched on. Consider Plateau One as the plugging into the wall-socket. This means you have the connection, you know where you're at.

But unless you "switch on", the potential lies dormant. Wouldn't it be a shame to leave a beautifully efficient washing machine plugged into the wall socket without ever turning it on?

What is the catalyst that will actualise *your* potential? Is it the person pressing the switch? Is it someone who knows how to press all the right buttons to make you respond? The amazing thing about the human being is the fact that we have the ability within ourselves to actualise our own potential, without the need for any outside influence. When we come to discuss the spiritual dimension in great detail, you will more fully understand this, but suffice to say that we can use our mental and spiritual dimensions to kick-start us into the process of actualising our own potential.

Your "vision" is what will help you to actualise your potential, and it will also help you to recognise and define your potential. In trying to reach your vision, and make it a reality, you will have to avail of every resource within yourself. Learn to recognise your own potential, and don't be negative or dismissive about your talents or abilities. However, unless you expand your horizons and push your boundaries, through experimentation, risk taking, and involvement, you will never learn to recognise your true talents and capabilities.

> *It is better to attempt something great, and fail,*
> *than to attempt nothing, and succeed.*

You will never know how good you are at anything until you try it. Think of what you consider to be your best talent or skill, and then ask yourself how you developed it to its present level. Somewhere along the line you had to begin with attempting, trying it out, and eventually you realised you had a particular flair for it, and you developed it. Use the same principle to discover all the other hidden talent and potential that you have! I love the Nike slogan — "Just Do It!"

Many years ago in the music industry I had occasion to employ a roadie to travel on the road with a touring band. This man was about thirty years of age, he was extremely competent in the area of sound and electronic equipment, and was generally considered to be an "ace roadie". He had developed his talent and ability to a very high level of competency, because it was the only job he had ever known. However, he went on holidays to Sweden for a winter break. During his time there, he decided to try his hand at skiing. The ski instructor asked him if he was an experienced skier, but the roadie explained that he had never even worn a pair of skis in his life. When the instructor watched him ski down the mountainside so skilfully, for his very first time, he was amazed at the natural talent that this man possessed. Three weeks later, he had given up his job as roadie and had become a full-time trainee ski instructor. To the best of my knowledge. he is still gainfully employed in that occupation. But if he had never ventured onto the ski slope, he would never have known the immense talent that he possessed in that area.

Some Self-Check Questions

- Do you feel that you are actualising your potential?
- Have you identified your potential in various areas of your life?
- Do you regularly expand your horizons and push your boundaries in an effort to discover your own potential?

PROACTIVITY

*Proactivity is more than just engaging in a project. It means
being actively involved in taking initiatives, reaching out, and
exploring ways to effect a successful conclusion to the exercise.*

As a natural progression from Potency and Act, we come to the
tremendous principle of proactivity. Once again the old Latin
comes to mind in dissecting the word, because the word "pro"
means "for" in Latin. The word proactivity really means "for activity", as opposed to "against activity", reactivity or simply pas-
sivity. We can allow our behaviour to be continuously conditioned
and restricted by external forces, or we can use our own initiative
and take the first step. "Behold the turtle, who only makes progress by sticking his neck out." We can be acted upon, or we can
act. "To act and not be acted upon" is activity in top gear, or the
principle of proactivity.

Every great leader was proactive; proactivity is one of the fundamental requirements of good leadership. The lethargic individual who sits back and waits for things to come will never make a
leader. Proactivity means taking the initiative, the first step, sticking your neck out, seeking positive alternatives, and just doing it.
In your language and actions, are you proactive or reactive? Instead of reacting with, "There's nothing I can do about that", do
you take the proactive approach and say, "Let's see if we can do
this another way"?

We have already mentioned conditioning in Chapter One, but,
in relation to the stimulus/response experiments, we must always
remember that we are human beings endowed with great intelligence, imagination, conscience and free will. We have the freedom
of choice. We don't have to follow any given path. We must

choose which path we take, but that choice only becomes a reality when we develop the principle of proactivity in our lives. In many instances, this will mean exercising the principle of faith, which we discussed in Chapter One, but sometimes you must take that step in faith!

How many times have you been in situations where people sit around complaining about the bad conditions, but as soon as a mention of doing something to change the condition is brought up, the old, "It's not my job", or "That wouldn't work", refrain is sounded? Corporate meetings can sometimes become most repetitive when the same problems keep presenting themselves for solutions. Effective use of the art of delegation, job description, teaching by example, and decision-making, could make life so much easier. All of these are proactive qualities and fundamental to the development of leadership skills.

Proactivity means forging ahead and getting the job done. The only way to write a book is to write it, the only way to dig a hole is to dig it, the only way to do anything is to get involved in the activity of actually doing it, working it and accomplishing it.

Some Self-Check Questions

- Are you proactive in your behaviour?

- Do you tend to take a passive interest in projects, or do you become actively engaged in using your own initiative?

- Do your activities engender proactivity or do you always play it safe?

- How have you developed your capacity for proactivity?

Dreams

"The future belongs to those who believe in
the beauty of their dreams."
— Eleanor Roosevelt

When I talk of "dreams" here, I am not referring to sleeping dreams or daydreaming, but rather to a graphically real vision/ dream of how things could be. Let me reiterate the importance of thoughts at this point, because dreams are really just great big thoughts. Take a look at the flow-chart in Figure 9, which demonstrates the progression from thoughts to character.

FIGURE 9: FROM THOUGHTS TO CHARACTER

Thoughts ➡ Action ➡ Habits ➡ Character

You are where you are and what you are
because of the dominating thoughts that occupy your mind.

Every time I talk about dreams in my seminars and courses, I show the video clip of Martin Luther King giving his famous dream speech. "I have a dream," he thundered! It illustrates in audio-visual format the conviction that this man had to his dream. But how many of us are so powerfully proactive about our dreams? The vision you have is your picture of what you would like to see happen in your life in the future. But this vision begins with a thought, and that thought grows into a dream, and that dream will form the basic drive for all of your actions in the future, if you nurture it, encourage it and don't neglect or abandon it.

Do you ever hear of great pioneers, explorers, mountain climbers and space explorers talk about their achievements as if it was just something they suddenly decided to do?

"Gosh, I think I'll go climb Mount Everest today!"

Of course not; these great feats of human endurance had their origins in the thoughts of these great people and then they became dreams. And only then did they become the driving forces that pushed them onwards and upwards to achieve that vision, to make that dream a reality.

However, the dream will remain just a dream unless it moves onto the next stage — the action that makes that dream come true. To realise a dream, you must exercise the principle of proactivity, take the step, devise a plan and make the dream come true.

Beware of the "dream-stealers" who lurk behind filing cabinets and appear at the table in conference rooms! You're familiar with that noxious breed of individual who vents his or her own inadequacies, frustrations and insecurities upon anybody who seems to be striving to achieve anything. The typical exclamations from these dream-stealers would be something like, "You must be crazy, that would never work"; "Don't tell anyone you're thinking of doing that, they'll only laugh at you"; "Not at all, I tried that myself, it's impossible". All solid negative conditioning! Positive, constructive criticism is always welcome, because it sharpens our skills. But negative, destructive criticism has no value.

We mustn't allow ourselves to be conditioned by these negative forces. Isn't it easy to see how easily our children can be negatively conditioned by such comments? That's why we must spend time with our children, talk with them and try to discover their dreams. Then we must encourage those dreams, build on those dreams, and help them to make those dreams a reality.

> *"Sow an act, and you reap a habit.*
> *Sow a habit, and you reap a character.*
> *Sow a character, and you reap a destiny."*
> — Charles Reade

I couldn't leave this section on dreams without mentioning the word sacrifice. The ability to adopt the principle of singularity of purpose is particularly important in relation to making dreams come true, in realising the ambition that is built into the dream. The law of the harvest — "You reap what you sow" — is poignantly applicable to making dreams come true, because of the amount of sacrifice and self-denial required.

The lack of self-sacrifice is what stops most people from becoming the people they are capable of becoming and of actualising their true potential. Sacrifice is very often the principle of foregoing the pleasure of the moment for the joy of the future. Take the example of a student studying to become a lawyer. He or she knows that there are many years of diligent study required to pass the exams and obtain that degree. So it means that there will be many times when his or her friends may be going off for long leisure weekends of golf or skiing, but they have to stay home and study. But sacrifice brings forth the blessings. The student has to learn to focus on the end result of these long hours of studying, the tremendous growth in knowledge and understanding of the legal system, and ultimately a successful career as a lawyer.

What makes great leaders? Surely they don't have to be involved in the mundane incidentals that we have to endure? Well that's exactly how most of them came to become great leaders, by doing the mundane and apparently insignificant things. It's by doing the little things well, by enduring the awkward and inconvenient moments, and by taking care of the small details, that leaders develop their acumen, knowledge and wisdom to lead. Sacrifice is a major part of leadership at every level. There is a price tag on everything in this life. "There are no free lunches!" If you want to pass an exam, then you must pay the price of sacrificing that afternoon of golf for study. But the secret of achieving success and making dreams come true is to make that dream such a powerfully dominant and driving force in your life that it becomes the foremost objective of every activity in your life — to bring the dream closer to reality. When we come to Plateau Five, Commitment, you will realise the importance of having dreams. Commitment is built on dreams.

Happy is the man who has a dream,
and is willing to pay the price to make that dream come true.

Some Self-Check Questions

- What are your dreams?
- Do you encourage your children, your colleagues, and your staff to have dreams, and to build on those dreams?
- Are your dreams vivid, or just vague notions?
- Are you trying to make your dream a reality, and is your dream a powerful driving force in your life?
- Are you willing to make sacrifices in the short term so that your dreams can come true in the future?

BEHAVIOURAL BLOCKS

If your progress is blocked by some physical object or force,
it is your responsibility to seek ways of removing the
obstruction, or finding an alternative route. But when

your own behaviour becomes the source of the blockage,
you have the power to remove that obstacle to your progress,
simply by changing that behaviour.

In Chapter One, we talked about the mental blocks and false assumptions that can hinder your progress. But, as we work on this Plateau of Vision, we must also address a more tangible obstacle that can become a block, and that is our *behaviour*. I came across a marvellous book some time ago called *Eliminate Your SDBs* by Jonathan M. Chamberlain. The SDBs refer to "self-defeating behaviours". Our behaviour can be a major obstacle that we sometimes unconsciously allow to restrict our progress. We can have the greatest intentions in the world, and draw up the most meticulous plans. But, due to a particular behavioural trait or habit, we just never get around to bringing those plans to fruition.

Do you recognise anything in your behaviour that could be an obstacle? Let me take a simple concrete example of the person trying to lose weight. This individual has drawn up an excellent workout routine, joined a gym, devised a diet plan, enrolled in the local slimming club and has the greatest expectations of achieving the desired weight-loss. However, at eleven o'clock each morning, everyone in the office meets in the canteen for a cup of coffee and a chat. But this canteen boasts the most delicious selection of cream cakes imaginable, and our dieter is absolutely addicted to cream cakes! Instead of avoiding the canteen every morning, at least until some of the weight starts to come off, this dieter religiously joins the group every morning, and indulges in just two cream cakes (instead of the usual five). On the one hand, the plans and aspirations are in place, but on the other hand, the behaviour defeats the whole purpose of trying to lose weight. Inferiority complex, depression, fear, compulsive eating, alcoholism, dependence, defensiveness, time-wasting and lack of confidence are just some of the behaviours that can impact negatively upon our progress.

It is not easy to change behaviour, but this book is all about changing how you think and how you act, so at some stage along the "Plateaus of Progress", you will need to address any behaviour that could prevent you from making adequate progress. You must identify their cause, the effect they have on your life and decide what action you must take to change them. As Stephen R. Covey says, "You can't *think* yourself out of situations that you *behaved* yourself into."

I believe that procrastination can be one of the most destructive behaviours that stops people from achieving success. Procrastination is the art of keeping up with yesterday. Once again, the Latin origin of the word can help to clarify its meaning. The word "pro" in Latin means "for". The word "cras" in Latin means "tomorrow". So *pro cras* means literally "for tomorrow".

> *Procrastination is a sin, it causes me much sorrow.*
> *I'll really have to chuck it in, in fact I'll start tomorrow.*

On my seminars, I often distribute the "Round Tuit" for delegates to use as a visual reminder that procrastination is the enemy of proactivity.

A Round Tuit

This is a Tuit. Guard it with your life, as Tuits are hard to come by, especially round ones. This is an indispensable item. It will help you become a much more efficient person. For years we have heard people say "I'll do this as soon as I get a Round Tuit". Now that you have one you can accomplish all those things you put aside until you got a Round Tuit.

Some Self-Check Questions

- Are you aware of any behavioural blocks in your life?

- Do you fall into the trap of procrastination?

- How are you trying to eliminate these habits?

ROLE IDENTIFICATION

Through role identification we clearly define who we are,
for what we are responsible, and to whom we are accountable.

The question of measuring success comes up quite often when we talk about progress and personal development, and it's one that evokes a mixed response. The typical example would be the high profile writer or politician who seems to have all the material trappings of success, enjoys an exciting and glamorous lifestyle, and seems to be enjoying the rewards for reaching the top rung of the ladder of success in their particular field. Suddenly a scandal hits the tabloids and it appears that everything was not so rosy in the domestic garden. Spouse left with another lover, children expelled from schools, etc. You wonder, "What went wrong?"

A great religious leader, David O. McKay, once said, "No amount of success can compensate for failure in the home", and this is one of the yardsticks by which I measure success. Once again, it means taking a holistic approach to life, stimulating every dimension and relating your aspirations to what is important in your life. If we don't have a clear understanding of our roles in life, and our responsibilities in those roles, then we will weave a tangled web of confusion as we try to balance principles with practices, and we will inevitably build a large chasm of unhappiness in the process.

What are your roles? Father, mother, sister, brother, parent, son and daughter are roles within the family context, but we also have social and community roles, business roles, leisure roles, etc. Most individuals have many roles in life. You could be a manager, the earner of money for the family, doctor, mechanic, city counsellor, church official, member of the PTA at your children's school, Round Table member, choir member, and many other types of roles.

To go through life believing that you have one single role is to ignore the need for stimulation in each dimension of your life, and will eventually result in an extreme case of introvert behaviour. The person who is self-centred and concentrates solely upon their advancement up the ladder of social or business success cannot find inner peace and harmony. By its very nature, that type of behaviour is contrary to the practices and guidelines that correspond to living by correct principles. Sometimes it is only through working with people on different levels that we identify and define our roles in life. But in order to "capture the vision" on this Plateau, it is necessary to identify your roles, know who you are, take cognisance of your position in each role, and accept the responsibility and accountability that comes with that position.

This particular area requires constant reviewing, because circumstances and conditions are constantly changing. However, this raises the question of how many roles one person can handle, and I would caution again about spreading yourself too thinly or trying to be all things to all people.

We have the great gift of independent agency in this life, which means that we can choose what roles we want in life. This does not mean for one moment that we have the freedom to shed the responsibility of certain roles, just because we find them inconvenient to our lifestyles. Independent agency means that we have the freedom to choose in righteousness, and *nobody's role in life brings them above the law.* When we get married and have children, we automatically inherit the role of parents, and sometimes this role can be smothered by so many other seemingly important issues. We will discuss prioritising in greater detail in a later chapter, but parenthood is one of the most powerful roles we will ever have in helping to develop our emotional and spiritual maturity, as we learn how to deal with children growing up. You cannot change who you are, but you can change what you are. The identification of your roles in life is one of the most important steps to take on this Plateau of Vision in order to get firmly on track for personal development and progress.

It is the neglect of certain roles, and the responsibility and accountability that goes with them, that creates the Chasm of Unhappiness in the lives of otherwise ostensibly successful individuals.

Some Self-Check Questions

- Have you identified your various roles in life?

- How do you fulfil each of your roles?

- What levels of responsibility and accountability are attached to each role, and are you responsible and accountable?

- Do you prioritise your roles?

VISUALISATION

The art of visualisation draws on the right side of the brain,
and stimulates the imagination to create a vivid picture of
the achieved objective, long before the process of achieving
that objective has been completed, or even begun.

William James, the American psychologist, is credited with saying, "Whatever the human mind can perceive and conceive, it can achieve." At first glance, that sounds quite profound and logical. We'll be discussing perceptions in a moment, but let's look at the idea of conceiving the notion in the mind. This is where the painting of the picture comes in, the visualising, picturing just how the future looks in your vision. The conception also involves visualising an effective plan to realise that goal. Our visual perception gives us a mental picture, and it's this mental picture that we need to create in vivid colour in order to make the visualisation process work. Whatever your vision is, you have to see yourself achieving that vision, making it a reality. Remember the old adage mentioned in Chapter One:

"Think successful, look successful, feel successful,
act successful, BE successful".

When Marilyn Monroe asked Eva Braun to be her photographer, the latter was astonished at the power of visualisation that this young starlet had. She could see herself as a superstar, long before she became one. Her faith in herself was tremendous. But she could actually see herself being successful and it was because of this great faith and visualising that Eva Braun agreed to photograph her. Marilyn Monroe's tremendous faith and enthusiasm in her own ability and future stardom was so powerful that it was infectious.

Geoff Read, the founder of Ballygowan Spring Water, was a shoe salesman working in London. But he had a dream, a vision of how a water bottling plant could work in Ireland. He visualised the entire operation, and then brought that dream to fruition with his own diligent efforts. He bottled the water himself, and with his wife and mother-in-law he labelled them, and then he set off in his car selling them to individual retailers. That was just the beginning. Within a year, he was a major player in the bottled water market, and within a further two years he was operating a multi-million dollar international operation.

Anita Roddick, founder of The Body Shop, was also a woman with a dream and a vision. She visualised exactly how her small rural manufacturing business could become a major international company, and she made her dream a reality through convincing her bank manager to believe in her vision. She shared her vision with the bank and they could see how she visualised the concept. She subsequently turned The Body Shop into a lucrative international trading operation and still remains head of that corporation.

It takes sacrifice to bring any dream to reality. Let me take a simple example of purchasing a car. If you're thinking about saving up to buy a new car, and in the back of your mind you think you would really like a particular top-of-the-range model, then go for it! Bring that thought to the front of your mind, make it into a dream, visualise yourself driving that car. Then go to the showrooms and test drive the car, check out the exact price, credit repayments, availability and colour. Take home the brochure, cut out a picture of the car and stick it on your wall! This is visualising — bringing the vision centre-stage on the screen of your mind, and playing it constantly. This will help you to save more diligently, work harder and make the appropriate sacrifices required to accumulate the cash. Of course, such a dream must fit in with what is truly important in your life — hence the need to prioritise. But unless you can actually see yourself in the final stage of achievement, by visualising the entire scenario, then there is a danger that the dream will slide back into the recesses of your mind, and die.

The principle of visualisation lies at the very heart of this Plateau — Vision. The ability to see things from the top of the mountain, before you actually arrive at the top, is the ultimate exercise of visualisation. And it's this type of visualisation that drives the great leaders of the world to inspire and encourage others to capture this vision for themselves. We will be discussing shared vision when we come to Plateau Five, but it's important that you understand at this stage how essential it is to develop the principle of visualisation in order to build the dream and solidify the vision. You can use role models to help you identify the type of person you want to become, but you have to see yourself fitting that role precisely, before it will begin to become a reality.

Some Self-Check Questions

- Do you visualise exactly how you are going to make your dream a reality?

- Is the exercise of visualisation helping you to achieve?

- Are you regularly exercising your powers of visualisation to put meat on the bones of your dream?

PERCEPTIONS

We can view life through rose-coloured glasses or a dirty
window pane. We choose the spectacles of perception through
which we view the world. Whether we have a clearly focused
picture, or a distorted image, depends on that choice.

I am not going to get involved in long explanations about the
complexities of the five senses and their varying types and degrees
of perception, but suffice to say that the human organism perceives with all of the senses. Perception is the sorting out, analys-
ing, interpreting and integrating of the various stimuli by our
sense organs. We hear, see, taste, smell and feel things. But have
you ever noticed how two people can attend a lecture and both
can hear two different stories? Are your perceptions accurate and
do you update your perceptions from time to time?

"Two men looked out at night through bars,
One saw darkness, the other saw stars."

Take a look at the human brain (Figure 10).

FIGURE 10: THE HUMAN BRAIN

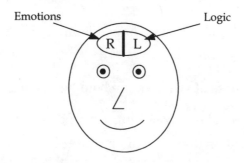

In the course of a series of seminars to second-level students, I
used the following diagram to indicate the difference between

how the left side of the brain (the logical side of the brain), and the right side of the brain (the intuitive, or creative side of the brain) interpret things. The left side has a very black and white, logical perception. But the right side adds colour, dimension, feeling, etc. to the concept. "Whole-brain thinking" perceives the full concept.

FIGURE 11: PERCEPTIONS BY THE RIGHT AND LEFT BRAIN

When you look at this diagram initially, it registers with the left side of the brain as being five irregular black shapes. But then the right side of the brain develops the visual image and creates the concept of the word "FLY". Remember, fly is not actually written on the paper. It's only the negative shadows of the area sur-rounding the word, and then the right side of the brain develops the empty white areas into the familiar shape of the word fly.

Harry Chapin wrote a beautiful song called "Flowers Are Red". In the song, a little boy is drawing a picture in the classroom, using his imagination, his creative powers and his visualisation. But the teacher tries to make him paint the flowers red and the leaves green, saying,

> *"There's no need to see flowers any other way*
> *than the way they always have been seen."*

Can't you just imagine the child painting blue houses, yellow trees, multicoloured grass? Just letting his imagination take full creative flight. He answered the teacher by describing how he could see all the colours of the rainbow, all the colours of flowers. What a beautiful sense of perception that child had, and what a stifled, narrow perception the teacher had!

Through the medium of visual perception, it is easy to demonstrate how easily we can be mistaken, but it's not always that easy to recognise when our perceptions are off course in other areas. The famous Muller-Lyer illusion (Figure 12), in which the upper line seems to be longer than the lower line, is a perfect example. In visual perception, we don't just passively respond to stimuli, but we go beyond it and try to create a meaning and sense to the situation. Unfortunately, we don't always try to ascertain the true meaning of situations in other spheres, and that's why there is always the other point of view.

FIGURE 12: THE MULLER-LYER ILLUSION

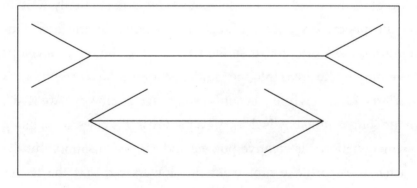

The story about the "duck shoot" amply illustrates the differences in perception of two people in the same situation observing the same action.

The Duck Shoot

Two men are out on a lake in a boat, waiting to shoot the next duck that should fly by. A second boat approaches close by, and the men in that boat have a dog with them, which is obviously to be used for retrieving the duck. Suddenly a duck appears in the sky and one of the men in the second boat shoots it. As it falls into the lake, the dog hops out of the boat and runs on top of the water, *retrieves the dead duck, and runs back* along the surface of the water *to the boat. The two men in the first boat just look at one another in dumbstruck amazement. Suddenly there's another duck, and another shot rings out from the second boat. Out hops the dog again, runs* along the top of the water, *retrieves the duck, and runs back* along the surface of the water *to the boat. In sheer disbelief, the two men in the first boat look at one another, and one says to the other, "Did you see that?"*

"Yes, amazing," replies the other man.

"Did you notice anything strange about that dog?" asks the first man.

"Yes, it can't swim," says the other man.

You must examine your perceptions, because your vision of the future will be determined to a large degree by your perceptions of the present. It's the inability to see the other person's point of view that stifles dialogue and leads to intransigence and stalemate at the negotiating table. If we cannot see the other person's point of view, we can never hope to have an overview of the situation. Hence, our judgement of the situation will always be biased.

Some Self-Check Questions

> - Do you have a true picture of exactly how things are at present?
>
> - How do you view your life domestically, socially, emotionally, and do you need to correct any erroneous perceptions that you may have developed?
>
> - Are your perceptions accurate?
>
> - On what are your perceptions based?
>
> - Are you aware of any false perceptions in your life, and are you doing something positive to correct those perceptions?
>
> - Do you regularly check your perceptions for accuracy?

CONCEPTS/INTEGRITY

Conceptual thinking is the epitome of whole-brain thinking.
If we can grasp the concept, then we can gain a clear
perspective on the matter.

When we talk about the whole concept of "The Five Plateaus of Progress" we know what that means. But lets put it into perspective with a little bit of technical knowledge on the background of concepts.

In order to develop conceptual thinking, we need to think of the whole brain coming into play. That means taking the facts and figures, passing them to the right brain for colour, perspective and expansion, and then together we have a concept. It means that we see the whole picture instead of just the black and white information slip. The resource of the right brain is immeasurable and we should learn to tap into it on a regular basis. The principle of visualisation is a perfect example of using the power of the right brain to expand the perception into a concept.

The brain is very often compared to an enormous computer with almost limitless storage capacity. In the brain we also have the memory. The function of the memory is to record, retain and retrieve information. Because it is such an astonishing piece of equipment, it actually records far more than we will ever need, and even records things we don't really want to retain. Remember the reference to "subliminal learning"? Apart from consciousness, there is one other major difference between the computer and the brain, and that is the ability of the computer to erase any piece of information by pressing a "delete" button. You can't do this with the human brain! So be careful what you absorb, because it records and retains the information, but it may retrieve the information at a most inappropriate time when you least expect it, or when you don't want it.

Essence Radiates

"Into the hands of every individual is given a marvellous power for good or for evil — the silent, unconscious, unseen influences of his life. This is simply the constant radiation of what man really is, not what he pretends to be. Every man, by his mere being, is radiating sympathy, or sorrow, or morbidity, or cynicism, or happiness, or hope, or any of a hundred other qualities. Life is a state of constant radiation and absorption; to exist is to radiate, to exist is to be the recipient of radiation. . . . Man cannot escape for one moment from this radiation of his character, this constantly weakening or strengthening of others. He can select the qualities that he will permit to be radiated, by developing such."
— David O. McKay

You should feed your mind and brain with positive affirmations, think positive thoughts, and avoid negative thoughts or actions. The things we listen to, using our aural perception, the things we watch, using our visual perception, the things we feel, using our emotional perception, the things we do with our actions, and the concepts we develop as a result of all of these activities, are all absorbed by the brain. You can't feed the brain with negatives and expect to get positive results. Did you ever watch a horror movie before going to bed, and then wonder why you're awake all night with nightmares? How can you have a pure and virtuous relationship with your spouse or partner if you fill your mind with scenes of sexual depravity by watching blue movies? These behaviours are incompatible with developing a healthy positive attitude to personal development and progress. We should develop wholesome and worthwhile occupations, hobbies and leisure pursuits. Wholesome thoughts breed wholesome conversations, which develop wholesome behaviour, and create wholesome character.

The very word "wholesome" denotes good, positive and complete. It relates directly to the creation of integrity in the individual. Integrity comes from the root "Integer", which means whole or complete. In mathematics, integers are whole numbers and fractions are parts of numbers. Are you going to live a fragmented existence or a whole existence? The modern meaning of the word integrity refers to a person of honour, accountability, reliability, honesty and trust — a whole and complete person.

> *"The man of integrity cannot be perplexed or frightened.*
> *He goes on at his own pace, whether in fortune or*
> *misfortune, like a clock during a thunderstorm."*
> — Blaine L. Lee

Some Self-Check Questions

- Are you aware of how much you use, or don't use, conceptual thinking?

- Do you try to develop the idea of whole-brain thinking to your concepts?

- Are you conscious of certain thought patterns that could be harmful to your development of wholesome concepts, and are you trying to eliminate them?

FOCUS

"Obstacles are the only things a person sees
when he takes his eyes off his goal."
— E. Joseph Cossman

Another essential leadership quality is the ability to focus upon the challenge at hand. In other words, to be able to get the job done without being distracted and side-tracked. When we talked earlier about Linford Christie and his "tunnel vision", that was an example of concentrated focus. Sometimes you may think that you don't have to focus upon anything, but the fact is, your focal point is like the needle of a compass, it never stops, it has to be pointing at something, and your job is to hold it in position long enough to do the job!

Wherever you are, be there!

If you are engaged in conversation with someone, but wishing you were speaking with someone else, thinking of something altogether different to the subject of the conversation, or wishing you were somewhere else, you'll have a very unproductive and frustrating life.

Focus involves the mental dimension, because it draws on our ability to concentrate. Mental concentration is essential to progress and productivity. We must learn to concentrate on what we're doing, until the job is done. This means that at times we must treat the subconscious mind like a spoilt child — ignore it, don't listen to its promptings.

The ability to focus on a subject or project for lengthy periods of time can be difficult, but it can be developed. Have you ever noticed the short attention span of children when you're trying to teach them a principle? A general rule of thumb for a child's concentration is one minute for each year of its life. Unless you translate your information into a story format with graphic descriptions, you could lose them after just three minutes! It's the same with adults in trying to focus upon a particular study, project, goal or priority. We have to be able to develop that Linford Christie type of "tunnel vision" by closing off the distractions, and concentrating our efforts on the challenge at hand until such time as it is completed. This is where the ability to say "no" comes into play.

Until you learn to say "no" to the unimportant things in life,
you will never be able to say "yes" to the important things.

We constantly hear about shifting trends, paradigm shifts, etc., and this also applies to our ability to shift our focus. However, until we develop the capacity to focus, we cannot develop the ability to shift that focus. The world is full of examples of marketing successes due to the ability of the marketing executive to shift focus at the appropriate and crucial time. But remember, it's a shift of focus, not a shift of gaze. I remember in the days I practised

Wado Ryu Karate, we used to practise the art of *Tamasheware*, or wood-breaking. This is a most spectacular exhibition of the art of control, power, concentration and focus in Karate training. It's exciting to watch the wood smash to pieces as the fist, or foot, makes contact. However, the ability to concentrate all the power into a single point of impact, and to focus precisely upon that point of impact, is the key to success in this demonstration. If you lose concentration or focus, you will fail. Similarly, in the business and corporate world, the ability to focus, and to shift focus, is a key principle of leadership.

Some Self-Check Questions

- Do you consider yourself to be focused?
- Are you aware of any areas in your life in which you are out of focus?
- How do you use focus to help you achieve?
- Are you consciously working on the elimination of distractions?

MENTAL DIMENSION

Self-discipline and our ability to overcome,
persist and endure, depends to a large degree
upon how well we have developed our mental capacity.

This is the second of the four dimensions that we will be discussing with regard to stimulation and growth. How many of our problems are only mental, and how often do we attribute our lack of achievement or accomplishment to the mental dimension? The stimulation of the mental dimension is important to the development of PMA — Positive Mental Attitude. I do not subscribe to the school of thinking which suggests that the development of PMA can happen without any great involvement of the other three dimensions, and neither do I agree that strong PMA solves all problems. But it has a major part to play in the personal development of the individual, because without it, the going gets really tough.

The mental dimension is stimulated by reading, visualising, planning, writing and absorbing things of an intellectual nature. It happens through expanding our awareness, increasing our knowledge, making decisions, and becoming more "in control" of our emotions, our appetites, desires and passions. It is like a control panel in the human organism, and we have to become proficient at using this panel. In a sound studio, the mixing desk is an essential piece of equipment used in converting all the raw material (the recording of voices and instruments) into a finished product. But if the sound engineer is not competent, no matter how good the desk is, the result will be dreadful. Imagine your mental dimension as the control panel or mixing desk; it's only by learning how to use it efficiently and effectively that it serves its real purpose.

Some Self-check Questions

- Do you stimulate your mental dimension?

- Do you read, write, or engage in similar intellectually stimulating exercises?

- Do you recognise the importance of stimulation in this area?

TIME MANAGEMENT

We each receive the same number of hours in a day.
How productively we use that allocation is determined
by our ability to manage wisely that elusive element — time.

I have included this topic in this chapter because it seems to be one of the great stumbling blocks for individuals on almost every course I conduct. "Time management" is really a misnomer, because the problem really is about how to manage our behaviour within certain time constraints. We all have 24 hours in each day, so the cry of, "I've no time to do that" is really irrelevant. It should be: "I've done something else with the time that I should have allocated to that project."

FIGURE 13: 24-HOUR CLOCK

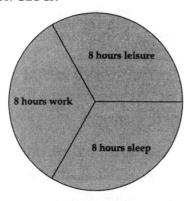

The principle of time management is:

To organise your behaviour around your priorities,
within the time constraints that exist.

To lead a balanced life we must understand what is important to us, learn how to prioritise according to our different roles and focus upon stimulating each dimension as we go about achieving our ambitions. The term "crisis management" crops up almost daily in the corporate sector, but the crisis is very often created in the first place by bad time management. It's not important to adhere strictly to a rigid form of documentation or elaborated filofax systems in order to achieve good time management. *Learning the principle is more important,* and then you choose the support system that best suits your style of management. Prevention is better than cure; many a stressed-out executive has learned this lesson too late.

We hear a lot of talk about prioritising, but unless we know what's important to us, how can we possibly prioritise effectively? A crisis occurs when things become urgent and important. In order to avoid a crisis, we need to prevent things becoming urgent and important, which means that we have to deal with matters before they become too urgent. This can be done very effectively if we learn how to prioritise.

> *"Things which matter most must never be at the mercy of*
> *things which matter least."*
> — Goethe

The best method of ascertaining what's really important to you is to revert to your values. Your values will immediately determine what you should do first. Eliminate procrastination from your life, learn to prioritise, develop precise methods of procedure, and you will avoid the stress of crisis management.

To avoid falling into the crisis management mode on a regular basis, you need to take control of your behaviour and your actions. Don't allow trivia to take up your time, don't allow interruptions to affect your focus, don't fall into the trap of having meetings for the sake of meetings. Learn how to delegate effectively and take time for yourself! In the case of athletes training for a race, they always reserve some rest days for themselves. This gives them time to recuperate and allows the muscles to repair themselves. If we don't allow specific time for ourselves we eventually suffer from the "burnout" syndrome.

In order to use your time wisely and effectively, you need to go beyond the stage of "post-it" notes stuck all over your desk and computer, the checklists, the appointment books, the schedules and plans, the organisers, targets, goals, etc. You need to get the overview in order to be able to focus upon your priorities, to develop your relationships, and ensure that you are being stimulated in every dimension without the whole world falling down around you. When you capture the vision of what you want to be, and where you want to be in the future, this will harness your energies and focus them upon what's important right now.

Keys to Successful Time Management:

- Make every minute count. Constantly ask yourself, "What am I doing with my time right now?"
- Focus on the challenge at hand and don't allow yourself to be distracted.
- Put first things first, prioritise your daily activities on the previous evening, and do them in that order!
- Plan your work, and work your plan.
- To prevent "burnout", allow some time in your schedule for yourself to relax and recuperate.
- Balance your time between your different roles.
- Avoid procrastination, do it now, and stick with the project until completion.

Roles, values, visions and goals are all important considerations in relation to effective time management. But the real key to successful time management is the development of the art of selective prioritising. Unless you first determine what things are really important in your life, you cannot possibly exercise the principle of prioritising.

Bear in mind that the principles of time management are useless, unless followed up with practical application.

> *The essence of time management is the productive use of our time, not the constant study of the principles.*

Advance planning, organising, using "Things to do today" lists, prioritising, avoiding procrastination, and leaving the trivia until last, are all essential elements of successful time management.

Some Self-Check Questions

- Do you constantly manage your time with the use of a diary or organiser?

- Have you taken the time to ascertain what's really important to you in relation to time management?

- Do you find yourself falling into crisis management too frequently?

- Are you taking steps to avoid crisis management?

- Have you developed the art of delegation, and do you use it effectively?

- Do you prioritise your daily, weekly, monthly tasks?

PLANNING

To go through our day, week or month without a plan is
like embarking on a fresh journey without using a road map.
Effective planning sets parameters, offers guidelines, defines
objectives, enforces the discipline of time management,
ensures enhanced productivity and achievement and
gives solid purpose to our endeavours.

Proper prior planning prevents poor performance. The subject of planning is as simple or as complex as you wish to make it. But it is an essential principle to develop in order to make progress. I remember attending a training course for sales consultants many years ago, and the course instructor spent about eight hours explaining the merits of his exciting new system of categorising clients, prospecting for new clients, and filing them in a unique way for quick referral. A colleague of mine was quite mesmerised by this great system. At the end of the week-long course he decided to reorganise his entire filing cabinet and client bank. Unfortunately, he got so tied up with this complicated method of rearranging his own relatively efficient system, that he lost sight of the purpose of his job, which was *to sell*! Two years later I had occasion to meet with this old colleague, and to my horror he was still hooked on this compulsion to organise his business by means of the system which he had learned. Having been caught up in the "perils of perfectionism", his business had declined rapidly, leaving him almost destitute.

The systems must never be confused with the principle, and the principle of planning is to plan with a purpose! It represents the second stage of setting and achieving goals, and it should be an integral part of your progress. Schedules, organisers, charts, diaries, electronic mail, etc., are all useful *support systems* that can help you to plan effectively. But take care to plan effectively, not just efficiently. Your charts, plans and schedules may be extremely efficient, but highly ineffective unless they effectively serve the purpose for which they were invented.

> *"Programmes blindly followed bring us to a* discipline *of*
> *doing good, but principles properly understood and*
> *practised, bring us to a* disposition *to do good."*
> — Glen L. Pace

In the following chapter, I give you a sample of my monthly goal-chart, and in relation to planning I think it is vitally important to have a monthly overview. With regard to my work, I have an annual view of what I intend to be doing at each particular time of the year, I slot in engagements, projects, holidays, etc. But then I plan my *month* in detail. Perhaps I may have a course that runs into eight weeks, which will necessitate making it a two-monthly chart, but essentially I need to have the monthly overview. Then I can plan my week in more precise detail by filling the particular time schedules, dates, functions, etc., and organise things around my priorities. The last thing I organise is my day. If I organise in a daily perspective I will find myself thinking in a daily mode, and I need to think in a monthly mode!

Planning should be used as a positive reinforcement of the principle of prioritising. Every successful game must have a good game plan and life is no different. We must develop an efficient and effective game plan to accomplish the things that we wish to accomplish. If you take the time to plan, you can pre-empt the crisis, prevent the pressure from becoming stressful, and it will go hand-in-hand with developing the principle of time management.

Four Keys to Effective Planning

1. Check your annual calendar every month — confirm special dates, vacation, projects, etc.

2. Check your monthly calendar every week — confirm specific times and arrangements, etc.

3. Check your weekly calendar every day — this means confirming times, appointments, etc.

4. Always review your daily plan on the previous evening, and refresh your memory every morning with a brief review — this will clarify your plan, help you develop the art of prioritising, and give you a sharp sense of focus and purpose for the day.

Sometimes people get caught up in the idea of goal-charts. Because of their visual appeal and built-in reporting procedure, they seem to be the answer to cultivating good habits, achieving goals and generally "making things happen". However, the goal-chart on its own is not sufficient; it must always fall into the broad overview of the game plan. I never use a goal-chart without using my weekly schedule/organiser alongside it, because occasionally I may need to make adjustments to my schedule. But as I use it in conjunction with my goal chart, I can still keep on track with my goals.

If you're failing to plan, you're planning to fail.

Some Self-Check Questions

> • Do you regularly plan your month, week and day?
>
> • Have you a clear picture of how your next week is shaping?
>
> • Do your plans include time for stimulation in every dimension of your life?
>
> • Do you always have a nightly review of your plans for the following day?

PERSONAL POWER

"The degree to which the opportunity to use power effectively
is granted to or withheld from individuals is one operative
difference between those companies which stagnate,
and those who innovate."
— Rosabeth Moss Kanter

Power can be ennobling or degrading, according to how it is used and administered. In recent years, we have seen some horrific examples of injustice and human suffering because of the abuse of power in governments and countries, where people were reduced to living in subhuman conditions. This type of power is an insult to humanity, to the dignity of mankind, and must be avoided, stopped and eliminated from our society. I categorise power under three broad headings:

• Coercive Power

• Utility Power

• Persuasive Power.

Coercive Power is the most dangerous and addictive, and the one that creates the megalomaniacs of this world. When people are coerced into situations, there will always be resentment. The person wielding the power is always in danger of deriving some perverted pleasure from the exercise. It's the thrill of exerting this unrighteous dominion over others that brings out the most base and inhuman qualities in those who indulge in this despicable exercise.

I remember listening to someone interviewing Olive Braiden, the founder of the Dublin Rape Crisis Centre, and how sickened I was to hear about the dreadful atrocities being carried out by men and women within the home. Husband battering and wife battering. Incest and rape. Physical, emotional, sexual and mental abuse of children and spouses. But the one common denominator was the pleasure that the perpetrators got from their sense of power over their victims.

During my early school days, before the abolition of the barbaric system of corporal punishment in schools, I was exposed to this type of unrighteous dominion and coercive power, which was wielded by teachers. A new teacher arrived into our classroom, pulled out the first row of students and proceeded to give each of them six smacks of his hard leather strap. (These leather straps were supplied for the precise purpose of inflicting corporal punishment on unruly students.) The students were mortally wounded emotionally, embarrassed by the physical display of brute force and ignorance, and mystified as to what they had done to deserve having this gratuitous violent punishment inflicted upon them. Then the teacher said, "That's just to let you know who's boss in this classroom. Okay?" How could he expect to have the respect of any of his students after such a display? Although corporal punishment was abolished shortly afterwards, that man never regained my respect or that of the other students whom he terrorised.

However, it is not only confined to the classrooms. I have experienced similar scenarios within the corporate sector. There are certain immature, insecure, ignorant and abusive individuals who somehow find themselves in positions of authority. Some of these, because they are unable to administer any physical force, do so in more subtle ways. They create a climate of fear in the workplace. A climate where it is difficult to speak out and stand up for your constitutional, personal, civil and human rights. This is coercive power at its most deadly, because it intimidates individuals, destroys confidence, distorts their thinking, and stifles growth and development.

Bullying in the workplace, sexual harassment, and the imposition of unreasonable penalties are all examples of unrighteous dominion, misuse of power, abuse of the position of authority, corruption, moral degradation and maltreatment of human beings. Don't be fooled by the fancy wrappings and flowery language. Learn to recognise coercive power, and don't allow yourself to be coerced.

Fear is one of the greatest tools used in the administration of this type of power. People do things out of fear. But when the fear is removed, the power is removed. This is always temporary power, because it only lasts as long as the person who wields the power is in a position to administer the punishment for non-compliance. Typical examples of this type of power would be:

"Do this, or else I'll see to it that you never get promotion!"

"You have to do it because I said so, and I'm the boss!"

"If you don't do it, you won't get paid!"

Utility Power is allocated to the individual because of their bargaining power, or position that they hold, whether it be in a corporation or public body. An individual can have the power to direct others because they are the elected representative of that body. But unless that individual is a person of integrity, there is a danger of engaging in abuse of authority, which leads to corruption. The "You scratch my back, and I'll scratch yours" syndrome represents utility power. We are all only too familiar with the traditional compensatory/reward systems that operate in most of our major corporations and this is also a perfect example of utility power. However, this type of power is also quite transitory, because as soon as the reward or compensation is removed, the power is also removed. If people become conditioned to work only for the rewards and compensations, how will we ever get them to work when we don't have rewards or compensations to offer them?

"If you work really hard and reach your goals, we'll send you on a holiday to Barbados!"

"If you finish the job on time we'll give you a bonus!"

Persuasive power is the term I use, for want of a better word, for this most effective, legitimate and permanent type of power. This is where people do things out of consideration, respect, and desire to accommodate the individual exerting the power. The person receiving direction always retains dignity and respect. This type of power belongs only to the person of integrity, the person of principle. To convince others to subscribe to your philosophy by gentle persuasion guarantees loyalty and sustaining support. But this will only happen when they see by your actions, your behaviour, your lifestyle and how you treat ALL people, that you have the qualities of character worthy of a leadership position. We've seen the horrible failures of fascism and dictatorships throughout history, and it's sad to see how history keeps repeating itself, even in our present time.

People in positions of authority should always endeavour to entreat and persuade in exerting their power. The abuse of a position of authority leads straight back to coercive power, diminished integrity, and eventual corruption.

When I think back to my childhood, I never forget how my mother taught me the principle of obedience. There was no threat of beatings or deprivation. She simply appealed to my sense of honour. Whenever she was in doubt about my explanations of dubious situations, she would always ask me, "On your word of honour, is this a true account of the incident?" Whenever she was leaving me in charge of a situation, or on my own, she would always add the powerful statement, "I'm leaving you on your word of honour to behave." It reminds me of a term that was much used in business many years ago, "My word is my bond". And I wonder whatever happened to the "Gentleman's Agreement"?

This type of power engenders strength of character, love, respect, honour, concern, compassion, willingness to serve, integrity, honesty, sincerity, and the desire to exercise your right as a human being to assist another human being with their needs. To exercise and respond to persuasive power is a most ennobling experience, a far cry from the selfish indulgence of coercive power. The principle of gentle persuasion must be used with discernment, however, because we couldn't have the law-enforcement agents gently trying to tell a hell-raiser to slow down from driving 100 mph in a residential estate crowded with little children! The development of your own personal power is the main consideration at this point, and that comes about by developing the following four qualities. The ability to:

1. Act decisively — make decisions.

2. Exert a positive influence on others.

3. Control the influence of others on you.

4. Achieve results, and make things happen.

If you examine these four aspects of personal power, you will see that they focus upon being "in control" of yourself and of your situation, regardless of external influences. Can you imagine a person in a position of leadership who cannot make decisions, cannot exert a positive influence over anybody, cannot control other people influencing his or her decisions and actions, and who never achieves anything? Not a very effective leader. As with every principle along The Five Plateaus of Progress, all of the above aspects of personal power are interlinked.

The development of this personal power comes through exercising correct principles. The development and proper use of personal power makes us feel good, gives us greater confidence in our abilities, helps us to achieve more, and makes us more productive individuals through our willingness to contribute our time, talents and efforts to worthwhile causes. Can't you see how accurately they relate to persuasive power?

Some Self-Check Questions

> - Are you "in control"?
>
> - Do you actually make decisions?
>
> - Do you find it easy, or difficult, to influence others?
>
> - Do you find yourself the victim or perpetrator of coercive or position power?
>
> - Do you act, or are you acted upon?

ACHIEVEMENT

*Nothing builds self-confidence like achievements. It is only
by achieving that we discover our ability to put our talents
and skills to productive and effective use. But achievement
is an action word, it means doing it!*

What do you hope to achieve in your vision of your future? Have you set out certain objectives on each Plateau along the way, or do you intend to take things as they come? Very few things have ever been achieved by accident, but most great achievements involved great motivation, planning, preparing, etc.

In working out how to achieve something, I believe we should look at the motive for achieving. The more powerful the motivating factors, the more quickly our vision comes to fruition.

Are your objectives based upon your values, or are you driven by an ulterior motive? The driving force that helps you maintain the momentum, as you come closer and closer to achieving your goal, must be strong, positive and realistic in its relation to your whole area of achievement and development. The basic drives like hunger and thirst are powerful driving forces, but achievement is a secondary drive which requires a superior motive in order to make it really worthwhile. I use the system of Disgust, Desire, Decision, Resolve to set and achieve my objectives.

- "I'm *disgusted* with the situation as it is, I just can't stand another minute of it; I really have to do something about it.

- The *desire* is burning inside of me, now that I've decided, and I really want to change.

- So I've *decided* to change it; I want to change this situation, which disgusts me so much.

- My *resolve* is final, and I am going to make this change happen, no excuses, no delays!"

Three Keys to Achieving Successfully:

1. Set your objectives, which must be based upon your vision and your values.

2. Clearly define your motives, which should be of a superior nature.

3. Take the necessary course of action, which means doing it.

In other words, you say what you're going to do, why you're going to do it, and then you just do it! But avoid the diseases of attitude that could knock you off track. Don't allow weeds to grow up and choke the beautiful flowers in your garden. Nothing builds self-confidence like achievement, and nothing bridges the chasm of unhappiness like the little building bricks of achievement. Don't expect major achievements immediately; build slowly on the small achievements as you progress from Plateau to Plateau.

Achievement is the accomplishment of an objective. The daily achievements are what build up our confidence, and increase our ability to achieve further. A simple "Things To Do Today" sheet, or a variation on that principle, is a concrete method of measuring our progress, and helping us to prioritise our daily activities. It's such a gratifying feeling, at the end of a long hard day, to tick off the accomplished tasks and items on your "Things To Do Today" sheet. A visual reminder of a day's work well done, and an encouragement to do the same the next day.

Some Self-Check Questions

* Are you aware of your achievements?

* Have you listed your achievements?

* Do you use your past achievements to help you achieve?

* Do you set goals and objectives?

* How do you achieve?

PERSONAL MISSION STATEMENT

As an individual human being, you have a unique mission
to accomplish in this life, in order to fulfil the measure of
your creation. The discovery of your talents and skills will
fuel your aspirations and ambitions, and channel all your
efforts into rising to the challenge and responding to the
driving force of your own personal mission statement.

Although you are only at the very start of this beautiful voyage of discovery and only becoming aware of so many facets of your personality and behaviour, it's important at this stage to start drafting your own Personal Mission Statement (just a first draft; you can build and develop it later). In pondering upon the purpose of life, and all the other topics covered in this book so far, you will have to come to a state of realisation with regard to what you really want in life. Every individual in this world is unique (and that means you too!), and nobody else can accomplish *your* mission.

You have a unique mission in this life, and you have talents, qualities, skills and intelligence to be used in this endeavour, but you must write *your own* Personal Mission Statement. Nobody else can write it for you, because nobody knows the innermost feelings of your heart, and nobody knows the deepest thoughts within your mind. You know yourself better than anyone else in the world, so who better to write your Personal Mission Statement than yourself! In very broad terms, your mission statement is a statement of what you want to be, what you want to do, and what you want to have in this life. The ingredients for that mission statement depend on you, but they have to be based upon your values, and they have to be honest, practical, and also reflect the nature and purpose of your existence.

In drafting a mission statement, it is helpful to use a *role model* as a yardstick. Is there someone in your life, or perhaps an individual in public life, who particularly inspires you to strive for excellence? When you finish reading this book, you will hopefully have drafted a more final mission statement, and that mission statement should be a driving force in your life, it should lift you up each time you read it, it should inspire and motivate you to make that statement a reality, to achieve, and to accomplish your mission. Take care in writing your mission statement, because it should put meaning and purpose into your daily life, enhance your character, and give you firm direction. Don't write a Personal

Mission Statement just for the purpose of writing one. This must become your own personal Charter, your own personal Constitution. When you read your Personal Mission Statement, you must feel uplifted, inspired, motivated and filled with the desire to fulfil your dreams, realise your ambitions, and accomplish your objectives in life.

Only when your personal mission statement becomes a sufficiently powerful driving force in your life, will you develop the missionary zeal required to successfully achieve your goals and objectives.

Some Self-Check Questions

- What is your personal mission statement in draft form?
- Does it uplift, edify, encourage and inspire you to achieve your mission?
- Does it relate to all areas of your life, or just to a few areas?
- Do you use your personal mission statement regularly?

ASSIGNMENTS FOR PLATEAU TWO

1. Using the basic three divisions of the 24-hour clock, identify specific activities and behaviours in your leisure time that are obvious time-wasters, and devise a method of consciously eliminating them. For example, list the number of hours you spend each day/evening watching television.

2. Having regard to the sections on The Mind, Dreams and Visualisation, write your own personal vision of your preferred picture of the future, and graphically describe how you visualise yourself in that picture.

3. List three specific areas in your life in which you recognise untapped potential, and how you propose to implement the principle of proactivity to actualise that potential.

4. Write your plan of how you can consciously deplete the amount of distractions and interruptions in order to implement the principle of focus in your work assignments, projects and daily tasks.

5. Examine your perceptions of yourself in your work, domestic and leisure environments and discover whether or not they need to be adjusted in order to align your perceptions and concepts with your vision of your future.

6. Identify and list your key roles, as you see them at present, in relation to your home, your work and your personal responsibilities; list the responsibility and accountability associated with each role, and how you propose to become more effective in each role.

In order to derive the maximum benefit from this chapter, you should be actively engaged in doing these assignments for a minimum of one week before proceeding to Plateau Three.

3

Plateau Three
DISCIPLINE

"He who reigns within himself, and rules passions,
desires and fears, is more than a king."
— David O. McKay

The word discipline can sometimes be a little bit overpowering, and very often conjures up ideas of strict military regimes or Zen Buddhist monks in the hills of Tibet. It is true to say that both of these employ a great amount of discipline, but it has a more far-reaching and all-encompassing meaning than that alone. The word discipline comes from Disciple, which means follower. One who adheres to a particular discipline is one who follows that particular code of practice. It really means getting on track, providing guidelines, setting parameters and striving to adhere strictly to that designated code of conduct. Asceticism is not a fundamental requisite for a disciplined lifestyle.

We frequently use the word as a verb when we talk about disciplining our children or disciplining ourselves into a particular way of thinking or acting. In the context of this Plateau, we will use the term in its widest possible meaning, because this Plateau is, for many people, the most difficult one to complete in every dimension. Talk is cheap, and we can discuss principles forever without ever truly understanding them. Our knowledge of the principle may be excellent, but it is only by applying the principle that we come to fully understand it. True understanding of a principle can only be gained through experiencing the practical application of the principle. This practical application requires discipline. It's discipline that makes us get up and go — it makes us do it! The practical application of persistence and endurance in every dimension requires the quality of discipline.

The topics covered in this Plateau are all relevant to discipline and essential to personal growth. This is the Plateau where you need to get *in control*, use the knowledge gained from the two preceding Plateaus, and prepare for changing your behaviour and your thinking. If you hit this Plateau, but don't tackle it successfully, you cannot expect to make progress to Plateaus Four or Five.

The development of self-discipline comes through the process of self-denial. The ability to deny oneself an indulgence is the beginning of a lifelong character-building exercise. It takes great effort to be in control of our appetites, desires and passions, but we *must* be in control of them, otherwise we can very easily become slaves to our emotions. Undisciplined people are those who always get what they want, do what they want, go where they want, without ever stopping to examine the cost or consequences to themselves or others. This is the epitome of selfish behaviour and a most destructive trait in anyone's character. The principle of "Effort and Reward" can never be fully understood until we exercise the principle of *working*, putting in that effort, for the reward.

Look at the world's greatest athletes, and see the great rewards of self-denial in their achievements. They had to learn to control their desires, curtail their habits, change their bad habits into good habits and endure long hours of training. Could they overcome the fatigue, the mental anguish, the bad days when they didn't feel like training, if they hadn't developed the ability to deny themselves the luxury of self-indulgence, procrastination or just sheer laziness. The problem is that self-indulgence, like most drugs, is absolutely *addictive*.

I remember waking up one winter's morning, looking out the window at a dark, wet, windy and cold day. My immediate thought was to return to the comfort of my warm bed, curl up and sleep on for an extra hour. However, I had committed myself to a fairly rigid training session, part of which was an early morning run and workout in the gym. Without allowing myself the luxury of another single negative thought about returning to bed, I gathered my gear and drove straight to the gym. When I returned to the gym, after a five-mile run in the cold, wet and windy day, I noticed a slogan on the wall, which read, "There'll be more bad days than good days!" Gosh, I felt good for having run, and I felt ready for a good workout. By the time I left the gym, I was ready to take on anything that day. We can't lay plans that are only geared for fine weather conditions. That's allowing ourselves to be "outer directed" instead of "inner directed". I apply the NMW principle here — do it, *"No Matter What!"*

It's by overcoming the desire to indulge that we gain greater strength of character. There *will be* withdrawal symptoms, just as there are withdrawal symptoms in giving up drugs, but the alternative is that we remain slaves to our emotional weaknesses. Self-denial builds great strength of character, self-control, integrity, honesty, health, self-respect and self-confidence.

Remember: "The thought is father to the deed". Every action has its origins in the mind. If we are not in control of our thoughts, we will have to face the consequences of the actions that will inevitably follow our thought patterns. How can a man possibly remain faithful to his wife if he constantly engages in watching pornographic movies? As soon as the opportunity presents itself for him to engage in any of these depraved sexual activities, he will succumb to temptation, because he has already considered these actions in his mind. The pornography was enough fuel to stimulate his imagination, but because we don't have a "delete" button for our minds, those thoughts took root and festered in his mind.

The principle of "no pain, no gain" applies to the development of self-denial in the individual. But it's worth it! Consider the many areas of self-indulgence that have become addictive in so many people's lives. All of these help to diminish character, reduce our ability to resist, and seriously hamper our growth and development.

Let me state this axiom loud and clear:

Addictions are fed by indulgence.

The longer we indulge, the greater the pain will be of eventual withdrawal. The sooner we develop the principle of self-denial in our lives, the more control we have of our lives. We speed up our growth and development in so many areas of our lives, as we build strength of character and integrity.

But remember, it doesn't happen overnight. It's a slow process to develop discipline in any dimension of our lives.

- When we learn to discipline our minds, we no longer engage in useless daydreaming. Instead, we develop the art of *mental focus*.

- When we discipline our bodies, we enjoy the fruits of health and fitness and the ability to enjoy our leisure-time more effectively.

- When we discipline our habits, we develop our self-confidence, increase our capacity to achieve, and enjoy greater inner peace and harmony.

- When we discipline our use of time, we experience the great joy of achievement and increased productivity.

- When we discipline our emotional dimension, we enjoy greater and more enriching experiences in life through relationships built on emotional maturity.

Wherever we endeavour to introduce the principle of discipline in our lives, we must initially *enforce* the discipline. Discipline doesn't just happen, we have to make it happen in our lives, therefore we must force ourselves to adhere to the particular code of discipline to which we agree to subscribe.

Take, for example, the salesman who decides that he is going to change his lazy habit of sleeping too long in the mornings. So he enrols in the local gym, decides to embark upon a programme of early morning workouts to increase his level of fitness, and to get himself up early in the mornings. However, after the initial enthusiasm of the first week, he falls prey to the lure of the blankets, and the desire for just another ten minutes in bed. He should have enforced the discipline by making a solid arrangement to meet someone else at the gym, and if he didn't show, they should have permission to call him and make him turn up for the appointment.

I remember many years ago, when I was training a team of salespeople, I came across one individual who always found it difficult to get his week off to a good start. I encouraged him to develop the discipline of early rising and then showed him how to enforce that discipline by always having an important appointment (preferably to close a sale!) first thing every Monday morning. He eventually got into the habit of having an 8.00 a.m. breakfast meeting with a client every Monday morning. Within a few months, he became the top producer on the team.

Some Self-Check Questions

- Do you lead a disciplined life?

- Are there areas in your life that are badly in need of more disciplined behaviour?

- How are you trying to introduce the principle of discipline into your lifestyle?

- Are you aware of areas in your life, emotional, mental, physical, social, etc. that require a more disciplined approach?

- Do you find it difficult to control certain passions, desires, or fears?

- Have you introduced any new habit or work pattern into your life that will enforce the discipline?

CHOICES

The degree to which we have success or failure in life is not solely dependent upon our environment, circumstances, colour, race, creed or domestic situations. It is our attitude to these things, and the ability to make the right choices, that ultimately

determines our success in overcoming obstacles, and
actualising our potential. We are born to succeed,
but we choose what we become.

I mentioned in an earlier chapter about how we obtain the greatest freedom through obedience to the natural laws. And it's through maintaining the discipline we set for ourselves that we eventually have the greatest freedom of choice. Have you ever noticed a child in a sweet shop, when asked to choose a bar of chocolate from the vast display of sweets? You could expect to stay there for about five hours if you were to wait for the child to decide, because children have not developed the discipline of making choices.

The choices we make can determine what happens in our lives, and often they can have a devastating effect upon our futures. We must learn how to make choices. But on what do we base our choices? We base our choices on the knowledge that we have of the situation at the time, and sometimes that knowledge can be based equally between faith and fact. However, we must also look at the consequences of choices and remember that when we make the choice, the consequence goes with it.

Let me give a graphic example. Suppose you're standing on the roof of a ten-storey building. You really have two choices:

- Choice number one would be to walk down the stairs and out of the front door. By making this *correct choice,* you have the freedom to make multiple future choices.

- Choice number two would be to jump off the roof. This *wrong choice* would eliminate all future choices, because the consequence of that action would mean instant death, thus depriving you of any future choices.

Every action has its own consequence, so don't start dwelling in the realms of unreality by imagining that *your* action will have a different consequence. You can't jump off the building, and then decide not to accept the consequence of being smashed to pieces. The consequence is already an inseparable part of the action. You choose the action, but the consequence comes with it!

Back to this word "motive" again, and how our motives can affect our choices. Do we act out of an ulterior or a superior motive? Let me give an example of what I mean by ulterior and superior motives.

Suppose that you push a child roughly to the ground, and the child grazes his knees, cuts his elbows, and bruises his head. The first consequence of that action is that the child has been injured and hurt.

The *ulterior* motive was that you didn't like the child, and anyway he was in your way, so you pushed him roughly to get him out of your way, hoping that the push would in fact hurt him.

However, the *superior* motive would be if you saw a car speeding towards him with no time to swerve or stop, so you immediately push the child to safety in order to save his life. In both cases, the child is hurt and injured, but in the latter case it was for a just cause, a superior motive, and resulted in minor injury rather than instant death.

As adults we must constantly make choices, and our choices may not always be as obvious as we would like them to be. Sometimes we have to utilise the old brain cells to think seriously about choices, but we *must* make them. No doubt you've come across the person who moans all night about having to attend a social function, whereas in fact they had the freedom to choose whether or not to attend the function in the first place. The discipline of making choices may not be easy to implement, but make the choice now to start implementing that discipline!

Our success and our ultimate joy and happiness in life is all about the choices that we make — the right and wrong choices. We must learn to make the right choices, and we will deal with that aspect later in the chapter when we discuss decision-making. But we must also learn from the wrong choices that we make. The choices we make affect not only our own lives, but also the lives of every other person with whom we come in contact. The consequences of our choices, and the influence our choices have on other people are immeasurable.

Anyone who has read Victor Frankl's marvellous book, *Man's Search for Meaning*, cannot avoid being touched by the vast influence his attitude and choices had on all of those people who were incarcerated with him in the concentration camps. Can you just imagine the hopelessness of the situation? But it didn't stop him making the right choices.

> *"Man can preserve a vestige of spiritual freedom, of independence of mind, even in such terrible conditions of psychic and physical stress. . . . We who lived in concentration camps can remember the men who walked through the huts comforting others, giving away their last piece of bread. They may have been few in number, but they offer sufficient proof that everything can be taken from a man but one thing: the last of human freedoms — to choose one's attitude in any given set of circumstances, to choose one's own way."*
> — Victor Frankl, *Man's Search for Meaning*

Some Self-Check Questions

- Are you aware of any wrong choices you have made, and have you learnt from them?

- Do you realise the importance of making correct choices?

- Are you aware of the repercussions or consequences when you make choices?

- Do you find it difficult to choose?

- Are you "inner directed" in your choices, and do you work from a superior motive?

- Are you happy with most of the choices you have made in your life?

THE LAW OF GROWTH

*Personal growth comes from our ability to endure and survive
the hardship of unpleasant experiences, re-evaluate our
situation, learn from the experience and adjust accordingly
in order to avoid similar unnecessary experiences. Every
experience in life can become a positive learning experience,
if we develop the capacity to adopt a positive attitude to it.*

The fear of failure, the fear of rejection, and the fear of the unknown are all reasons for not trying. But in reality they are very often cop-outs. I love the title of Susan Jeffers' book, *Feel The Fear, And Do It Anyway*. I know it's not always quite as simple as that, and I will deal with this element of fear in greater detail in Chapter Five. Some fears are very deep-rooted and may require professional counselling to resolve them. However, I'm talking about the normal situations that we face in our day-to-day living — the type of situation that creates imaginary fears as a reason to avoid doing them. This is very often the case in situations which have to be addressed, even though it is a distasteful or painful job. Don't tell me that everyone loves going to the dentist!

However, there's nothing like failure to keep a good man down, and it's not easy to lift yourself up, brush yourself down, and start again. There is a certain stigma attached to failure. But I applaud people who experience failure, because it just shows that they had the guts to go out and try it in the first place! The spirit of free enterprise will never die, as long as people take a positive approach to the risks involved and accept failure for what it really is — just an obstacle to progress. How many successful entrepreneurs do you know who have never experienced failure? So don't allow failure to stop you making progress, just use it as a stepping stone, another brick in the wall of experience.

The Law of Growth (see p. 12 of the Introduction) does not say that we should fail, try again, fail, try again, because that way you are almost guaranteeing continued failure. The key word is "*adjust*". But unfortunately it is the word that is ignored by so many people who are travelling at such speed that they forget this simple action, *adjusting*.

Remember that *direction is more important than speed*. Let me illustrate the point with a simple example. Suppose you are trying to fix a puncture in the wheel of your car, but the car is parked on a slight incline. Every time you have the car fully jacked up, it starts to slide slowly backwards. Do you just keep jacking it up and hope that somehow it will stop sliding backwards? No: you *adjust* the situation by placing a brick behind the rear wheels of the car or by applying the handbrake fully, and then you try again.

Some people can feel so deflated and put down by other people's opinions that they never even try again. Originality, creativity, ideas and innovation are among the most powerful commodities, and are the keys to success in today's world.

"A righteous man may fall seven times and rise again."
— Proverbs 24:16

Some Self-Check Questions

- Does the fear of failure ever prevent you from embarking upon a project?

- Have you been disillusioned with your efforts because of adverse comments from others?

- Have you ever given up without adjusting and trying again?

- Do you feel confident or apprehensive about attempting something new and original?

COMFORT ZONES

Comfort zones can envelop us as swiftly as a mist on a mountaintop. To escape from the mist and find our way home, we need a compass. Our compass is our vision, values, and the correct principles by which we should strive to live. We drift into comfort zones, but we have to use considerable force and willpower to break out of them. But break out of them we must. Otherwise we will remain on the same Plateau indefinitely.

Practically every topic that we've discussed in this book relates to
the dreaded area of "Comfort Zones". Remaining in a comfort
zone guarantees no growth! It really means remaining on the same
Plateau without making any effort to move forward or upward.
The principle of growth and progress means constant striving,
pushing boundaries, expanding horizons, reaching out, stretching
yourself, going the extra mile, and living by the *spirit* of the law,
instead of the *letter* of the law. When we stop doing these things
we stop growing, and we fall back into our nice little comfort
zones. No wonder they are called comfort zones, because they require no effort, no work, no exertion, no uncomfortable chores or
meetings, no reaching out, no overcoming of habits or behaviours,
and no mental effort in making difficult choices. Nothing. Just lie
back and relax. It may not be quite that extreme in most cases, but
whatever, or wherever, your comfort zone lies, it will definitely
stop your progress. It's the unreal approach to life by imagining
that there is a "status quo", and that you *can* remain the same
without improving or making progress. There is no "status quo",
but there *are* comfort zones, many of them!

Consider the mental blocks, the behaviour blocks, the HITS
Syndrome, and try to identify your comfort zones. They may be
easily recognisable in your business environment, but perhaps not
so easily identifiable in your domestic situation. Comfort zones
exist in every dimension and, as part of Plateau One, Awareness,
you should have a fairly clear knowledge of what they are. During
Plateau Two, Vision, you should have recognised how they are a
hindrance to your progress in capturing that vision. But here on
Plateau Three, you have to develop a discipline in your thinking
behaviour that will help you to break out of them. At every level,
and in every dimension, if you enter a comfort zone you cannot

possibly progress to the next Plateau without breaking out of that comfort zone. Remember the Edward de Bono puzzle on lateral thinking? It was only by going outside the self-imposed limitations that it became possible to connect the nine dots correctly.

I cannot emphasise strongly enough the need to recognise and break out of comfort zones. I have witnessed the most horrific psychological trauma and distress in people's lives, as a direct result of them remaining in comfort zones and refusing to expand horizons and stretch themselves in a particular direction. A major part of our growth and development as human beings comes from our interpersonal relationships. How can we possibly hope to acquire and develop social graces or communication skills if we never even bother to speak to people? For some people it may be the most difficult thing in the world to greet a new neighbour. For others it may seem almost impossible to approach their boss on a personal or domestic issue. It may be uncomfortable at first, but we must endure the initial discomfort. This is breaking out of our comfort zone.

It's good to have a dream. But if we only think about that dream, and do nothing to make it a reality, then we are dwelling in the realms of unreality — we're only daydreaming! We must make it happen. The way to make it happen is by breaking out of the comfort zones that lull us into a false sense of security, and prevent us from realising our goals, achieving our ambitions, and ultimately becoming the person we are capable of becoming.

Being alive to the needs of others, and having the capacity to reach out to others, are qualities that require a great degree of unselfishness, and a deep conviction of the value we should place on our own individual contribution towards making this world a better place in which to live. Of course, this involves inconvenience, upsetting schedules, sacrifice, discipline, etc. But the joy experienced by the exercise is immense! You can't make an omelette without breaking eggs. You cannot grow and develop emotionally without social interaction. Breaking out of comfort zones is mandatory.

There was a man on a working committee, of which I was part, who learned about the principle of sacrifice and inconvenience for a cause. We were at the final stages of planning a major event, and it was necessary to fix a mutually convenient time for our next meeting immediately prior to this important event. However, he explained that he would be unable to attend because that was the night of a World Cup soccer match. I suggested that in this age of advanced technology, perhaps he could record the match on his VCR, and then he could watch it later that evening, after the meeting. But he said, "It wouldn't be the same. I need to watch those games live." A typical comfort zone.

I remember another occasion where an individual failed to attend a late-night business meeting because he would have missed a concluding episode of his favourite soap opera on television. These are typical examples of comfort zones, and manifest a selfish and sometimes warped sense of values, commitment and prioritising.

There are other types of comfort zones. A friend of mine, recently widowed, came back from her first continental holiday. Throughout her 35 years of marriage, her husband never took her on such a holiday, because he had no interest in travelling abroad. She had broken out of that comfort zone.

There are also plenty of examples of people not visiting friends in hospital, simply because they find hospitals "depressing".

Some Self-Check Questions

- Do you recognise comfort zones in various aspects of your life — domestic, business, social?

- Are you doing anything to break out of any of these comfort zones?

- How do you feel about comfort zones?

- Have you broken out of comfort zones in the past?

- What, in your estimation, is your greatest comfort zone?

- How are you dealing with it?

DECISIONS

If we go through life like Abel's ass, we will never know the
wisdom of our thoughts, because we will never translate them
into action and put them into practice. Making decisions
indicates the existence of courage and confidence, and the
ability to accept responsibility for our actions. The very essence
of true leadership is the ability to make decisions, and to stand
accountable for those decisions.

To make a decision is to arrive at a point of no uncertainty. But how often we see people think that they are making decisions, while confusion still reigns.

You can't please all of the people all of the time.

Sometimes it's hard to make decisions, knowing that someone is going to be upset at your decision. But that's what makes great leaders. They are capable of making decisions. Of course, you will sometimes make the wrong decision, and sometimes you will have to reverse a decision. But isn't that better than never deciding in the first place? At the end of your life, the only real regrets that you will have will be for the things you never did, rather than for the things you did. I always remember a lovely line from an old Kris Kristofferson song:

> *"I'd rather be sorry for something I've done,*
> *than for something I didn't do."*

So make the decision, and start doing things.

In relation to addictions, *you* decide to take the substances, *you* decide to indulge in the habit, *you* decide to allow that mental block to affect your actions. By not deciding to do something, you have already made the decision to "not do" that thing. Wouldn't it be far more beneficial to you if you made the proactive decision to take positive action?

Let me just focus on two aspects of the decision-making process at this stage. Another look at the Latin as we dissect this word "decision". I don't want to get caught up in an elaborate etymological exercise, but in some instances, examining its origins can help to clarify the true meaning of the word. It comes from the Latin word *decidere*. *De* means "from" in Latin, and *cidere* means "to cut", so together it means "to cut from". When you are faced with a decision, you must have options, otherwise it would not require a decision. You examine each option on its merits, and then you "cut" the least attractive options away from the group, and you're left with one option. That should be the point of no uncertainty, and the option that remains is the one to run with.

The second aspect of decision-making forms an integral part of the whole procedure, because once you have arrived at this point of no uncertainty, there is no room for ambivalence — "murder the alternative". Don't keep thinking, "What if I had chosen the other one?"; "Maybe I should have discussed the matter more thoroughly?" . . . STOP! You've made the decision, cut the other options, and now you should run with it. Yes, RUN with it. Can you imagine a player on the football field being ambivalent about what he should do with the ball once it lands in front of him? "Eh . . . maybe if I just run around for a while as I'm deciding what to actually do with the ball . . . no, perhaps I should just kick it . . .or maybe . . ." By this stage he would probably be pulverised by his own team for destroying the game! The principle of singularity of purpose is very pertinent to the process of decision-making.

Three Key Principles of Decision-Making

1. Examine all your options.

2. Eliminate the least viable, don't procrastinate, and make a decision to run with the best option.

3. Murder the alternative, and carry out the decision.

The ability to make and carry out decisions is a key
fundamental principle of leadership, and a mandatory
requirement for people who hold positions of leadership.

Nobody is going to be absolutely right all the time. No matter how knowledgeable you are, and how experienced you are, there will be times when you will make the wrong decision. So what? Mistakes can be rectified, and the competent leader will accept responsibility for their decision. Accountability is an integral part of leadership. But at least a decision has been made. There is nothing as infuriating as waiting for endless hours and days on a decision to be made.

How many times have we witnessed the snail's pace of the crawling bureaucracy at work, as yet another project or initiative grinds to a halt because the proposal is still lying on the desk of some bureaucrat who is incapable of making a decision? One of the major restraining forces in an organisation can be the length of time it takes to get decisions from those in a position of authority.

Some Self-Check Questions

> - Do you make decisions easily, or do you need to dissect and analyse every available piece of information beforehand?
>
> - Have you lost out on situations because of your inability to decide?
>
> - Are you aware of your level of competence and action in making decisions?
>
> - What are you doing to make yourself a more effective decision-maker?

GOALS

In the game of life, how can we tell whether we're winning or losing if we don't have goals? Capturing the vision means setting goals and objectives to achieve that vision and make it a reality. If we have nothing to aim for, it is difficult to be inspired, motivated or enthused. Setting and achieving goals will stretch you to accomplish more than you ever thought possible.

When people first start playing the game of golf they are always mystified at how often they keep missing the ball as they try to tee off. The problem is that they ignore one of the first principles —

"Keep your eye on the ball". As soon as they grasp this principle, and practise it, the problem of missing the ball disappears. The same principle applies with goals. You only see the obstacles when you take your eye off the goal.

This is the plateau on which you should start identifying the goals that you wish to set for yourself. The reason that we set and achieve goals is to monitor our progress. As we review each year, we can gauge our progress by the number of goals we have achieved during that year. Could you imagine trying to play a game of soccer without goalposts? How would you decide the winner? If we don't set and achieve goals for ourselves, we will never know whether we are winning or losing!

A goal can be a place, or state, or level of progress that we wish to achieve. It can be a position in business, or it can be the development of a situation within the family. Whatever the goals may be, it is essential that we set them and try to achieve them. The sense of achievement, self-fulfilment, success and self-confidence that we enjoy when we arrive at our goals is something that can carry us through the valley periods of our lives. We can look at the goals we have achieved, and those accomplishments can inspire and drive us to continue striving and achieving.

Our goals can be long-term, medium-term or short-term, and generally we will find ourselves striving for a mixture of goals at any one time. They can apply to each dimension of our lives, the physical, the mental, the emotional or the spiritual. We can have domestic goals, business goals, leisure goals, as they relate to our various roles in life. But whatever our goals relate to, they should all conform to the criteria of making us better people in some way, of enhancing our lives, of helping us to recognise and use our talents and skills, and to actualise our potential.

FIGURE 14: ACHIEVING GOALS

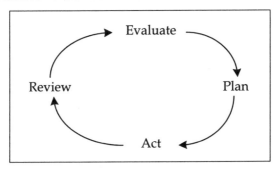

In Figure 14, I have illustrated a system that I use for achieving goals. The first part is the *evaluation*. This must include examination of the motivating factor. If the "why" is not strong enough, the "how" will be a hard struggle. So you must ask yourself:

- *What* is my goal?

- *Why* am I setting this as a goal?

- Will it *benefit* me or my family or my business?

- Is it *important* to me?

- Is it based on my *values*?

- Is it part of my *vision* for my future?

- Will I be a *better person* for achieving this goal?

- Is it *realistic*? and

- Should it take *priority* in my life?

Then you must clearly identify the goal in specific terms without any vague generalities. To set a goal like, "I'm going to keep fit" is far too vague. That could mean that you will go for a bicycle ride about once a week! You should really say something like, "I'm going to increase my stamina and strength, so I'll start with 15 push-ups per day, and increase by 2 each day until I reach the stage of doing 50 push-ups per day. I'm going to run every day, starting with 10 minutes per day, and increase each week by 10 minutes until eventually I'm running 40 minutes per day." These are specifics, putting the meat on the bones! Now WRITE IT DOWN, because it's only a wish until it's written down.

Another part of the evaluation is setting an objective for your goal. Identify precisely "why" you want to achieve this goal. Your objective, or "why", will become the driving force in helping you to achieve the goal. Remember that your objective is the reason for setting and achieving the goal. To set a goal without clearly examining its objective is like setting off on a journey without fully realising your destination.

If the "why" is strong enough, the "how" becomes easy.

Next comes the *planning*. This is where you put a time-frame on the goal, work out the best way of achieving it, and draw up your daily schedule accordingly. Then use the principles of time management by organising the schedule around your priorities in your daily lifestyle. You can't have an open-ended goal; you must work to a deadline, put some pressure on yourself to accomplish the exercise by a given date and time. Part of the planning is to use a goal-chart; I have outlined a very simple one that can be used for almost any type of goal setting (see Figure 15). I have used this particular chart for the past six years with great success. With goals lasting longer than a month, I just enlarge the chart, and join two charts together. Don't hide the chart; place it in a prominent place as a constant daily reminder to yourself. And don't be ashamed of it, you're making progress! Control the influence of others on you, and develop that personal power! I write out my goal in great detail, and then I transfer a shortened or coded version of the goal to my goal-chart at the bottom, together with the date on which I hope to achieve the goal. In the little daily squares, I write an abbreviated word for each goal, and immediately beside it I draw a small blank box. Every day I mark a tick or a zero in each box for that particular day, depending on whether I have done it or not. This is the greatest monitoring tool for me, because I have to face that goal-chart every day and mark in my performance! The goal-chart is a visual aid, a visual motivator, a practical monitor that you have to check with every day. Use it!

FIGURE 15: GOAL CHART

Goal Chart				Month:			
Mon	Tues	Wed	Thurs	Fri	Sat	Sun	*% Done*
				1	2	3	
4	5	6	7	8	9	10	
11	12	13	14	15	16	17	
18	19	20	21	22	23	24	
25	26	27	28	29	30	31	

	Goals	Symbol		Achievement Date
1	_____		1	_____
2	_____		2	_____
3	_____		3	_____
4	_____		4	_____
5	_____		5	_____

Now that you've evaluated and planned your goals, you must *act* on them, and that means taking the appropriate action to make these goals happen. All the evaluating and planning will not accomplish your goals; you have to go out there and do it! This is where your weekly or monthly schedule should be co-ordinated with your goal-chart to make the practical implementation of the goal effective. Don't allow your feelings, change of circumstances, or external influences distract you from implementing your goal. You must forge ahead with diligence, develop a tunnel vision about it and make it happen. Remember that it's your goal, your purpose, you are in control, and *you're* the only one that can make it happen!

The aspect of REPORT/REVIEW is another essential element in successfully achieving our goals. If we don't report or review, we are deficient in the area of accountability. Ultimately, we're accountable to ourselves, but in the absence of a spouse or companion with whom we can share our goals, use the goal-chart as the reporting instrument, and report to it daily. A weekly review of your progress is also advisable, as it can be a tremendous boost to your self-confidence as you watch yourself coming closer to the achievement date. The review is the monitoring aspect of measuring performance. It's what accelerates our rate of improvement. Remember the importance of having a firm objective in achieving the goal? The review/report should refer directly to the objective to see that our progress and improvement is in line with our objectives, to ensure that we're not being side-tracked.

You can break down your goals into different categories, but always remember that they are all inter-linked. Such a breakdown could be: short-term goals (this week); medium-term goals (this month/quarter); long-term goals (this year, three-year plan, five-year plan). Very often, your success with short-term goals can be an extremely positive encouragement to achieve the medium-term and long-term goals. However, don't set your goals in concrete. There may be situations or circumstances that could necessitate the adapting or restructuring of your goals. In Chapter One, we talked about values, and your goals must be based on your values and vision. Always try to keep your priorities in line with your values, and you *will* achieve your goals.

Some Self-Check Questions

- Do you set and achieve goals regularly?

- Have you reviewed your goals and achievements recently?

- Do you use a goal-chart or any other visual aid?

- Have you set goals in each area of your life relating to your various roles in these areas?

- Have you a clear picture of your goals for the next twelve months, and have you carefully planned how to achieve them?

- What is the most recent goal that you have achieved?

TALENTS/SKILLS

Everyone in this world is born with inherent talents, but it is only by expanding our horizons and pushing our boundaries, in an effort to find those talents, that we can hope to turn those talents into skills. By using our talents, we become skilful, and the repetitive skilful use of them will turn them into an art.

A brief word about talents and skills is warranted at this point along The Five Plateaus of Progress. Some people think they have no talents or skills, and consequently don't bother to strive in any direction because they believe they lack the raw material in the first place. The parable of the Ten Talents in the New Testament is something that should awaken us to the realisation that we must use our talents. Along with the old adage of "No pain, no gain", should also go the other adage, "If you don't use it, you'll lose it".

FIGURE 16: THE DEVELOPMENT OF TALENT

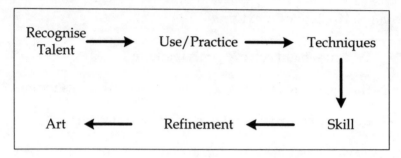

In Figure 16, I have illustrated the progression in the development of a talent. The first thing is to recognise the talent that we have, and the only way to recognise it is by observing it in use, and the only way it will be in use is when we expand our horizons, explore, attempt, and push boundaries. Let's take the example of a musical talent. By sitting down at the piano and attempting to create tunes and music, you suddenly realise you have a talent for making music! So you learn the various techniques in playing the piano, you practise, you study and learn more advanced techniques and now it becomes a skill. But you want to utilise that skill to its very limit, and in dedicating your efforts and your time to the advanced study and practice of the instrument, you become an accomplished artiste.

The talent is the raw material, the skill and the art are developed by working on that raw material, refining it, polishing it, and creating something excellent out of it. How do you know you're not a great fiction writer, or a fabulous skier, or perhaps an outstanding actor, or anything you would like to be, unless you try them? Recognising the talent is part of the Plateau of Awareness, but sometimes it doesn't surface until a later Plateau when you start reaching out, experimenting, exploring, etc. But the development of the talent is definitely a "Plateau Three" exercise in disciplining yourself to build and nurture the talent.

Whenever I hear people complain that it's too late to do anything about developing or discovering a new talent, I'm immediately reminded about the great story of Grandma Moses. This was the professional name of Anna Mary Robertson Moses (1860–1961). She started painting at the age of 67. With no formal training and very limited education, she persevered with her artistic endeavours and eventually had her paintings exhibited at the Museum of Modern Art in New York City in 1939. In 1952, at the age of 91, she published her autobiography. It wasn't too late for her to start a whole new career at 67, and yet I hear people in their 30s complaining that they're "over the hill, past it, no sense in trying something new at this stage"! It's never too late to start, and it's never too late to change.

Some Self-Check Questions

- Do you know in what areas your talents lie?
- Have you a talent in music, art, business, sport, writing, administration?
- Have you identified your talents yet?
- Are you actively engaged in developing your talents?
- What is your most precious talent?
- How have you used your talents in recent years?

ROUTINES/REINFORCEMENT

*Routines develop self-discipline. It's through the dutiful
exercise of essential routines that we develop the ability to
persist in our efforts to accomplish the task and reinforce
in our minds the initial inspiration which motivated us to
undertake the task in the first place.*

The subject of routines very often evokes a rather negative response, and a reluctance to become involved in a routine, humdrum existence. But routines, in the context of Plateau Three, are anything but boring, and they are essential in establishing order and discipline in your life.

Can you imagine a neurosurgeon going into the operating theatre without certain specific and essential routines already in place for the operation? The surgeon doesn't sit around the operating table with their associates discussing which type of scalpel they should use, or whether or not a human being can exist for more than sixty seconds under anaesthetic without oxygen! They know that there are certain procedures or routines in place, with which they must rigidly comply in order to operate successfully. An airline pilot doesn't sit in the cockpit of the aeroplane before take-off, and ponder about which dials and safety features they will check. A professional dancer doesn't decide on the spur of the moment what steps they are going to use in the performance. That has already been worked out precisely in the rehearsal, and that's why it is called a dance routine.

Routines develop self-discipline!

Don't expect an easy ride when it comes to self-discipline. It only comes from the continuous repetition of routines. The discipline of routines will *make* the goal happen for you. Let me give you an example. If early rising is something that doesn't come naturally to you, yet you find it important to you in achieving your goals, then you must establish a routine to develop the discipline of getting up early. Set your alarm clock to sound at exactly the same time *every* morning (no excuses for public holidays or anything else) *for a minimum of 30 days*. Now here's the secret — get up the very second the alarm sounds! Don't you dare get back into that bed, but stay up; go for your run, or have your shower, get dressed, but at all costs stay up, wake up! This is a routine to develop the self-discipline of rising at the same early hour every morning and it's also a positive reinforcement of the discipline by using the alarm clock. I guarantee you that after 30 days you can leave your alarm clock switched off, and on day 31 you will awaken at precisely the same time as you have done for the previous 30 days. It becomes a conditioning process and it's based upon the principle of self-suggestion and the internal clock. Furthermore, the reinforcement of the discipline will also make you aware of your times for retiring to bed at night time, because you can't burn the candle at both ends. Can you see how such a disciplined behaviour would help to create order and discipline in your life?

Your monthly goal-chart is a perfect example of daily routines, and I cannot emphasise strongly enough the importance of introducing these effective daily routines into your lifestyle. Routines in family life, business life or leisure pursuits should only be used as long as they are effective, and until the discipline has been introduced and firmly established. There is nothing as bad as systems or routines in place for no apparent reason. If a routine or system supports your efforts to progress, then use them, but if they are ineffective, you should abandon them.

In the corporate sector, there are many processes and procedures, but sometimes they can be superfluous, and it is important to examine the systems in place to ensure that they are what they are supposed to be — support systems. A process is really putting something into practice, and a procedure is the effective development of that process. But don't allow systems, processes, or procedures become obstacles to your progress and growth.

Some Self-Check Questions

- Have you introduced any routines into your life?

- Do you use daily routines to develop your self-discipline?

- What daily/weekly routine has been most successful in developing your self-discipline?

- Have you found it difficult to maintain the repetition in keeping to a routine?

- Is your self-discipline becoming stronger as a result of these routines?

DAILY MONITORING

"When performance is measured, performance improves.
When performance is measured and reported,
the rate of improvement accelerates."
— Thomas S. Monson

As we become aware of things we can sometimes do something about them on the spot, but I believe the more frequent scenario would be that we recognise a certain behavioural trait or verbal cliché, and say to ourselves "I must remember to work on that".

But as the days go by, and in the hustle and bustle of daily living, how are we going to monitor our progress in that regard? Do we tick it off on our wall chart, send ourselves a memo on e-mail, or tie a rubber band around our wrists to remind ourselves?

When we're discussing growth and development, it is essential to monitor progress, especially in an area of personal development where you're dealing with so many intangibles. At the end of Plateau One, I suggested you begin keeping a journal to monitor your progress. However, it is really on this Plateau, Discipline, that the benefits of your journal writing can be truly felt. I believe that recording feelings, thoughts and accounts of the day's activities in a daily journal is the greatest way to monitor progress in your life.

A journal is not a diary, an organiser or a daily planner. It is simply an account of what you have done, or what you plan to do, how you have responded, or reacted, to the things you have done, and how you feel about these things. It's something deeply personal, subjective, and completely honest. If it's anything less than that, then you're wasting your time. Could you imagine how well you would know your great-grandfather if you were to find one of his old journals?

In order to accelerate the rate of improvement, report to your journal every day! I have been keeping a daily journal for many years, and it is marvellous to look back on events of a few years ago, see how you felt, what you did, and then consider whether or not you have grown, developed or changed in any way since then.

Have you ever noticed how difficult it is to write something down when it relates to your innermost feelings? The test of how well a concept is assimilated in your mind is in how well you can translate it onto paper. You must develop the ability to marshal your thoughts to walk on paper. Become accustomed to expressing your feelings in writing and you will be amazed how this will stimulate the other dimensions of your life.

I always give written assignments to participants on my courses and seminars, for two reasons. Firstly, it will show me how well, or how badly, the individuals can express themselves in writing. Secondly, it is an accurate assessment of how well they have assimilated the concepts or ideas. You cannot possibly write an account of a concept unless you have first fully assimilated and understood the concept clearly in your own mind.

Journals always start off with brief accounts of the activities of the day, and perhaps just a hint of how you felt about certain situations. However, when you persist and eliminate the inhibitions that stop you from expressing your feelings on paper, your journal becomes like a dear and trusted companion in whom you can confide, and to whom you can pour out the deepest feelings of your heart in daily sessions.

Journal writing comes in three distinct stages. The *first stage* is the simple recording of events, just like diary entries. The *second stage* includes descriptions of these events, with the addition of times and places, etc. This begins to add colour to your journal. The *third stage* is when you start to describe how you felt about these situations, circumstances, people, etc. This is where you are opening up and beginning to express your feelings on paper.

The very exercise of writing a daily journal stimulates every dimension, the physical, the emotional, the mental and the spiritual. Your daily journal is your own personal progress monitor. It will help you to identify, and overcome, any recurring problems in your life. It will encourage you to become more accomplished at expressing yourself in writing. And it will give you a tremendous overview of your progress.

Some Self-Check Questions

> • Do you keep a daily journal?
>
> • How do you monitor your progress?

ACTIVITY, PERFORMANCE AND PRODUCTIVITY

*Practice makes perfect, and it's the activity of "doing it" that
develops our quality of performance, and ultimately increases
our productivity. Improved performance and increased
productivity come not from the lethargic, but from inspired,
motivated, and active individuals.*

Many years ago, I managed a team of sales consultants in the financial services sector and, in an effort to monitor their performance and production effectively, I introduced a "Weekly Reporting Sheet". This report highlighted their daily activity, performance and productivity. By the end of the first month, we had solved the problems that the low achievers were experiencing, which were all due to a low level of activity.

To illustrate the point, let's take the example of the salesperson who wants to sell photocopiers on the open market. Leaving aside the obvious research, marketing, promotion, advertising, etc., that goes into the sales operation, the important thing for the salesperson is that they make contact with and talk personally to as many people as possible. This increases the chances of making a sale. The more people who know about me, the more people are likely to buy my product. The actual sales presentation should improve because it's being practised so often with each appointment. The result is that sales figures increase; in other words, the salesperson's productivity increases.

This same principle applies to many other areas of business, domestic and social life. If you increase your activity, it improves your performance, and the amalgamation of the two results in enhanced productivity. But please don't get caught up in activity for the sake of activity, because that becomes a fruitless exercise, and eventually becomes a source of frustration rather than satisfaction. The activity must be worthwhile and it must have purpose. The activity represents to a large degree what we are putting into something. Our activity should be the sowing of the seed and the nurturing of that seed. And there must be an objective or a goal at the end of the activity. Remember the adage, "Direction is more important than speed." When it comes to activity we must also remember that "more haste, less speed" can become a reality if we are not focused on what we are doing. We don't run around like the headless chicken. We must keep our heads, and remain in control of what we are doing. I have discussed planning in more detail in an earlier chapter, but let me just mention here that planned activity is infinitely more productive and rewarding than random activity. The principle of the "Things To Do Today" sheet will guarantee productive activity, and help you to prioritise.

However, the problem with people in relation to increasing activity is the lack of discipline. Take, for example, the salesperson who knows that she should be out on the road making those evening calls, the ones that were impossible to make during the day. But the draw of the crackling log fire, the comfortable chair, the smell of dinner cooking on the stove, and besides all of that it's raining hailstones outside, is too much of an enticement for her, and she doesn't make those evening calls. Does it take discipline to break out of that comfort zone and increase the activity level? You bet it takes discipline!

I had the opportunity to spend 18 months travelling to schools and colleges around Ireland and England with my son, Julian, presenting the "Ray of Hope" drugs awareness seminars to students and parents. We produced the seminars with the appropriate visual aids, etc. But Julian was initially quite nervous about his ability to present the seminar effectively, this being an entirely new departure for him. He used about four pages of notes during his first day of seminars. However, by the end of the first week, he was delivering his 75-minute presentation with all the hallmarks of a seasoned veteran, with no notes whatsoever! Bear in mind that we were presenting three two-hour seminars per day to capacity audiences. Because of the daily activity of presenting the seminars, his performance improved dramatically, and this resulted in an extremely effective seminar. Can you imagine trying to hold the attention of students at a seminar for two hours? During the "Ray of Hope" seminars, you could hear a pin drop — the students hung on every word he spoke. There's nothing as boring as listening to a soporific speaker who reads his entire speech from his notes, with little or no inflection in his voice.

The old adage, "practice makes perfect", applies perfectly to this principle. How do you improve your performance in swimming? By the repetitive procedure of swimming. The more you swim, the better you become as a swimmer. The same applies to all sport. I have spoken with many athletes who have successfully applied all of the principles contained in this book into their training schedules and lifestyles. The results have been excellent. But this principle of increasing the right activity, thereby improving the performance, has remarkable and tangible results at the productivity end of the scale.

Some Self-Check Questions

- In what activities are you engaged on a daily basis that will help to improve your overall performance?

- Are you aware of any aspect of your performance that would improve with increased activity?

- Have you observed how this principle works, how your performance improves through increased activity?

EMOTIONAL/SOCIAL DIMENSION

It is only when we have learned to subordinate our feelings
to our will that we can fully enjoy the highest level of
emotional maturity.

Here lies the crux for most of our failures in life. It is this emotional dimension that gently leads us into our comfort zones. It is because of our emotional weaknesses that we indulge rather than resist. The greatest confusion in relationships has been caused by the lack of understanding of our emotional dimensions. Everything in life should not be subject to our feelings at the time. Possibly more than any other dimension, it is the control of this dimension that helps us to be in control of our behaviour.

In the course of a conversation over dinner with some friends, one of the men expressed his anxiety about the uncertainty of the future, especially in regard to personal and domestic relationships. I asked him to elaborate and he explained that, for instance, in his own relationship he didn't know how he would feel about his wife in five years' time. I looked at his beautiful wife and thought how insensitive and utterly childish his remark had been. This was an intelligent and very successful businessman. I was quite shocked at his low level of maturity, and his lack of emotional understanding in areas like commitment, love, sacrifice, self-discipline, control, etc. But it epitomised an increasingly prevalent attitude in our society — the hedonistic attitude. As long as people continue to subscribe to the raw basic pleasure/pain principle, they can never aspire to the finer qualities in life and they will never build strength of character.

This is one of the reasons why it is often so difficult to teach correct principles to our children, because they have seen this type of childish behaviour in adults. So many times they ask, "Why should I have to do it if I don't feel like doing it?" We only make real progress in this world by overcoming our feelings of the moment and doing some of the more distasteful things. If we based everything on our feelings and emotions we would become totally egocentric, worthless, miserable individuals. Could you imagine if nobody got up out of bed in the mornings, nobody went to work, nobody bothered to control their appetites? The world would virtually come to a standstill. Remember the sport slogan, "There'll be more bad days than good days". Most of the great things in this world have been achieved by responsible people who didn't always feel like doing certain things, but did them anyway.

As human beings we have one tremendous guiding influence in our lives and that is our own independent will. This is what brings us to a higher level, to a different plane, to a more noble and fulfilling existence. We cannot afford to be slaves to our emotions. We cannot base every action on our emotional feelings. It is

through our conduct and behaviour in our interpersonal relationships with other human beings that we eventually grow and develop. There is nothing more frustrating and infuriating than to
come across an individual who is in a senior management position, but who has never grown or developed emotionally. The
"spoilt child" syndrome is still evident in their behaviour.

I remember witnessing the demise of a marriage many years
ago. It was a most distressing and sad occasion, because so many
people were deeply hurt by the situation. This man was extremely
successful in business and his family situation had all the hallmarks of a happy marriage. He loved his wife and four children
dearly, and to see them all together, it was obvious that they were
a very content family unit. However, his business necessitated him
travelling quite often and also working late into the evenings. As
part of his working team, he had a very professional and efficient
female personal assistant who travelled with him frequently and
also worked with him at the late evening meetings. Without any
intention of infidelity to his wife, or any ulterior motive, he became very close to his assistant because of their constant physical
proximity. However, an emotional attachment began to develop
because of the many shared moments, experiences, and unusual
incidents that they witnessed together. The emotional involvement
began to grow, and eventually it left him emotionally drained
when he returned to his wife. On one occasion, he was away from
home for four weeks — four weeks that nurtured and fed the
emotional relationship with his assistant. Before he returned
home, the relationship had become a physical and sexual one.
Were it not for the powerful emotional bond that had developed
between them, there might have been some hope of reconciliation.
But unfortunately, it had all gone too far, and his marriage col-

lapsed. I don't have to give you the gory details of the amount of pain, sorrow, grief and devastation that followed.

All of this could have been avoided if this man had realised that *any* emotional or physical involvement with his assistant was tantamount to infidelity to his wife. To share special moments, to enjoy dinner together, to have that drink at the end of a long meeting, or to discuss details of any domestic situations can all be part of the beginnings of infidelity, unless the individual is solidly in control of the emotional dimension.

I had occasion to help a colleague of mine overcome a problem with alcoholism some time ago. In the course of our many discussions, the word HALT took on a whole new meaning for me. It represented the words Hungry, Angry, Lonely and Tired. These were the danger areas where the weakness of drinking was concerned. Whenever this person was hungry, angry, lonely or tired, the alarm bells went off and she contacted a friend or associate immediately to help talk her out of the temptation to drink. Can't you see how the HALT principle applied to my business friend? It was during the times of loneliness, tiredness and hunger that his assistant was always there for him. It was with her that he shared his feelings, instead of with his wife. No wonder an emotional attachment developed.

Whether it is in domestic, business, or social relationships, sport, academics, industry, etc., we must learn to subordinate our feelings to our will. Otherwise, we are doomed to failure in our endeavours. If we are not "in control" of our feelings, emotions, appetites and driving passions, we are no better than the animals. We are human beings, created in the image and likeness of God. We are the highest of all the species in this world, and we should act accordingly in a manner befitting this noble lineage.

There is such a need for men and women of integrity in today's world of advanced technology and progress. But integrity can never be achieved without strength of character, and that can never be achieved until we are firmly "in control" of our lives and have learned to subordinate our feelings to our independent will.

Some Self-Check Questions

- Have you ever tried to subordinate your feelings to your will?

- Do you feel that you are "in control" of your life, or are you a slave to your emotions?

- What areas of your life are most seriously affected by your emotional weaknesses?

- Are you making progress in any area of controlling your emotions?

INDEPENDENCE

When we finally "let go", and learn to stand on our own two
feet, we can develop our own independent perspective on life,
and face the future with confidence.

In Chapter One, we discussed the harmful effect dependence can have on our progress. Once we overcome our tendencies to be dependent, we learn to become independent, and eventually we can stand on our own two feet. The whole process of raising children is to make them ready to become independent human beings in their own right. Until a child reaches the age of 21, they can be dependent on their parents in varying degrees. However, as the independent will of the rebellious teenager proves, they quickly develop their independent opinions, goals, ambitions and attitudes in life. If they don't develop this independence before they enter a marriage relationship, major problems can develop very quickly.

The section on Comfort Zones is also relevant here. We can allow ourselves the comfort of remaining on the one plateau for a long time, but the penalties are quite severe. The expression "he is his own man" refers to the individual who has broken away from areas of dependence, broken out of comfort zones, and is now successfully standing on his own two feet. From that position of independence, he is capable of making more accurate judgements and is unhampered by comfort zones or dependence.

Young people who live at home during their 20s and depend upon their parents for financial support will never achieve independence. They need to break out of the comfort zone of living at home and see what it's like trying to make ends meet without depending on parents to help them out.

Possessiveness can be another source of dependence. I'm sure you're familiar with the "magpie mentality" of the hoarder. The hoarder is one who wants to keep every item they have ever received in their life. This is the type of person who eventually ends up buying for the sake of possession. This develops a dependence upon material possessions. Never letting go, just in case you may need it. It's similar to the narrow-minded focus on money and wealth, the sole preoccupation with accumulating as much money as possible, to be as rich as possible. Why? It's a dangerous road to go down, because we allow the things of the material world to possess us. We become slaves to our appetites for more material things. This does not breed independence; it creates a greater dependence, we can't do without certain things anymore. Of course, money is essential to provide for our needs, but not for every vague desire and want that we have. How profound the following saying:

> *"True possession is proved only by giving.*
> *All that you are unable to give possesses you."*

The subject of independence is particularly applicable to teenage youth, who are exposed to all sorts of temptations. They need to "stand on their own two feet" and be able to resist peer pressure that would encourage them to do things which they know are not right. The development of this type of independence comes from raising their self-esteem and self-confidence. So often, young people embark on crazy paths to destruction for no other reason than their low self-esteem and lack of self-confidence. They want to be one of the gang, not to be the odd one out, and fear ridicule by their peers. We need to encourage our young people to develop a strong sense of values and then to make up their own minds and make their own decisions. We shouldn't get too upset and disappointed if they don't follow the career paths that *we* have chosen for them! Freedom of expression is part of making their own decisions based on the knowledge they have gained. All we can do is teach correct principles, but they must govern themselves.

Independence denotes freedom. We read of the various wars of independence, when the people of a country fought valiantly to obtain their country's independence. To be independent means to be free from the shackles and chains of dependence; free from the dependence that could sway you to make the wrong decisions. The step from dependence to independence is a major transitional step from a lower to a higher plateau.

Some Self-Check Questions

- Do you consider yourself to be independent?

- Are there still areas in your life in which you rely too heavily on others?

- How do you encourage independence in your staff or your children?

- What steps are you taking to become more independent?

TRAINING

"Train up a child in the way he should go,
and when he is old, he will not depart from it."
— Proverbs 22:6

At times, the corporate sector seems to be top-heavy with training courses of every description. In this age of information technology and rapid technological advancement, it is necessary to regularly upgrade people's knowledge of various programmes or procedures. The lack of tolerance from the public for inefficiency is a driving force for training managers to ensure that their staff are fully trained in the correct processes and procedures.

However, training for the sake of training is absolute nonsense. I remember talking to a prospective employer one time about the need for quality and effective training for his sales teams. His answer was, "Training is a cop out." This answer gave me a very clear understanding of how this man viewed his sales teams, and his obviously bad experiences with training methods. I subsequently had the opportunity to talk with many of the consultants on his sales teams and I realised that the standard of training they were receiving was absolutely abysmal and archaic.

Training has to have a firm objective in mind. What are you training for? Let me again take the example of an athlete. A runner's training schedule will be completely different to a swimmer's training schedule. Both are training to compete in high energy sports, but the training involved is to tone and strengthen different muscles. The whole area of sports coaching has become a highly sophisticated and very scientific profession. The training now encompasses diet, nutrition, sleep patterns, stamina training, speed training, techniques, psychological approach, etc. To even contemplate a career in sport without adequate training would be absolutely ludicrous. Training is essential for success.

The principle of education is to equip us with knowledge about our particular chosen field. But then we need the relevant training in order to apply that knowledge to our job. Can you imagine a medical student on his or her first assignment after qualification being landed in the deep end in an intensive care unit? Training is part of our education, it's knowing how to apply our knowledge. Training is the honing of our craft, making us more efficient and effective at what we do.

We will deal with Change in a later chapter, but unless we train ourselves to become competent within the new parameters set by the rapid changes of modern life and business, there is a serious danger of our qualifications becoming obsolete. Fortunately, we get plenty of advance warnings in most sectors of the workplace and we can plan our training strategies.

As I said at the beginning of this section, our training must have a firm objective. If you're a 100-metre runner, you don't train by swimming 50 lengths of the pool every day! If you're in sales, you don't train by studying your monthly calendar. Training has to be specific. The purpose of training is to increase the efficiency and effectiveness of an organisation or of a section within an organisation. First, we need to know what type of training we require and then we find the professionals who can deliver that type of training. Selective and effective training will sharpen our competitive edge, and increase our levels of competence and confidence.

Some Self-Check Questions

- Is regular training an integral part of your organisation?

- How effective has your training been in the past?

- Are you training at present?

- How do you propose to introduce effective training into your schedule?

- Who conducts the training for your staff?

- Are you up to speed in all aspects of competency in your field?

SELF-MASTERY

True integrity is only attained when self-mastery has been achieved. The outward manifestation should reflect the diligent "cleansing of the inner vessel", and a thorough realisation of the inner self, and its immense capacity.

The ultimate goal on this Plateau of Discipline is to achieve self-mastery, but don't get too worried if it takes a lot longer than you anticipated. In many cases, it takes a few times through each plateau in various dimensions before the state of self-mastery is realised. Nothing will build strength of character as quickly as the development of self-mastery in our lives. The more you indulge in a habit or weakness, the weaker your character becomes, your confidence suffers and your mind is not at peace. The more you resist and overcome the desire to indulge, the stronger your character becomes, your confidence increases and you develop great peace of mind.

Resist and build, indulge and weaken!

Your level of control over situations, people, events or circumstances will correspond to the level of control you have over yourself, your emotions, your passions, your desires, your habits, your behaviour and your appetites. If you reach the stage of being "in control" of just one aspect of your character at a time, and then build on that, you will slowly but surely arrive at the level of self-mastery. It isn't easy, but it *is* worthwhile. Cleanse the inner vessel. This is what it's all about. Walk your talk. If you want trust, be trustworthy. If you want a disciplined workforce, be self-disciplined — achieve self-mastery.

OVERCOMING WEAKNESS

"When a man wages war on his weaknesses, he engages in the holiest war that mortals ever wage. The reward that comes from victory in this struggle is the most enduring, most satisfying, and most exquisite that any man ever experiences. The power to do what we ought to do is the greatest freedom."
— Gordon B. Hinckley (quoting his father).

When we talk about developing skills, we can also use the term "mastering the art" of a skill or a sport. Being a master of anything means having abundant knowledge on the subject, and in many instances becoming shining examples of the practical implementation of that subject in our lives. This only comes from long hours of study, dedication, self-denial, resisting temptations and focusing upon the objective of gaining a thorough understanding of our subject. So when you consider yourself, with all your talents, skills, ambitions, aspirations, desires, habits, etc., how much "in control" are you, and what aspects of your personality or character have you mastered?

Isn't it a sad situation when we see people lose control of themselves in any context or situation? The parent who lashes out at the child through frustration and bad temper; the manager who cannot conduct an interview with a member of his or her staff because of an emotional involvement; the alcoholic who leaves his or her family destitute because of a selfish drinking habit; the husband who beats his wife because of frustration and misunderstanding; the wife who cheats on her husband because of emotional starvation; the teenager who destroys his life because his drug habit got out of control. Although sad to observe, and at times heartbreaking to experience, all of these should serve as incentives for us to strive constantly to maintain that level of self-mastery at all costs. Once again, it gives one great freedom when self-mastery is attained through obedience to a higher law than that of self-gratification or social pressure. To take control of our lives, our environment, our domestic and business situations, our families, and our futures, we must first take control of ourselves on this Plateau of Discipline through developing the art of self-mastery.

To obtain a Master's Degree in any subject, it is necessary to prove that you fully understand the subject, and that you have great mastery of it. If you were questioned on any aspect of that subject, you would feel confident that you could respond and ex-

plain satisfactorily. In order to attain self-mastery, it is equally important that we get to know ourselves, our strengths and weaknesses, our abilities, talents, capabilities and capacities in various
dimensions of our lives. This requires absolute honesty on our
part. We have to be honest enough to recognise all of these facets
about ourselves, and then we have to have the courage to take
control of our lives. We are *masters*, not *subjects*. We have been
given our talents, our emotions, our brains, etc. to develop and use
wisely. We must be in the driving seat, we must take charge. This
inevitably means that there will be an element of sacrifice, but the
personal growth and development achieved through self-mastery
represents the supreme actualisation of our potential in every dimension. Remember the quote at the beginning of this chapter by
David O. McKay:

> *"He who reigns within himself, and rules passions,*
> *desires and fears is more than a king."*

Some Self-Check Questions

- Are you "in control" of yourself?

- Have you achieved self-mastery in any area of your life?

- Are you aware of the areas that need to be addressed on
  this issue?

- Do you have a firm plan in mind to overcome any of your
  weaknesses? Have you grasped the reality and extreme
  importance of this concept of self-mastery?

ASSIGNMENTS FOR PLATEAU THREE

1. Identify one comfort zone that you recognise in your life, and illustrate how you intend to break out of it. Indicate what choices you will have to make, and how you must adjust certain situations in order to exercise the Law of Growth in this instance.

2. List your present goals, how they relate to your roles in Chapter Two, and how you propose to achieve these goals through exercising the principles discussed in this chapter. Design a goal-chart and set about monitoring your progress and achievements daily.

3. Introduce just one new daily routine into your life to reinforce the principle of discipline and self-mastery. Write this down, be very specific about it, and incorporate it into your daily planner/organiser and monthly goal chart.

4. Apply the principles of activity, performance and productivity to your daily work, and monitor the improved performance and enhanced productivity through increased activity.

5. Identify a specific area of your life in which you are emotionally immature and, by applying the principle of self-mastery, work out exactly what steps you can take to develop a more emotionally mature approach to the situation, and then take those steps.

In order to derive the maximum benefit from this chapter, you should be actively engaged in doing these assignments for a minimum of one week before proceeding to Plateau Four.

4

Plateau Four:
CHANGE

*"The Changemasters are those people and organisations
adept at the art of anticipating the need for, and of leading
productive change."*
— Rosabeth Moss Kanter

I f you have been using this book as a type of manual, and doing
the assignments at the end of each chapter, you will realise that
the first visible signs of progress have been manifested through the
implementation of Plateau Three, Discipline. As you discipline
your mind and your behaviour to make choices, break out of comfort zones, make decisions, identify goals, and introduce routines
into your life, it must bear some immediate fruit.

However, as the progress gets better, the plateaus get that little
bit harder. But always remember that they *are* worthwhile! Plateaus Three and Four are the testing of your mettle, because they
necessitate getting "in control" of your life, with firm action. The
grey areas of general notions and ideals are translated into a pattern of action to implement the principles.

At this stage, you should clearly know exactly where you're at,
you should have captured the vision of where you would like to

be, and you should have introduced sufficient discipline into your life to enable you to make the necessary changes. This Plateau is also the one that evokes the most apprehension and fear from individuals, because somehow there is this great reluctance to, and fear of, change.

To live *is to change, and to live well is to have changed often.*

I detest hearing the old cliché, "That's the way we've always done it", because it epitomises everything that is stagnant about our society. It is one of the most stifling attitudes prevailing in our social and corporate sectors today. Many people will sit and ponder about their plight, and wish that things would change for them. As long as they only *wish*, things will never change. But if they really want things to change, they *can* do something about it.

For things to change for you, you've got to change.

This can mean a change of attitude, a change of perception, a change of environment, a change of job, a change of behaviour, but the key word is *change*. Things around us are continually changing and moving on and if we don't change we could be left behind.

Can you imagine if everyone in the computer industry decided that their success was final when the first computer was invented? "Okay guys, take it easy, we've invented the computer, the latest innovation in information and communication technology, so sit back and relax, we've arrived!" Would we ever have seen the PC, interactive systems, modems, compact disc compatibility, e-mail, and the myriad of high-tech inventions that have been launched on the market in the last ten years? All of these things came about through the diligence of the people working on them, and the ability that these people had to change, to adapt, to alter perspectives, to "boldly go where no man has gone before"! That's what pioneering is all about. Changing, moving on, not accepting the mediocre and the mundane, but reaching out, stretching forward and upwards in search of excellence in every dimension.

Of course, it isn't always easy to change. There can often be considerable inconvenience and pain attached to change. But sometimes you just have to realise one very important aspect of change. The pain of changing now will be significantly less than the pain of remaining the same.

One of the most poignant examples of the urgent need for change was in the aftermath of the fall of the Berlin Wall. For the world, it was a great and historic event, but for thousands of people it meant that their qualifications and skills would now be redundant in the new hi-tech world to which they were exposed. The decisions were hard, but they had to be made. Change was happening all around them, so they had to change or be left behind. It was painful, humiliating, frustrating, wearying, but it eventually paid dividends. Those who changed can now enjoy a productive and prosperous life. Those who didn't change suffer the ongoing frustration and pain of being non-productive, feeling useless, with low morale and a miserable lifestyle.

Some Self-Check Questions

- Do you feel as if you're stuck in a rut and unable to change?

- Are you aware of the need for change in your life?

- How recently have you exercised your creative or innovative qualities to implement change?

- In what areas of your life do you intend making changes?

HABITS

*As human beings we are naturally creatures of habit. However,
the degree to which we control our habits, or allow our habits
to control us, will determine the measure of our character.*

Let me focus on one aspect of the flowchart in Figure 9 (page 100)
for a moment: the subject of HABITS. They can either build tremendously strong character, or they can be the means of creating
incredibly weak character. When you reflect upon the reasons why
you haven't made enough significant progress, you can always
identify a few habits in there that have served as major stumbling
blocks, or, in some instances, brick walls! "I'm sorry, I can't participate in that fun run, I'm too unfit, and I smoke." So where's the
personal power when it comes to allowing our habits to control
us? If you really wanted to compete in the fun run, you would
have prepared for it by giving up the habit of smoking and then
training to become fit enough for it. But isn't this so often the case?
We allow our habits to prevent us from making progress, and
sometimes from just enjoying ourselves and getting the most out
of activities or events. Most of the habits that you now possess
were just thoughts at one time. But by entertaining them, and allowing them to take centre-stage in your mind, and then talking
about them, they turned into actions. When actions are repeated
consistently, they become habits.

Imagine that your mind is a hotel and everything that wants to
stay in this hotel has to register at the reception desk in the foyer.
Our minds are always being exposed to thoughts, but if we don't
allow the negative and bad thoughts past the foyer of the hotel to
register with reception, then they can't stay in the hotel. So you
really have to nip them in the bud, don't allow them to take proper

form in your mind, don't even let them past the foyer of your mind, throw them out!

It is imperative that you successfully address the area of habits if you want to exercise any sort of significant change in your life. In Figure 17, I have drawn a table with good habits (things I need to cultivate) on one side and bad habits (things I need to eliminate) on the other side. This is simply a list of "things to do" in relation to habits. But unless you identify them and write them down, they will never become part of your game plan, or appear on your goal chart. They will just remain *wishes*. As you work on this list, initially the good habits will represent the opposites of the bad habits, but as you get to grips with this problem of habits, you will gradually break from that stark contrast. You will begin to identify good habits worth cultivating, and your focus will eventually shift from the bad habits and focus upon the good habits.

FIGURE 17: IDENTIFY BAD AND GOOD HABITS

Bad Habits (Things I need to eliminate)	Good Habits (Things I need to cultivate)

The golden rule of habits states: "If an action is performed consistently and consecutively more than 20 times, it becomes a habit." That rule applies equally to good and to bad habits. But the second part of that rule states: "If we refrain from the action on three consecutive occasions, it can break a good habit, or give us breathing space to break a bad habit." Isn't it interesting how it affects the good and the bad in slightly different ways? The reason is that we have to be *proactive* in cultivating good habits. It has to be a conscious decision to develop a certain habit that will be for our ultimate good and well-being. This very often involves the principles of discipline, change, visualising, decision-making, self-mastery, reinforcement, etc. Whereas the bad habit just seems to creep into our lives through the back door of the mind, sneaks into the "live action" department, and bingo, it's home safe and sound, and protected by a beautiful comfort zone!

> *Habits begin as cobwebs, and end up as chains.*
> *But the chains of habit are too weak to be felt,*
> *until they are too strong to be broken.*

The natural state of man is one based upon instinct. But, unlike the animals, we are the most intelligent of the species, and we have a powerful spiritual and mental dimension in our lives. By developing good habits, we help ourselves gain control of our lives. We must not allow ourselves to be bound by the chains of habit. I don't want you to focus too much on the bad habits, but we must understand how they came about in the first place. Bad habits are developed through laziness, lack of concern, lack of enthusiasm, lack of commitment, not being in control of our appetites, desires, or passions, conditioning by our families, society, environments, and lifestyles. Habits relate to our behaviour, and you should cast your mind back to the discussion on behavioural patterns in order to recognise any behaviours that may be self-defeating blocks to your progress. However, it's not just a case of deciding to eliminate the bad habit, because, like the section on focus, it is essential to create an alternative for ourselves. Whatever dimension the bad habit is feeding, that dimension will be depleted in stimulation when the bad habit is removed. So we must create an alternative form of stimulation for that particular dimension. Bad habits are often formed for no other reason than the *lack of alternatives*. Just look at many of the socially deprived areas of any city, and observe the lack of facilities to occupy the youth, and the resulting abundance of bad habits that abound in these areas.

Good habits are developed by cultivating good qualities, introducing order and discipline into our lives, focusing upon our true values in life, and getting "in control" of our thoughts and behaviours. We work at developing good habits by introducing routines, self-discipline, consistency, planning, evaluating, setting goals, and cultivating an "above-average" attitude. Rise above the level of subservience, or compliance with what you know to be wrong, and strive to bring the "actual" closer to the "ideal" by developing the techniques to implement the principles that will help you in your pursuit of excellence along the Plateaus of Progress. Most of the bad habits to which we have become addicted had their origins in our emotional dimension, but the good habits always have their origins in our spiritual or mental dimensions. Strength of character is only developed by being "in control". Bad, or weak, habits put us out of control, because in effect they are controlling us — we are slaves to our habits.

Three Key Principles on Habits

1. Identify and list your good and bad habits. This will help you to clarify your position in relation to habits.

2. Start eliminating your bad habits by providing alternatives. This will strengthen your resolve, increase your confidence, and free you from the grip of your bad habits.

3. Focus on the cultivation of new good habits. This will renew your enthusiasm, put distance between your new habits and the old ones, and accelerate your progress.

Some Self-Check Questions

- Are you aware of any bad habits in your life?

- What are your good habits?

- Do you strive to eliminate bad habits and cultivate good habits?

- How do you propose to eliminate your bad habits, and provide alternative stimulation?

CHANGING PERSPECTIVES

Inaccurate perceptions can create distorted perspectives.
To acquire a broad perspective, we need to be in possession
of as much information as possible, and view from
the highest possible vantage point.

Your perspectives depend to a large degree upon your vantage point. For example, if you are looking at the main street of a city from inside an office building, you will have a narrow perspective of the physical features of the street. But if you were to stand on a rooftop and get an overview of the street, feel the atmosphere, and see the life in the street, then you would have a broader perspective of that street.

In endeavouring to develop a comprehensive perspective on situations, your vantage point is initially your perception of what the situation seems to be. However, in order to gain a proper perspective, it is important to investigate, relate it to circumstances and events that may be contributing factors, experience it, become involved in trying to understand it, and then you develop a proper perspective on it. When a particular incident is described out of the context of its origin, it is very difficult to give any sort of judgement, because you cannot possibly gain a proper perspective on the matter. In the film *Yentl*, I was impressed by the lovely song, "A Piece Of Sky", sung by Barbara Streisand. From her window, she could only see a piece of sky, but when she stepped outside and looked around, she never dreamed it was so wide or even half as high. She had to try her wings, to reach out, to explore, and she realised that the more she lived, the more she learned, the more she realised the less she knew. So why should she settle for a piece of sky, when there is so much to see, so much to learn, to question, to believe?

As we go through life we have the opportunity to develop *fresh* perspectives on situations, people and circumstances, if we really want to see things from a different vantage point. But it takes effort, and sometimes a little bit of risk. But it always takes courage to take that step and use every opportunity for growth and development, to progress rather than regress.

I remember a friend of mine who was having great difficulty in reading, and he just didn't have time to drop into an optician, or optometrist, to have his glasses changed. However, one day he lost his reading glasses, and for two days he couldn't read anything. Now he was forced to attend the optician, and within a couple of hours he was back in action with a new pair of reading glasses. "What a pair of glasses!" he exclaimed. "I've never had such glasses, I can read everything, even the small print!" He was seeing things from a fresh perspective. It's even more astonishing in real life situations when we adopt a different perspective on things; we can sometimes be pleasantly surprised. This is the Plateau on which you should examine your perspectives and, if you feel it necessary, endeavour to change them, to adopt a fresh perspective. Reflect upon how you examined your perceptions, attitudes, conditioning, concepts, roles, goals, choices and comfort zones, and see if a fresh perspective would affect any of these areas in a positive manner. Change also means seeing things in a different light and this different light can be a fresh perspective.

Some Self-Check Questions

- Are you aware of the accuracy of your perspectives?

- Do you always strive to gain the highest vantage point in order to gain the broadest perspective?

- Do you regularly alter any distortions in your perspectives?

- How do you plan to develop broader perspectives on situations in the future?

CREATIVITY

*The ability to create something new, fresh, innovative, useful
or educational from the raw materials and knowledge we
have at our disposal is a talent upon which the world has
relied since its creation. Without the creative talents of the
men and women who are engaged in invention, research,
innovation, exploration and pioneering, our progress
would be severely diminished.*

Have you ever watched an artist draw or paint a portrait? I have often stood for hours watching one of the many sidewalk artists, dotted along the promenade of the Spanish Costa del Sol, execute magnificent portraits on a blank piece of paper or canvas. This is an example of artistic talent, used and practised until it has been refined into an art. With skilful use of pastels, capturing the varying degrees of light and shade, the artist can create the character and expression of the individual on paper.

When I study the various corporate mission statements, I very often find the word "creativity" conspicuous by its absence. I believe that creativity should be a core value in every organisation that is serious about learning and progressing. The nature/nurture argument always arises when we discuss this topic, but it's almost irrelevant, because the very nature of the subject, creativity, pertains to innovation. It is this preoccupation with the origins of the word or idea of creativity that sometimes stunts the growth of creativity in organisations and in individuals. The focus of management is too often upon production, bottom-line issues, and on maintaining the efficiency of the organisation. But the very reason why so many of these organisations are in existence is because someone had the creative spark to start the company!

If we don't nurture the creative inputs, ideas, opinions, and concepts of our workforce, we will be responsible for the drought that will inevitably result from such negligence. The most powerful commodity in the world today is "idea power". This power only develops when we allow, and encourage, our workforce to utilise the creative side of their brains and come up with innovative "brainwaves".

Creativity denotes change, innovation, new, different, fresh, movement, progress, and anything to do with development of, or elaboration on, something. Throughout the centuries, we have always applauded the one who came up with the bright new idea.

Businesses, industries and societies, thrive upon this great gift of creativity. The great inventors, innovators, researchers, pioneers, and explorers are all people with tremendous creative ability. They have used their creative imaginations to think, and then to dream, and then to turn the dream into reality through the creative implementation of their concept.

No matter where we travel, how we travel, what we watch, what we hear, what we buy, how we communicate, how we obtain information, how we produce, how we manufacture, how we live, we constantly take for granted the latest modern conveniences, the latest high-tech machinery, the efficient building and heating systems, our transport, our computers, our televisions and our telephones. All of these are the results of creativity in action. Change can be creative, but we must use our imaginations, our minds and our talents to be creative in our use of change. The changes that we implement in our lives must be creatively positive in order to change our lives for the better and help us make greater progress.

During the 1970s, I worked as a record producer for about eight years, and I found it one of the most rewarding aspects of my musical career. It was a tremendous feeling to go into a studio with absolutely nothing but an idea and to emerge 12 hours later with multiple tracks of sheer musical creativity. I always chose session musicians, not only on their technique and ability, but on their "feel" for music, and their ability to contribute creative music that would complement the song being recorded. Once the basic tracks were laid down, it became like a piece of tapestry on which to weave the musical nuances and mix them down to create a finished product. As each track was added, the tapestry began to take shape. As the tracks were mixed, the tapestry gained depth. At the final mix, the tapestry took on a life of its own, a new creation, made up of the multiple musical contributions from the various musicians, singers, engineers and producers. I'm sure it must be even a greater thrill to create a movie!

Some Self-Check Questions

- Are you creative in your work formats?
- Are you creative in your business and domestic planning?
- Do you recognise creativity in your workforce, and do you nurture its development?
- What creative ideas have you utilised in recent months?

TEMPTATIONS

When we experience the wonderful feelings of triumph, success and self-confidence that flow from our decisive action to resist temptation, it helps us to strive more diligently to overcome our weaknesses. It is only through resistance to temptations that we strengthen our will power.

Oscar Wilde once wrote, "I can resist everything except temptation!" Wouldn't it be great if there were no temptations to knock us off track? Actually it wouldn't, because it's only by overcoming the opposition that we strengthen our resolve, build our character, and develop the resilience necessary to overcome obstacles in the future. Unfortunately, there are many temptations in every dimension of our lives, but living by correct principles makes us more prepared for them, and our ability to overcome them increases. The old adage, "If you can't resist it, avoid it", is sound counsel with regard to avoiding the places or circumstances where we know we will be tempted. The alcoholic who is desperately trying to kick the habit should never agree to meet friends in the pub, because that's just walking into temptation.

Temptations, like opportunities, are all around us. Our success depends on our discernment in recognising the empty promises of temptation and our ability not to succumb to the enticements of temptations to engage in activities which we know to be wrong, evil, harmful, underhand, or in any way detrimental to our well-being. We must never allow our emotional weaknesses to dictate our behaviour. Our feelings must be subordinated to our independent will.

There are four steps to avoid, if we really want to overcome these obstacles to our progress:

- The first step is *enduring*. We will endure the inconvenience of the temptation, even though we have no intention of giving in to the temptation. This is a most deadly occupation!

- The second step is *tolerating*. We have endured it under duress, but now it's not as bad as it seemed. So we content ourselves with tolerating it, even though we have no intention of giving in to the temptation. We're now becoming indifferent and apathetic, another deadly occupation!

- The third step is *accepting*. Because it's not affecting anyone else and it's not too bad. So we accept that it's going to stay with us, even though we have no intention of giving in to the temptation. Don't ever accept it; eradicate it at all costs!

- The fourth step is *embracing*. Because after all, everybody's doing it, and having endured, tolerated and accepted it, "If you can't beat them join them", is the attitude that prevails. So we might as well embrace it, enjoy it, give in! This is the end; you've lost the fight.

Endure, tolerate, accept and embrace are the deadly steps that will guarantee a fall, where temptation is concerned.

> *"Vice is a master of so frightful mien,*
> *As to be hated, needs but to be seen.*
> *Yet seen too oft, familiar with her face,*
> *We first endure, then pity, then embrace."*
> — Alexander Pope

We should make every effort humanly possible to rise to the *third level* of temptation as quickly as possible (see Figure 18).

FIGURE 18: THE THREE LEVELS OF TEMPTATION

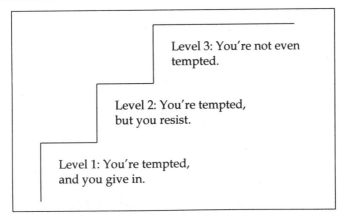

These could be called the Three Levels of Temptation, because invariably we always seem to stay on Level One the longest, but then we break the comfort zone and move to Level Two. The first level of temptation is when we are tempted, we resist initially, but then *we give in*. The second level of temptation is where we are tempted, but *we resist* more strenuously than on the first level, and we don't give in to the temptation! The third level of temptation is where we should strive to be. This is where we have risen so far above the very notion of the temptation that *we're not even tempted!*

The one great temptation that we all face is to avoid the actualising of our potential, because we are inherently lazy as human
beings. We don't really like to break out of comfort zones — we
like our comfort! The temptation is to *remain the same*, to keep our
old habits (which we convince ourselves aren't that bad anyway).
We try to avoid burning up the grey matter and being creative. We
convince ourselves that we're satisfied with the talents that we
have already discovered without having to find out what else
we're good at. We want to leave the goals alone (we're not going
too badly). We don't want to introduce any more routines into our
lives (we've enough to do already). At all costs, we want to avoid
having to make choices and decisions. We'd rather keep to our list
of "things to do" (that's not bad time management). We'd like to
put this physical dimension stuff on hold until such time as we've
got enough time to fit it into our hectic daily schedules. And we'd
just like to observe our progress at a more leisurely pace . . . after
all, what's the big rush? This type of behaviour is guaranteed to
result in rapid regression!

Remember that you will always have *two choices* in determining
your level of progression. Change or justify! You can change and
stop the bad behaviour, or justify your failure by continuing with
the bad behaviour! The obvious choice is to repent, turn over a
new leaf, give up the bad habit, and break out of that comfort
zone. Temptations are the things that will constantly put you off
course, knock you off track, and unless you build up a strong resistance to them, you will always remain on Level One. This is not
progress, because there is no "status quo", which means that you
will start regressing. Recognise them, identify them and be prepared for them. But at all costs resist them!

Some Self-Check Questions

- Do you recognise areas of temptation in your life and do you try to avoid them?

- Are you aware that temptations always promise more than they can deliver?

- Do you follow your feelings or are you directed by your will power?

- Are you aware of any patterns in temptations, and have you learned how to break those patterns?

SYNERGY

When the efforts of many individuals are fused together in the principle of synergy, the enhanced rewards are commensurate with the subsequent power of team effort.

The credo of Gestalt Psychology is that "the whole is greater than the sum of its individual parts". This epitomises the principle of synergy, where 1+1=2+. If we take the human body as an example, we can see how every organ in the body has separate functions, but they have to use the principle of synergy, because they cannot function separately. When all the organs function together, they form the human organism, the incredible human being. But if we were to take the heart out of the body, it would be useless on its own and its absence would render the rest of the body useless.

The construction industry has used the principle of synergy for decades. Take three beams of wood in an upright position, and lay another beam across the top of the three beams. Now let's suppose that this construction can carry a weight of 600 pounds. If we double up on the three beams supporting this structure, to make it six beams in the supporting role, will it now take a weight of 1200 pounds? No, it will take a weight of about 2,400 pounds!

The principle of synergy is to synchronise the energy available to us, to gather all available resources, and to pull them together to form one unit. In order to implement the principle of synergy effectively, it is important to learn another principle also, the principle of *prioritising*. We must learn to recognise what's important to us, what things, people, situations and circumstances should take precedence over others. To work on consensus of opinion in all situations can make us "outer directed". But if we constantly revert to our vision and values base, we can quickly identify what's important to us. Our Personal Mission Statement should be the inspiration for our motivation and, if we're driven by a motive that's strong enough, we can encourage the principle of synergy by our very enthusiasm and determination.

The principle of synergy is ideally manifested in the spirit of Zion in the scriptures.

> *"And the Lord called his people Zion, because they were of*
> *one heart and one mind, and they dwelt in righteousness,*
> *and there was no poor among them."*
> — *The Pearl of Great Value*, Moses 7:18

Can you imagine the power of just two people who are of one heart and one mind? Imagine the power of an entire organisation if they were all of one heart and one mind! We can implement the principle of synergy in the family, school, workplace, communities, corporations, organisations and anywhere we have the opportunity to utilise the resources available to us. By using the principle of synergy, we become more aware of the holistic approach we should use in developing our perspectives, in being able to see the whole picture, and realising that people working together can be a mighty force for good.

"Changes come from the power of many, but only when the
many come together to form that which is invincible . . .
the power of one."
— John G. Avildsen, *The Power of One*

Some Self-Check Questions

- Do you exercise the principle of synergy in your life?

- Is the principle of synergy evident in your workplace?

- How do you propose to adopt, or introduce, the principle of synergy to your workforce?

COURAGE

In this great and abundant world of advanced technology,
excellent amenities, and comprehensive facilities for our
growth and development, we are privileged to enjoy the fruits
of our labours. But the reason we have such an abundant life is
a direct result of the great men and women of this generation,
and previous generations, who had the courage of their
convictions, the courage to sacrifice, the courage to take
risks, the courage to stand for right, and the courage
to speak out in defence of truth and justice.

Those with courage find a way; those without find an excuse. Yes, it does take courage to move from one Plateau to the next, but the rewards for having courage are great indeed. Have you ever heard of a successful leader who didn't have courage? One of the greatest gifts that we have in this world is the gift of Free Agency, the ability we have to make our own choices. The one thing of which we are deprived when we break the law is our free agency. We lose that privilege, we are locked up, and our freedom is curtailed. So we have the freedom of choice to enter the battleground, or stay on the sidelines, or maybe even just listen to it on the radio! What stops us going forward when we know that we are right? We have the idea, we want to make an impact, we know we *should* open our mouths and go for it, but we just can't.

Is it the lack of self-confidence, the lack of knowledge, or perhaps the fear of the consequences? Having the courage to accept the consequences of your actions is what makes the difference between the adult and the child. If you know it's right, and you've examined the circumstances, gauged the reaction and possible consequences, then you have to develop the *courage* to act on principle, and go for it!

- It takes courage to stand up again when you fall.

- It takes courage to adjust when you have failed.

- It takes courage to accept that you were mistaken.

- It takes courage to apologise.

- It takes courage to admit that you were wrong.

- It takes courage to express your feelings and emotions.

- It takes courage to be "in control".

- It takes courage to stick to your principles when you're in the minority.

- It takes courage to speak out against injustice.

- It takes courage to say "no".

- It takes courage to face the future alone.

- It takes courage to "hang in there" when the chips are down.

- It takes courage to take the lead.

- It takes courage to change.

> *"The credit belongs to the man who is actually in the arena,*
> *who strives valiantly; who knows the great enthusiasms, the*
> *great devotions, and spends himself in a worthy cause; who, at*
> *the best, knows the triumph of high achievement; and who, at*
> *the worst, if he fails, at least fails while daring greatly, so that*
> *his place shall never be with those cold and timid souls who*
> *know neither victory nor defeat."*
> — Theodore Roosevelt

It was Calvin Coolidge, the thirtieth president of the United States, 1923–1929, who said the following:

POD

> *"Nothing in the world can take the place of persistence. Talent*
> *will not; nothing is more common than unsuccessful men with*
> *talent. Genius will not; unrewarded genius is almost a proverb.*
> *Education will not; the world is full of educated derelicts.*
> *Persistence, optimism and determination alone are omnipotent.*
> *Press forward . . . is, and ever shall be the cry."*

I call this the POD principle, and it's one that takes great courage to implement. To have the courage of your convictions is to stand on the peak and survey the valley, equipped with the knowledge and understanding of *where* you must go, *why* you must go, and *how* you must go. But that courage only comes through living by these principles, developing firm concepts and convictions, and coming through these five basic plateaus. You develop that courage as you take step after step in faith, climb that mountain, reach that peak, and experience the magnificent overview.

Indeed it does take courage to change. Courage involves minimising and avoiding unnecessary risks. It means being able to address and resolve conflict situations at meetings. This requires an acute awareness of the prevailing perceptions, values, expectations and power. Important parts of successful negotiation are the establishment of trust and communication, and designing options for action. It takes courage to do these things, and that's why good leaders are men and women of great courage.

Some Self-Check Questions

- Have you got the courage of your convictions?
- Do you have the courage to speak out against injustice?
- Are there times in your life when you lack courage?
- How do you propose to develop the quality of courage in your life?
- Do you recognise the need for courage?

ADAPTABILITY

It is by developing our capacity to adapt to the vicissitudes of life that we considerably lessen the amount of stress and pressure, and eventually restore normality to our lives. Our inability to adapt only increases the stress and pressure.

The ability to adapt plays a major role in identifying the mental health of the individual. Our hospitals and asylums are full of people who just cannot cope, who can't adapt. The inability to adapt is very often related to the individual's fear of change. We live in a finite world where time moves on, and the world is in a continuous state of change. This means that from time to time we have to adapt to different situations, conditions, circumstances and environments. Adaptability is being able to work, rest and play in balanced measure.

We are all familiar with the trauma experienced when we move house. The upheaval, the fuss, the panic, the adjustments, etc. The same type of trauma exists when a long-term relationship breaks down; the stress and trauma that parents and children experience when a marriage breaks down, or when a spouse dies. It can be absolutely harrowing. Some people never get over these radical changes to their lives. Others have learned, through experience, that the only way to make progress is to identify the situation, adapt to the new parameters, and then move on and make progress. We must never allow these changes, no matter how traumatic or inconvenient they may be, to hamper or impede our natural progression. If we do allow these problems to impede our progress, then we are allowing that problem to expand and exacerbate, and we are allowing it to continue to influence our lives.

Who's in control here? The stressful situation, or us? How many times have we heard the sad account of people whose lives have been destroyed because of an incident in their childhood? How often we see an individual become a virtual recluse, withdraw from all social contact and eventually cease to work. All because of a broken relationship? This is an insult to our intelligence and to the immense capacity we have as human beings to deal with, and overcome, these various situations. We can allow an incident from our past to affect the present and the future, or we can take control of the situation, be "in control" of our lives, and adapt.

How many times have we seen men and women who were born into socially deprived areas, rise up, educate themselves, achieve great success in their field and make tremendously positive contributions to society? These were people who were acutely aware of their unfortunate circumstances, but who captured a vision of what life could really be like for them, developed sufficient discipline to change their lives, and in the process gained a greater level of commitment, broke out of the unsavoury environment, left the past behind, and achieved success. Unfortunately, we have many situations where class distinction is still a major issue, but most people can grasp the opportunity for education and change by adapting their circumstances.

Our ultimate success in life will be determined largely on how well we can adapt to change in our lives. Remember, Whatever your past has been, your future is always spotless. We are living in a fast-moving and rapidly changing world. There's no time for the luxury of brooding and licking wounds. Face the situation, deal with it as best you can, then adapt to your new situation by making the appropriate adjustments, and then move on — don't get stuck in a rut!

Some Self-Check Questions

- Do you adapt to change easily?

- Are there any situations in your life where you are deliberately avoiding adapting?

- How successful do you adapt to changes in your domestic and business life?

- Do you waste a long time bemoaning your changed circumstances, or do you adjust and adapt?

SPIRITUAL DIMENSION

*In order to accelerate our personal growth and development,
we must tap into our spiritual dimension. With proper
nurturing and stimulation it will become a powerful driving
force for all the other dimensions, and become our greatest
source of strength and direction.*

This is the final of the Four Dimensions and in my view it is the most important dimension in attaining that elusive state of inner peace and harmony. Have you ever noticed how many of the spiritual leaders in various religious denominations take time off to visit holy places, or travel deep into the mountains? Just to be alone, to have peace and quiet, to be able to reflect, meditate, ponder and perhaps pray without the distraction of the hustle and bustle of the world. The great mystics of our time seem to be constantly in a state of meditation and contemplation, seeking the inspiration from the inner self.

But what about the poor individuals who have to rise at the crack of dawn to catch the train, to link with the bus, to be on time for their first meeting at 8.30 a.m.? Then they have to rush through the busy day, and face the return journey by bus and train to get home in the evening. How do they get time to reflect, or go to the mountains, or even get away on a religious retreat for a few days to rejuvenate their spiritual batteries?

In discussing the other three dimensions, I mentioned the need to stimulate, nurture and feed each dimension in order to maintain balance. However, the spiritual dimension very often seems to be the one without any stimulation and it is the one that needs it most. Without the spiritual dimension to drive and inspire, the other dimensions will not function as effectively as they should.

This is the most personal dimension, the one that deals with the deep issues, that delves deep inside to reach the "inner self", the real you! Deep within the spiritual dimension lies the soul of the individual, because it is the aggregate of all the other dimensions. It encompasses the whole being. All other dimensions are merely attributes or appendages to the spiritual dimension.

There will be times in your life when you meet someone who touches you deeply. Not by what they say or do, but by something very deep and unquantifiable or indescribable about their character or presence. You've heard the term "kindred spirits". Have you ever noticed by a person's countenance how their spirit shines through and brightens your day? When you touch base with this part of another human being, you are in touch with their very soul. This is the ideal union in marriage, when two people really become as one, because their spirits touch. There is a misconception that the spiritual dimension pertains directly to organised religion, and sacred ordinances and rituals, but this is *not* the case. That misconception is one of the false assumptions that keeps people from attempting to touch base with their spiritual dimension, because of the fear and mental associations that go with their conceptions of religious experiences. Of course, your religious background will have an impact upon your spiritual dimension. Your spiritual dimension is an autonomous and separate dimension from your religious beliefs, but it is an integral part of your being. However, it is non-sectarian! Not believing in the existence of the spiritual dimension is like refusing to accept the law of gravity. It exists, it is part of you, but you have the free agency to choose whether or not to stimulate it.

I don't believe anyone is born into this world as a bad person, but through conditioning we can become bad people. Within our spiritual dimension lies the conscience, the knowledge of what is good and what is evil. This conscience can either be a lax or an informed conscience, depending upon our level of maturity, awareness and growth. An individual could be physically mature but mentally immature, or emotionally mature and spiritually dormant. These are the imbalances I talked about in earlier chapters.

The reason why people go on retreats and into the mountains is for *spiritual renewal*. This renewal comes about by meditating, contemplating, pondering, sometimes even just absorbing the beauties of nature, and getting in touch with yourself. The myth about going off *in search of yourself* stops right here! The "self" is waiting within you, waiting to be created, waiting to be ignited and to become a burning force that will drive all the other dimensions. If you haven't recognised your spiritual dimension yet, or just haven't bothered to stimulate it, then you have a sleeping giant inside of you just waiting to be woken up and unleashed upon your equally dormant potential!

We can only explain the almost supernatural feats of human endeavour and endurance by the strong spiritual dimension of the individual. What made a frail little nun like Mother Teresa keep going at such a pace, with such dedication, love and care, without any material or political gain? She walked to the beat of a different drum. She listened to the sounds of a gentle spirit and lived her life by a higher law, a divine law. The most noble aspirations of mankind have their origins deep within this spiritual dimension, and in the course of the busy day, you will sometimes hear that "still small voice" telling you that what you're doing is not in keeping with what you know to be right. But do you ignore that voice and put it down to idle thoughts, or do you listen and follow its counsel? If we take the time to listen to ourselves, we may be surprised at what we hear, but we will certainly be uplifted by the experience of just *listening,* even if we don't hear anything.

It was Pierre Teilhard de Chardin who said, "We are spiritual beings, having a physical experience." Doesn't this put it in clear perspective? Unfortunately, judging by our actions, we generally seem to consider the opposite to be true. Our spiritual dimension can be confused with the emotional and mental dimensions, but it is neither of these, it lies at a much deeper level. The mental dimension tells us what we *think,* and the emotional dimension tells us what we *feel,* but the spiritual dimension tells us how we *are,* what we should feel, what we should think and how we should respond. The spiritual dimension tells us what we should do.

Sometimes the forces of habit in all other dimensions of our lives can be subtle constraints that prevent us from really touching base with our spiritual dimension. One of the most effective ways of subordinating all other dimensions, and opening the way to explore the spiritual dimension, is through fasting. When we fast from food and water, the natural necessary ingredients which satisfy our basic primary needs, we can more clearly focus on things of a spiritual nature. However, depriving yourself of food and water for a given length of time, without any spiritual purpose, is merely starvation. Food and water are stimulation for the physical dimension. Love, conversation and social interaction stimulate the social/emotional dimension. Reading, studying and engaging in intellectual dialogue stimulate the mental dimension. But isn't it amazing how the absence of all these stimulants — just silence, no food or water — can be a powerful stimulation for the spiritual dimension. We are eager to feed all other dimensions, but we often forget that without spiritual food/nourishment, our spiritual dimension cannot function effectively. Could you imagine if you deprived the physical dimension of nourishment, how soon it would create an imbalance of crisis proportions?

Whilst writing this book, I spent many long hours walking along a deserted beach, trying to gather my thoughts into proper sequence and order. I go to a place called Curracloe Strand in County Wexford. It holds many fond memories for me of long hot summers spent there in my childhood days. We spent our carefree days during those long summers helping out with farmyard chores, making hay, playing on the sand dunes, swimming in the sea, walking in the forest and riding horses. It was an idyllic location with plenty of farms and fields, nine miles of beautiful golden beach and sand dunes, flanked by a green coniferous forest. Now it serves me as a place where I can go to retreat from the hustle and bustle of the city, the noise, the phones, the faxes, the interruptions. It's a place where I can gather my thoughts, contemplate, meditate and engage in a spiritual renewal.

To help me stay on track throughout the day, I strive to do three things every morning — write, read and run. I like to rise early in the mornings in order to have the peace and quiet to write my daily journal. This is a reflective time when I review my thoughts and actions of the previous day. In the freshness of the early morning, I can easily retrieve the information, formulate it in my mind, which is alert in the early morning, and translate it to writing for my journal. This exercise draws on the mental, emotional and spiritual dimensions. Then I like to spend some time in reading and studying the scriptures, and to take time to ponder their meaning in order to gain greater knowledge and understanding. This exercise clarifies my values in my mind and sets me on a clear path of progress for the day, whilst stimulating the spiritual, emotional and mental dimensions. Finally, I like to go for a 30-minute run to get the old endorphins going. As I run, I think about what I have written and what I have read, so this exercise stimulates the physical dimension *and* the other three. Now I'm ready to face the day with all four dimensions stimulated to some degree and my metabolism is up and running.

Our spiritual dimension is the very essence of our being. It's the part that determines how effectively all the other parts function. Brighten your *spirits*, be in good *spirit*, observe the *spirit* of the law instead of the letter of the law. All of these refer to our spiritual dimension. But the most important thing to understand about it is the fact that it encompasses all of the other dimensions, it is the interlinking adhesive that bonds them all together.

Knowledge at all other levels — academic, practical, experiential — are incomplete until they are fully internalised and understood at the spiritual level. The inherent knowledge of the basic difference between good and evil is spiritual knowledge. When a musician develops his or her talent to the level of artistic genius, their understanding and feel for musical overtones and chord structures is beyond the physical, emotional and mental. It has become part of their soul. It has become spiritual knowledge.

Have you ever been in a situation where you have examined something thoroughly, studied every aspect in detail, tested it on a practical level of complete understanding, and yet you somehow don't feel comfortable with it? Your spiritual dimension is giving you the signal that it's not right. If only we could more readily tap into our spiritual dimension and follow its promptings, the fewer mistakes we would make.

Whatever you have to do in order to find this spiritual dimension is irrelevant. But in order to find that inner peace and harmony, bring balance into your life and actualise your potential, you need to search for that spiritual dimension. When you find it, you will wonder how you ever existed without being fully aware of its existence. It will drive all of the other dimensions, and it will become the burning zeal within you that adds fire to your mission statement, and gives real meaning to your life.

Some Self-Check Questions

- Are you aware of your spiritual dimension?
- Does your spiritual dimension play a major role in your life?
- Have you tapped into your spiritual dimension yet?
- How do you propose to stimulate your spiritual dimension?

CONTRIBUTION

"The powerful play goes on, and you may contribute a verse.
What will your verse be?"
— From *The Dead Poets Society*

There is nothing more frustrating than to sit at a meeting with a group of individuals who say "yes" or "no" to everything, but who never make any positive contribution to the meeting. When Cecil Lewis (a founder member of the BBC) was asked to what he attributed his long life and success, he replied, "Three things: enthusiasm, enthusiasm, enthusiasm."

In relation to the opening quote from *The Dead Poets Society*, how many of us are willing to watch the play without contributing a verse? The play refers to life. Could it be a case of not having time to write a verse, or perhaps not considering our verse to be worthwhile? We need to change from a position where we take from life without giving, to an openness to contributing what we can to make life better for all.

> *"I am of the opinion that my life belongs to the whole*
> *community, and as long as I live, it is my privilege to do for*
> *it whatsoever I can. I want to be thoroughly used up when*
> *I die, for the harder I work, the more I live. I rejoice in life*
> *for its own sake. Life is no brief candle to me. It is sort of*
> *a splendid torch which I have got hold of for a moment,*
> *and I want to make it burn as brightly as possible*
> *before handing it on to future generations."*
> — George Bernard Shaw

Because we are all unique, we each have our own opinions, points of view and perspectives on whatever subject is being discussed. But in the interest of utilising the principle of synergy, it is only by contributing to the conversation, the discussion or the meeting that the whole actually becomes greater than the sum of its individual parts. If we don't contribute, then why are we there in the first place? In most circumstances and situations we will have an opportunity to contribute and the successful outcome depends upon the level of contribution being made. We can choose to be an observer or a participant, and whether to contribute positively or negatively, to increase and enhance, or to diminish the position.

Too many people just sit back and wait for things to happen — and when they don't happen, they complain. There is a very negative element that prevails at times in various industries — "That's not my job, I'm only responsible for the store until five o'clock". These are generally the people who constantly watch the clock. He who watches the clock will always remain one of the hands! To grow and develop in all four dimensions, we must use our powers of communication to make positive contributions to every situation and try to increase and enhance the position. We must become more involved in order to understand, share our knowledge and expertise and be a participant, instead of just an observer.

> *"Ask not what your country can do for you,*
> *but ask what you can do for your country."*
> — President John F. Kennedy

Don't just attend meetings, but *participate* in meetings, reach out, seek solutions, express opinions, give positive feedback and become an asset to your organisation, your relationship, your family. Whether we like it or not, we influence everybody around us just by our presence, just by being there. Why not make that influence an influence for good? Why not make a contribution instead of being an observer? The beauty of communication is that we can use such powers to share our vision, expound our ideas, discuss our problems, and make a contribution to the company, the meeting, the family, the organisation, the world.

Our contribution does not have to be monetary. This is very often a cop-out for people who couldn't be bothered giving of their time, talents or efforts. By contributing, you are voicing your opinion, playing in the game, giving something of yourself to the development of the greater good. Your contribution is the sharing of your knowledge, talents, expertise, skills, understanding, qualities and everything with which you have been endowed in this world. You are unique and individual, with specific attributes which nobody else has, because you have to accomplish your own mission in life with what you have. Nobody else in the world can accomplish the same mission as you, because you are unique. Now consider your contribution. Don't you realise that your individual contribution could be vital?

Some Self-Check Questions

- Do you contribute to conversations, meetings, discussions?

- How do you contribute to your children's development?

- Do you share your talents by contributing your efforts?

- What have been your greatest contributions to your family situation?

- How do you contribute to society?

- How do you contribute to your company?

EXAMPLE

"If you treat an individual as he is, he will remain as he is.
But if you treat him as if he were what he could be,
and ought to be, he will become what he ought to be."
— Goethe

People will rise to the expectations that others have of them, and what greater leadership quality can there be than that of leading by example? It epitomises the very essence of leadership by encouraging, inspiring and demonstrating. The very act of example is in itself an inspiration to those you wish to follow, because they can see that you are prepared to pave the way, to lead by example and to do yourself what you expect them to do.

This brings me back to the point that I made at the beginning in relation to using this book as a manual for a course. It is essential to be living by these principles before you can hope to teach them. Example is not just telling how, it's actually *showing* how, and by its nature it fulfils the third element in the teaching process, which is *involvement*.

The greatest teacher the world has ever known was the Lord Jesus Christ. Besides the use of parables and symbolic figurative speech, He taught most of all by His example. He asked His disciples to follow Him, to do as He did, to become as He was. "Come follow me." What greater instruction can you get from a teacher when you ask how you may make progress and increase in knowledge and understanding?

In order to create disciples who will follow your guidance and teaching, you have to become a leader who will inspire them to follow. Be the leader, take the initiative, express your opinions, show them how, and lead them by example. Your example covers more than just the issues at hand; it relates to your entire lifestyle, your behaviour, your language, your remarks, the way you treat people on every level.

The true character of a man can be measured by how he treats those who can do nothing for him in return.

The very essence of teaching is to demonstrate, and there is a three-part method of imparting knowledge effectively.

Three Keys to Successful Teaching:

- *Show* — what it is.

- *Discuss* — discuss the various aspects of what it is.

- *Apply* — demonstrate its practical application.

In order to encourage involvement and understanding, this entire process can be demonstrated by example. We have to reverse the old narrow-minded cliché, "Don't do as I do, just do as I tell you", and turn it into an adage for the future success of the individual,

"Do as I do!" You wouldn't really expect anyone to do something that you would not be prepared to do yourself . . . would you?

Our example can have more far-reaching effects than we could ever imagine. We don't know how people react or respond to our behaviour unless they manifest it in their behaviour in our presence. Do you ever stop to consider the extent of your influence on other people? We may never know the level of impact our behaviour has on others, but rest assured that the impact is there.

When we enter this life and begin to function properly, we become like drops in a pond. No drop enters a pond silently; it has to create a sound, a ripple on the surface. We cannot avoid breaking the surface and creating ripples. The ripples that we create can spread far beyond our recognised circle of influence. Every drop that enters the pond has an influence on the entire pond because of the ripples it creates. How we influence others will determine how they respond to us. When we influence them for good, we engender a tremendous bond of fellowship. It generates personal power of the highest order, because people will do things for us out of respect. They will recognise our sense of honour, and it will help them to rise sufficiently to respond with honour. What they do for us will not be out of fear or for some sort of reward, it will be for the superior motive of honouring our wishes, with a genuine desire to help and to live up to the expectations we have of them.

Sandra

I can still remember vividly the first time I met Sandra. As a member of the local church choir, I used to meet her regularly when we met to rehearse the hymns for Sunday. She usually arrived by bicycle, and her presence just brightened everybody's spirits. There was nothing false or pretentious about Sandra. She was a normal, extremely pleasant, genuinely helpful and considerate young woman.

The first thing I noticed about her was her smiling countenance. She never seemed to be in bad form, rarely if ever got upset about things, and always seemed to find the common ground in discussions. Most of all, she had the most gentle spirit. She was an extremely independent young woman, but asserted her authority with gentleness. Her compassion was extraordinary, and she was always looking out for the needs of others.

However, Sandra developed a rare type of osteoporosis, and it seemed to increase in severity quite rapidly. Within a few months, she was no longer capable of riding her bicycle without fear of accident. A year later her mobility was severely affected and she found it difficult to walk without the aid of a walking stick. During this time she was attending the best medical specialists and had undergone a number of operations in an effort to halt or cure this debilitating disease. Another year went by, and by now she was unable to walk without the use of a walking frame. She was wasting away before our very eyes, and there seemed to be no way to halt her deterioration. Finally she was confined to a wheelchair, unable to walk anymore, and required constant nursing care.

None of this stopped Sandra from participating in and contributing to events, functions, outings, dances or anything else that she had done as a normal young woman. She even operated her own small business and lived in her own house with a permanent helper. Obviously, she relied heavily upon all of her friends and family for transport to and from her engagements. But she was still an independent woman and she always arranged these things herself by phone. She was actively involved in church activities, and she was a marvellous fundraiser.

Throughout all of this, Sandra was in constant pain, only obtaining relief with the aid of painkillers. But in all the years I had known Sandra, I never once heard her complain about her predicament, and she never once greeted anybody without that radiant and genuine smile. She was always smiling, always contributing, always concerned for the welfare of others, and always willing to accept any assignments to help.

I had the privilege of knowing Sandra for many years, and she discussed her life, her goals, her concerns, and her aspirations with me on a regular basis. She always felt that she could somehow contribute more, and she felt so sorry for being a burden on us. What an incredible example of the most noble of human beings. Her humility, her sense of humour, her compassion, her willingness to contribute and help, her constant smiling face, and her lack of complaining, all made her one of the finest human beings I have ever had the good fortune and privilege of meeting and befriending. We all attended Sandra's funeral about three years ago. There was great sadness at the loss of such a wonderful human being and such a genuine friend. But there was great joy because of the legacy that she left to posterity. Her qualities of patience, endurance, tolerance, humility, honesty, compassion, and understanding, leave us with the fondest of memories. In terms of power, Sandra was one of the most powerful people I have ever known, because she inspired you to rise to her level of integrity, to do whatever she wanted you to do in order to please her, to respect and to honour her. She brightened our lives, and left this world a better place for her having been part of it during her short life. What influence, what contribution, what example. She enriched our lives beyond measure. Long may we all remember her, and strive to live our lives as she did.

"We ourselves feel that what we are doing is just like a drop in the ocean. But if that drop was not in the ocean, I think the ocean would be less because of that missing drop. I do not agree with the big way of doing things. To us, what matters is the individual."
— Mother Teresa

Some Self-Check Questions

- Do you lead by example?

- Are you aware of any areas where you may be showing bad example?

- How do you propose to develop the leadership principle of example?

- Are you aware of how vast your circle of influence can be?

UNDERSTANDING

Confusion is the enemy of action
– understanding precedes action.

Before I finish on the Fourth Plateau of Progress, I would like to clarify the subject of understanding in relation to everything that has been discussed up to this point. By using all four dimensions, we *can* increase our knowledge and our understanding.

FIGURE 19: STIMULATION OF THE FOUR DIMENSIONS

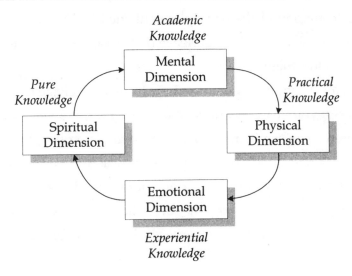

In Figure 19, I have illustrated the circle of interdependent exercises in stimulation that have to take place to gain effective understanding. The knowledge is initially acquired by intellectual stimulation of the mental dimension. The techniques involved in developing that knowledge are implemented by stimulating the physical dimension. The application of that knowledge occurs through the stimulation of the emotional dimension. The final stage is the involvement of the whole self, the stimulation of the spiritual dimension, from whence comes understanding.

The knowledge, techniques and applications of all the principles have already been discussed, but now comes the real testing ground — the involvement, utilising the spiritual dimension. From the very beginning in Plateau One, Awareness, you can see how every principle is interrelated, and as we come closer to the final Plateau of Commitment, they all start falling into place. You cannot possibly gain the full knowledge and understanding of any of these principles unless you become involved in them, test them, use them, and live them. To gain a testimony of swimming, you have to swim. To gain a testimony of saving, you have to save. To gain a testimony of the principles contained in The Five Plateaus of Progress, you have to experience them, use them, try them, test them and live them.

The most common refrain we hear from our teenage children is, "But Dad, you just don't understand." As I spent a year, with my son, presenting seminars on drug abuse to young people, I recognised that one of the biggest problems was the young people's perception of how much we don't understand them and their culture. We can never hope to solve the problem of drug abuse unless we earnestly try to *understand* this youth culture, and this drugs culture. Very often, understanding means just taking a look at the other side of the coin, *listening* to the other's point of view.

So often I hear the cry from some of my work associates, "But my wife doesn't understand me." How could she understand him when he's never at home long enough to have a worthwhile conversation? How could he understand his children's demands when he doesn't take the time to get to know them? To understand something or somebody, we have to get to know the thing or the person as intimately as possible. We must listen to learn, and we must learn to listen.

A change of attitude, approach, behaviour, thinking, perspective, perception, habit, or concept can bring about great understanding. You have the ability to change, you have the knowledge of why you should change, you have the vision of what that change could bring forth in your life. You should now have the understanding of many of the other principles, but ultimately the choice is yours, to *change*, or to *remain the same*. But remember the "status quo" fallacy.

It is not enough that we accept the language and ostensible
paraphernalia of change; we must adopt a change of behaviour
in order to effect the growth and development necessary
to bring us to the next Plateau.

Some Self-Check Questions

- Do you realise the importance of understanding?

- Is your knowledge merely academic, or do you really understand?

- How do you propose to increase your understanding?

Assignments for Plateau Four

1. Indicate the old habits you intend eliminating, and the new habits you hope to cultivate. Incorporate them into your planning, and with a fresh perspective identify how you will be able to bring your plans to fruition without being tempted to revert to your old habits.

2. Using your powers of creativity, identify specific ways in which you can utilise them in a synergistic manner within your family and within your organisation.

3. With heightened awareness of your talents and capabilities, and exercising the principle of understanding, list the ways in which you can increase your contribution to fulfilling your various roles more effectively.

4. Consider how you can be a better example in your behaviour and attitude, and actively try to gauge the extent of your influence on others. Being aware of that influence, take whatever steps are necessary to ensure that in future your influence will be of a positive nature and for the betterment of those being influenced.

5. Take the practical steps of finding and touching base with your spiritual dimension. Institute certain daily procedures in your life that will keep you more in touch with it and take time away from your busy schedule for spiritual renewal.

In order to derive the maximum benefit from this chapter, you should be actively engaged in doing these assignments for a minimum of one week before proceeding to Plateau Five.

5

Plateau Five:
COMMITMENT

"We must rise up from our valley of indecision,
through the plateaus of progress,
and climb the mountain of our commitment."
— Jeffrey R. Holland

No matter how successful you have been on each Plateau up to this point, it will never amount to absolute fulfilment unless there is the *commitment to follow through*. Commitment is that firm resolve to do it, to make it happen, "no matter what!" To reach this level, where you are ready to give such an enormous undertaking, you must have developed the qualities through implementing the principles discussed on the preceding Plateaus. By way of illustration, let me relate this to the physical level. The preceding Plateaus represent the long and gruelling training schedule, but now you're ready to run the marathon! You can run the 5K, or the 10K race without becoming over-involved, but to run the marathon you need *commitment*. It requires the dedication to engage in the routines, the regular training, the building up of stamina, the stimulating of the spiritual and mental dimensions in order to carry yourself "over the wall".

Do you find it difficult to get firm commitments from people? The ability to make and keep commitments manifests great strength of character, authenticity, confidence, integrity, direction, identity, discipline, and many other fine attributes in the individual. A person without commitment is shallow, empty, transparent, like the scarecrow blown to and fro by every wind, with no identity, and no real meaning or purpose to life.

People with commitment are reliable, thorough, finishers, and they work to a higher law that dictates their choice of action, and the responsibility to accept the consequences of those choices. Commitment is like service: the more you give, the greater the reward. I'm not talking in material or monetary terms; I'm talking about the growth and development of the individual, the increase in knowledge and understanding, and the raising of self-esteem.

Commitment establishes your values, sets your priorities, tests every talent and skill that you've got, puts order into your life, and makes everything that you're doing worthwhile!

When you have developed the principle of commitment in your life, you will be able to accomplish anything that you want to accomplish. Your qualities of persistence, optimism, determination, perseverance and endurance will all be greatly enhanced, because you will be constantly expanding your horizons and pushing your boundaries. It is only with commitment that you have the courage to put your thoughts on paper, to give your views in writing, to express your thoughts and feelings in your journal. This all comes with commitment, because it brings with it a higher level of thinking, a higher level of achievement, a greater sense of purpose and progress. Commitment will firmly establish your identity, and help you to become the person you are capable of becoming.

Commitment makes the whole person. True commitment is only obtained by stretching yourself beyond your natural capability, by going the extra mile, by continuing long after subjugating your feelings and emotions and physical exhaustion to the power of your independent will.

One of the most poignant examples of sheer commitment and love that I have ever seen was portrayed vividly in the movie *Lorenzo's Oil*. It documented the amazing true story of Lorenzo Michael Murphy Odone, who had contracted a rare disease called ALD. He went from being a young active boy to a most horrific state of semi-consciousness, lost his sight, control of his limbs, his hearing, and virtually all use of his muscles and senses. However, his parents, Augusto and Michaela Odone, would not accept a death sentence from the medical profession for their son. They dedicated their lives to finding a cure, and spent their entire waking hours caring for their beloved child. Through their tireless efforts, the famous "Myelin Project" came about, they discovered the healing properties of Lorenzo's Oil, and hundreds of other young children will now benefit from their sense of commitment to their child.

Involvement is mandatory if commitment is to be sincere. You cannot have commitment without involvement, but don't mistake involvement alone for commitment. Next time you have bacon and egg for breakfast, remember that the hen was *involved*, but the pig was *committed!*

Some Self-Check Questions

- How strong is your level of commitment?

- In what areas of your life do you feel that you have developed firm commitment?

- When it comes to the crunch, are you aware of the lack of commitment in others?

- How do you propose to develop a higher level of commitment in your own life?

BALANCE

To maintain good health of body, mind and soul, it is important to engage in our pursuit of work, rest and play in balanced measure. When an imbalance occurs in our internal system, the ensuing illness is quickly manifest. But when an imbalance occurs between our physical and mental, or between our emotional and spiritual dimensions, such illness is not so apparent, but it will manifest itself eventually.

The ability to lead a balanced and successful life seems to be the ideal dream of every person striving to achieve financial independence, social acceptance, career position, happy relationships and contentment. I often marvel at the many married, and single, parents who have developed the juggling act between baby-sitters, crèches, school pick-ups, job assignments, meetings, social engagements and family life. It's not an easy task, but balance *can* be achieved and maintained if you observe the principles, and make steady progress through each Plateau.

The famous Professor Suzuki discovered that children's minds are like sponges — but only when the information is supplied in a varied format and with the focus on the objective of the exercise. For example, the objective of learning the violin is to be able to create music, so he endeavours to help the student to create some music almost immediately. If the child was subjected to a Maths teacher for three hours at a stretch, he or she would not absorb the information. Anyone with children can tell you how short the attention span can be! However, if the principle of maths was introduced, discussed and then applied within a 15- or 20-minute session, and then the focus changed to table tennis for 20 minutes, and then to music for 20 minutes, etc., the child will *continue* to absorb and assimilate as fast as the information keeps coming.

Let me take the typical example of the overworked executive who arrives home at 7.00 p.m. from work, flops into a chair, eats a TV dinner and spends the rest of the evening in front of the television. Her reasoning is that she needs the break after such a long hard day at the office. But when she wakes up the next morning, she feels just as tired as she did when she came in from work the previous evening. The reason is an imbalance in the stimulation of the four dimensions. Her mental and emotional dimensions were stimulated during her work hours. But instead of stimulating her physical or spiritual dimensions to correct the balance, she resorts to the passive activity of minimal stimulation by watching television. This is not an activity; it is a passive exercise. If she had gone for a good game of squash or tennis, or perhaps a nice swim, she would have been refreshed by the physical stimulation, and it would have helped to correct the imbalance. If you're involved in a sedentary occupation, it is essential that you make the effort to get regular physical exercise in order to maintain a healthy balance, and to avoid the development of heart disease. This is where commitment comes in. If she had real commitment, she would ensure that her behaviour created the right balance in her lifestyle, regardless of how difficult, inconvenient or uncomfortable that may be.

I cannot emphasise strongly enough the essential need to stimulate every dimension of our lives. Gandhi made reference to the fact that all departments in life are inextricably linked. This is only another endorsement of that concept, because you cannot separate the mental dimension from the physical dimension, or the spiritual from the emotional dimension.

Don't get too frustrated in your efforts to balance your family life with your work life, your time with your behaviour, your leisure time with your family time, etc. Just go back to the principles and the four dimensions. Look at your values, your vision, your roles, your goals and your mission statement. Are they all compatible? If you have followed the instructions in each Plateau, you will be familiar with the art of adjusting in order to accommodate your desires and aspirations. If each dimension is being regularly stimulated, you will automatically achieve balance in your life.

Some Self-Check Questions

- Are you getting sufficient mental, physical, intellectual, emotional, spiritual, social stimulation?

- Are you aware of any imbalances that exist in your present levels of stimulation?

- Do you actually try to ensure that you stimulate each area?

- How do you maintain balance in your life at present? Are you taking regular, daily exercise, reading books, engaging in wholesome relationships and conversations, and taking time for spiritual renewal?

COMMUNICATION

In this rapidly changing world of high technology, advanced communication systems, fibre optics and satellite broadcasts, we must never lose our one most important and valuable life-skill: the basic art of conversation and personal communication.

We are gregarious by nature, but because of our sensitive natures and the negative conditioning that we receive, we can become introvert, inhibited, anti-social, and sometimes it can develop into a chronic condition resulting in becoming a recluse. The following words are taken from an excellent recording in 1988 by Mike and the Mechanics. They highlight the sadness experienced because of the lack of communication.

The Living Years
by Mike Rutherford & B.A. Robertson

(WEA Records)

Every generation blames the one before,
And all of their frustrations
Come beating on your door.
I know that I'm a prisoner
To all my father held so dear.
I know that I'm a hostage
To all his hopes and fears,
I just wish I could have told him,
In the living years.

Say it loud, say it clear,
You can listen as well as you hear.
It's too late when we die,
To admit we don't see eye to eye.

The language of the song speaks volumes on the principles of empathy, understanding, compassion, communication, reaching out, listening, proactivity, reality and being inner directed.

Stephen R. Covey calls communication "the most important skill in life", and I too believe it is the most important skill. No matter how much knowledge we have, we cannot share it unless we can communicate effectively. We cannot develop a lasting and loving relationship unless we communicate. We cannot lead or manage effectively unless we develop our powers of communication. We communicate through writing, reading, speaking, listening and body language. The only real communication is two-way communication, i.e. where one person talks and the other listens, and then they reverse the roles. We can communicate by empathising with people, by seeking to understand their point of view. My wife Marina gave me a beautiful definition of empathy — "your pain in my heart". Doesn't that describe it beautifully?

There is a danger in this world of advanced technology that we could become like robots, and start to communicate through our computers! This world of fibre optics, satellite communications, electronic mail, etc., can become a world of mechanical communication. We need to talk to one another, because that is the basis of all communication, the international language of speech communication! I always have to pull heavily on the reins when I open a subject for forum discussion in a corporate workshop seminar, because the delegates get carried away with talking to one another about the problems that I present for discussion. They are becoming so accustomed to sending memos by electronic mail, consulting their schedules and diaries on the computer screen, that they are starved of "face to face" verbal communication. I hate to hear the expression, "I communicated your information to the manager, and I'm awaiting a response." Why couldn't he just have talked it over with the manager to give him an idea of the concept?

Some time ago I conducted a seminar for a company on the mechanics of corporate re-engineering. The seminar was entitled "Changing Times/New Frontiers". We quickly identified one of the major sources of the problem, which was their inability to adapt to changing markets and territories. But the real source of the problem was their lack of internal communication within the company. The problem was highlighted by an incident involving the transfer of information from one section to another. The information was printed, bound and sent with a covering letter, *by first-class mail*, to the other section. This information was in report form and the section sending the information was urgently awaiting a response from the other section. However, the section sending the information was situated on the second floor of the building, and the section receiving the information was located on the third floor of the *same* building! The invisible barriers that had been created between the sections had become like solid steel walls. How could the principles of co-operation, synergy, interdependency or communication exist in such an environment?

We must use the comparison of the human body with the corporate body, and indeed with the whole of society, if we are to understand that we are not isolated individuals. We are all part of the one family of mankind. I have already made the comparison that all the organs of the body have separate functions, but they cannot function separately. As individuals, we should not try to function independently of the rest of mankind. We each have an important mission to fulfil in this life, and that mission cannot be fulfilled if we live our lives as hermits. If you haven't yet identified your own Personal Mission, then start at Plateau One in each dimension, and slowly it will dawn on you as you make progress along the Five Plateaus.

Sometimes we feel that the only relevant type of communication is verbal or written, and we neglect one of the fundamental methods of communication — physical communication. Did you ever long for a warm hug? My youngest son, Zachary, who is only beginning to put words together, frequently raises his hand to me and says, "Han . . . han . . . han". This is his simple request for me to take him by the hand, to hold his hand. He then takes me for walks around the room or around the garden. A very simple gesture, but it's his way of gaining comfort from the secure knowledge that he is making firm communication with me through holding hands.

Recently I listened to a lovely true story on the radio about the compassion and understanding of a midwife who cared enough to communicate and spend time with a new mother.

The Midwife

"I had been looking forward to having a child ever since we got married. I had enjoyed the nine months of my first pregnancy, and now I was in hospital preparing to deliver my first child who had been part of me for nine months. The nurses were so kind and gentle with me, and my doctor assured me that everything would be just fine. My initial examinations showed that everything was going according to plan, and that within a few hours I should deliver a fine healthy baby.

However, as I lay there in the hospital bed adjacent to the labour ward, I felt something wasn't quite right, and I called for the nurse. The midwife and doctor examined me, and they realised that the baby was becoming a little distressed. After constant monitoring for the next ten minutes they agreed that they would bring me into the labour ward and induce me to deliver the baby.

A sense of urgency and slight panic began to overcome me, but I was encouraged to relax and not to worry. Things got worse in the labour ward, and eventually I delivered the baby by caesarean section. I had been expecting a girl, but I received a boy.

My next port of call was the recovery ward, where I had been told by all of my friends and the nurses that I would feel like a queen with my new baby. The feeling I had was far from that. I felt numbed, torn, bruised, broken and overwhelmed by my sense of worthlessness, now that I had finished my job of carrying this baby. I felt redundant, defunct. Who needs me now? I've fulfilled my function as mother. I have never experienced such a feeling of black depression in my life.

This should have been a great moment of celebration for me and my husband. He arrived with my parents and some other relatives. There were hugs and kisses, congratulations, flowers, cards, great jubilation all around. The new baby had arrived. Eventually my visitors left and I sank back into this black hole of depression, fear, loneliness and blankness. As the midwife was leaving to go on her well earned break, I said to her, "Are you very busy right now and for the next few minutes?"

"Not at all," she replied. "What can I do for you?"

"Could I just hold your hand for a few minutes?" I asked.

That kind midwife sat beside me and held my hand, and we talked about nothing and everything for the next hour. I will never forget her kindness and understanding for my situation. She realised the importance of having somebody's hand to hold. She put her own needs aside and tended to my needs. She gave me the comfort that only a human touch can give, and which was much needed at that time.

Although I had been in a room full of visitors, nobody seemed to understand what I had gone through. Nobody could empathise with me. In the midst of all the celebrations, flowers, happy greetings and congratulations, I felt so alone, so afraid, and so much in need of comfort. This good midwife helped me overcome a major hurdle after experiencing the miracle of life. The trauma was so intense that I couldn't communicate it. All it needed was the human touch, a hand to hold."

There are two beautiful lines in a song recorded by Scottish singer, John Martyn, which highlight this great need for the comfort of physical contact and communication:

> *"May you never lay your head down, without a hand to hold.*
> *May you never make your bed out in the cold."*

Some Self-Check Questions

- Do you communicate effectively with your spouse, your family, your contemporaries?

- Is verbal communication difficult for you?

- Have you developed your powers of communication?

- Do you write to people regularly?

- Do you engage in worthwhile communication and conversation with people on a daily basis?

FEAR

Fear, a most subjective emotion, a state of mind, can create a
major problem to our progress. The fear of confrontation, fear
of failure, fear of consequences — we must not allow these fears
to restrict us from accomplishing our task.

A word about fears, whether real or imaginary, is warranted at this point, because fear is what stops many people from changing, or making a commitment. We talked about mental blocks and false assumptions in an earlier chapter, but the whole sensation of *fear* is a very real cause for concern.

I'm not going to discuss the type of fear that has developed through the experience of traumatic events like child abuse, rape, incest, and all other such abominations that can adversely affect the lives of the victims. These require professional treatment by doctors, psychologists and trained counsellors. And I would not suggest that fear created by such acts are anything less than horrific. The focus of this section is on how we recognise and deal with fear in general.

We must examine the cause of our fear, on what it is based, and whether it is a genuinely founded fear. Has the fear been caused by an experience, or by imagining the reality of the fear? Remember the "Lawnmower Syndrome"? The principle of "self-fulfilling prophecy" in psychology can actually happen. Expect the worst, you get the worst. Expect the best, you get the best.

In order to overcome the fear, it is often a good idea to *imagine* the worst possible scenario relating to the fear, envisage the most dreadful consequences, and then bring yourself through it as calmly as possible. This will only be a mental journey, but it can help to diminish the enormity of the fear, and perhaps reduce it to practical and manageable proportions. By facing the fear and drawing upon the strength of your inner self through your spiritual dimension, you can eventually overcome most fears. Don't allow your fears to have control over you, take charge of your situation, *you are in control*, you decide what actions to take. The fear of failure, fear of the unknown, and sometimes even fear of success, can be a stumbling block. If you want to make real progress, you have to face the fears, overcome them, and go for it! Yes, as Susan Jeffers says, "Feel the fear, and do it anyway." Remember that the opposite of fear is confidence, and we build confidence by achievement, by *doing it*.

Don't confuse this with foolhardiness. When someone asks you to accompany them on a white water rapids trip in a small canoe, don't throw caution to the wind and accept, just because you're afraid to let them see you're scared! It takes training and expertise to navigate those rapids.

As I mentioned in Chapter Two in the Personal Power section, there are people who will create a climate of fear in which you work, making it difficult to speak out and stand up for your constitutional, civil, personal and human rights. These are the evil perpetrators of coercive power. They are bullying, abusive, insecure individuals of whom you must beware. But don't allow them to increase your fear. Recognise them for what they are, expose them, and always remember that bullies are cowards.

I attended a seminar one time where the presenter was showing how to deal effectively with depression:

> *"Just wave your hands in the air, look up to the sky,
> and then say, 'I am depressed'. Difficult, isn't it?"*

I call that the "feel good" psychology approach, but it certainly doesn't address the real issue of depression. For anyone who suffers from depression, it can be the greatest insult to their intelligence. Environmental factors, chemical imbalances, and a multitude of other things can be the cause of depression, and it's not so easy to lift someone out of it. I wish it could be so simple, but unfortunately it's not.

I remember discussing this problem of/fear with a manager during an open forum session on one of my courses. He had a serious problem with a certain administration procedure within the company. However, this particular procedure had originally been implemented by the chief executive of the company. This manager just could not bring himself to raise this issue at his board meetings or at any of the meetings that he had with his chief executive. In the course of the discussion, we narrowed it down to one problem — fear. He was actually afraid to mention it to his chief executive. Every person on the session contributed in trying to solve this manager's problem, and in the final analysis we realised that the worst thing that could possibly happen would be for his chief executive to say no and to dismiss his suggestion.

The very next day, this manager went straight to his chief executive and raised the issue, which had been a major source of annoyance to him for over six months. To his astonishment, the chief executive thanked him for his suggestion and told him he himself had had doubts about its effectiveness for some time, but because nobody had bothered to enlighten him otherwise, he presumed that it was working. He furthermore agreed to dispense with the particular procedure and to investigate the possibility of introducing an alternative procedure that this manager had suggested.

I don't have to tell you how this affected this man's self-confidence. The positive affirmation from his boss, and his own sense of achievement in having the guts to bring it to his attention, left this man walking ten feet tall!

We can very easily allow fear to have an extremely negative affect upon us. We can succumb to fear and allow it to take us over. We can fear the consequences of change, the unknown, failure, and even success!

There was a man on one of my sales teams who was a top producer and excellent on one-to-one communication. However, he had an incredible fear of speaking to a large audience. He was given an assignment to address his contemporaries at an annual sales conference — an audience of about 1,000 delegates! He was petrified. So I gave him some pointers on the construction of his speech, techniques on delivery, and some deep breathing exercises to relax him before his address. Now he should have nothing to worry about. But he still wasn't very confident. However, when I explained to him that he only had to address one individual in the audience, he began to relax a little. All he had to do was focus on the happiest and most responsive face in the audience, and talk directly to him. The rest of the delegates are just listening in! As soon as he took the podium, he found a friendly face in the audience and directed his talk to him. He couldn't get over how relaxed he became, and he couldn't understand why he was afraid in the first place. He subsequently went on to become quite an accomplished public speaker.

Genuine fear of a potentially dangerous or life-threatening situation has to be taken very seriously. But most fears are ill-founded and are generally a result of an overactive imagination. We have to learn how to overcome these fears. This often means taking risks, going into the unknown, taking chances, but ultimately it means taking the lead. It takes great courage to lead where danger lurks, but that's one of the qualities of leadership that we need to cultivate. It's exercising the principle of having the courage to lead on, despite our own fears.

Some Self-Check Questions

- Do you have fears in your life?
- Have you identified the root cause of these fears?
- How do fears affect your life?
- Are you taking any steps to allay your fears?
- Have you overcome any fears in your life?

MOTIVATION

The cultivation of the inner self and the constant striving to align our behaviour with correct principles will help to make us more intrinsically motivated, or self-motivated individuals.

Don't we often wonder about situations that we thought were quite normal, but suddenly something catastrophic happens, somebody does something outrageous, and the question is always asked, "What was the motive? What made them do it?" In every crime/detective drama, the characters are always trying to identify a motive for the killing. I believe that we are inspired from time to time by various stimuli, and this inspiration takes root in our minds and affects how we think. We can be inspired by music, poetry, art, films, conversation, talks, scriptures, etc. But it's only when these inspirations are fully assimilated that they will manifest themselves in action or motion. This is motivation. We are literally moved to do something about it.

The final stage of motivation comes through our physical dimension as we actually go about doing the thing, but its origins are normally within our mental, emotional or spiritual dimensions. Our emotional dimension results in impromptu, reflex, and reactive actions to situations, but to be driven and motivated by something higher than just a feeling, we need to delve deeper into the other two dimensions.

There are two types of motivation: extrinsic and intrinsic. The most powerful and successful type is the intrinsic, because it comes from within, from a deep conviction. The extrinsic motivation is from an external source, e.g. "Sell 50 units this week and you will win a trip to Jamaica!" Therefore, in order to motivate people, we need to come up with all sorts of techniques, compensatory reward systems, bonus structures, etc. We will never know at the beginning of the exercise whether or not we have appealed to their desires. I believe we should endeavour to inspire them, to raise them up to see their capabilities, their potential, and let them motivate themselves with the desire to actualise this potential, and to be driven by their own inner force. When someone is inspired by some person, principle, ideal or cause, it takes root deep within their spiritual dimension, it becomes part of their soul. Just look at the thousands of examples we have throughout history of men and women who were inspired by ideals and by strong leaders, and who subsequently achieved far beyond their naturally abilities. That type of missionary zeal can only be obtained by inspiration. Can you imagine the powerful force we would have within an organisation if the leaders of that organisation inspired their workforces? This becomes intrinsic motivation, and intrinsic motivation is part of Plateau Five, Commitment.

Some Self-Check Questions

- Are you self-motivated?

- Do you inspire your workforce?

- Have you ever been inspired by someone or some ideal?

- What motivates you to accomplish things?

- Do you motivate others?

- Are you intrinsically or extrinsically motivated?

EMOTIONAL MATURITY

All the academic achievements, career success, universal acclaim,
physical prowess and artistic talent are wasted, hollow, empty
victories unless the individual has developed the emotional
fortitude to harness and channel these accomplishments into
worthwhile relationships without developing an inflated ego.

Physical maturity is easily identifiable because we can see the growth and development in the physical features of the body. Mental, emotional or spiritual maturity is a lot more difficult to detect, and in some instances it can be covered with layers of protective shields. There are three stages of development in the mental dimension, three distinct stages of mental attitude:

Child > Adult > Parent

These correspond to the physical growth from child to adult and parent, but at age 50, the mental state of mind could still be at the child stage. This also applies to emotional development, and we should try to reach the level of parent (not necessarily becoming a parent in a physical sense) as quickly as possible. However, this emotional growth, development, and maturation process only happens through social interactive experiences.

The term "emotional cripple" applies to the individual who cannot handle situations, can't get involved in games, sports, or any sort of communication exercises for fear of being emotionally hurt or upset. Can you imagine how restrictive this condition can be to your growth and development? Another example is those individuals in an organisation who have to be continually handled with kid gloves. I'm not talking about staff alone; it could be the general manager who just doesn't like to hear any adverse criticism in feedback. These are major stumbling blocks to the progress of that organisation. How could you expect to encourage and inspire a group of people in an adult way, when some of them are still children at heart? If we continually engage in the practice of "ego massage", how can we expect the recipient of such treatment to grow or develop emotionally? There comes a time for home truths, and it's up to the individual to learn how to accept reality, and then to grow from that experience.

Our emotional behaviour helps us to shape our future, it helps to regulate social interaction, and it prepares us for action. Our physiological, cognitive and emotional developments are all interlinked, but if we allow ourselves to be restricted because of our reluctance to overcome some emotional imbalances, then this can have an extremely adverse effect upon our progress. The Facial Feedback Hypothesis is a perfect example of developing emotional maturity — "Smile, though your heart is breaking". This is putting on a brave front, keeping the best side out, and dealing with the disappointment or upset.

This is not to say that we should constantly *repress* our feelings, but we should be *in control of* our feelings. The spoilt child will throw a tantrum in the supermarket because it can't have sweets. We may very often feel like throwing a tantrum when we have a game of tennis, but our emotional maturity enables us to handle the situation in a dignified manner. Every situation that we experience is an opportunity for our progression or our regression. We can choose to dwell on the negative side of the situation, go into a huff, take out our anger on everyone around us, and throw a tantrum. Or we can act like a mature parent, handle the situation with dignity, and grow stronger from the experience.

Some time ago I conducted a preview seminar for a group of senior managers in a major organisation and, due to a breakdown in *their* computer capacity, the start of the seminar was delayed for over an hour. I explained the situation to the assembled chief executives, managing directors and senior executives, and apologised for the delay, even though it was *their system* that had malfunctioned. The group decided to adjourn to another room for coffee and to await being called for the seminar. However, after 45 minutes, the most senior person in the group came back into the room, muttered something about how ridiculous this delay was, took his coat, and left in a very brusque manner. When I recalled the rest of the group, and started the seminar, the influence of that senior person's behaviour had changed the whole atmosphere of the seminar. He was obviously an emotionally immature individual, accustomed to regular helpings of "ego massage", and prone to that sort of childish behaviour. But his bad example gave some of the other executives a licence to continue in the same vein, and to offer indifferent and destructive criticism towards the seminar.

From the start of the seminar, I noticed that only one or two individuals decided to take any notes, and the amount of participation was negligible. The thing that struck me about the bad manners of the executive who had no patience was how he managed his time. Surely he must have originally allocated that three hours to attending the seminar, so what could have been so important to drag him away? Nothing except his ignorance, bad manners, lack of patience, and the need to display his position of authority by expressing his annoyance at being kept waiting.

I do not subscribe to the school of thought that makes special exception for people who have achieved fame and fortune to behave in an abominable manner in public. We have seen so many examples of this in the various media through the years — famous footballers hitting their wives in public, drunken orgies involving high-ranking politicians, physical, verbal and even sexual abuse carried on by people who hold positions of authority, and generally immoral conduct. There is no justification for this type of behaviour. It is simply childish indulgence, lack of self-control, and the abuse of position. The law is for all of the people, not just certain sections of the population. Everyone is accountable. These public manifestations of the "spoilt child syndrome" are merely examples of emotional immaturity. We really need to see more examples of emotional maturity in public life.

The manner in which the late Gordon Wilson dealt with the tragedies in his life will always stand as a powerful lesson on how a man of integrity can influence other people by example. His qualities of acceptance, forgiveness and dignity under duress were inspirational.

Some Self-Check Questions

- Do you feel that you are in control of your emotions?

- Are you aware of your emotional weaknesses?

- Are you engaged in any exercise to stimulate and strengthen your emotional dimension?

- At what level of emotional maturity do you consider yourself to be?

- Have you experienced this emotional immaturity in the workplace or in your domestic life?

- What are you doing to change it, or how are you dealing with it?

PRESSURE/STRESS

As we respond to various pressures in our lives, they can be a
great source of inspiration and motivation, and can serve to
accelerate achievement. But when pressure turns to stress, it
crosses the line, loses all of its positive values, and becomes a
negative source of enervation and debilitation,
which slows down our ability to achieve.

We live in a world full of pressures and we constantly engage in courses and seminars that investigate methods of alleviating the pressures to make them acceptable. Financial pressures, family pressures, emotional pressures, psychological pressures, work pressures, deadline pressures, target pressures, goal pressures, performance pressures, pressures *ad infinitum*. Some people cannot work under pressure and other people thrive on pressure to keep themselves in peak performance mode. Commitment is a pressure, because it forces us to complete the task, no matter what. This should be a good pressure and in my opinion most pressures can be a source of positive energy, if they are handled correctly. I would never write this book if I didn't work to a schedule, plan, and deadline. Sales figures would never increase if there were no pressures brought to bear on the salespeople to achieve targets.

Part of the emotional dimension is being able to cope with pressure, but it also spills over into the physical and mental dimensions. The pressure from the atmosphere or the environment can have a debilitating affect on some people. SAD — Seasonal Affective Disorder — can force some people to return to bed for the day because they cannot face the rainy and miserable weather outside. However, the systems in place that create deliberate pressure are the ones we have to deal with on a daily basis. Pressure on your performance is created by work assignments, targets, and managing your time effectively. Imagine if these systems were eliminated, and ask yourself if you would perform at the same level.

If pressures become too much to handle, if they become insurmountable, then they become stressors. Danger signals should immediately start flashing, because stress is not good. Stress can have such a debilitating effect on your health and is one of the chief causes of psychosomatic disorders. Don't be confused with the misconception that psychosomatic disorders are not real. They are very real and, unless treated, can become chronic disorders.

Prevention is better than cure. But I'm amazed at the number of "stress management" courses and seminars that are on the market. We're inundated with flyers from "stress management consultants". I would love to see more "stress elimination consultants" on the market.

The opposite to stressors are uplifts, and we should try to deliver as many of these to our friends, family, colleagues and associates each day. It's like the positive and negative situation; the more uplifts a person receives every day, the less drastic will be the effect of the stressors.

Some Self-Check Questions

- Do you experience much pressure in your job?
- How do you respond to pressure?
- Is there domestic pressure in your life?
- Are you aware of any stressors in your life?
- How are you dealing with them?
- What steps have you taken to prevent pressure from turning to stress?

RELATIONSHIPS

By using our time, talents and efforts to build an honest,
wholesome, working relationship, we will be engaged in one
of the most worthwhile, satisfying and rewarding endeavours
of our lives. A solid relationship will bring out the best in
each partner and help them to grow, achieve and realise
dreams together.

We are constantly reading about marriage breakups, extra-marital affairs, alimony payments, divorces, and all manner of reasons why these situations developed in the first place. This Plateau is the ideal one on which to discuss the subject of relationships, because the fundamental requirement for a successful relationship is commitment.

People can enter a marriage with great knowledge of what a *marriage* is supposed to be like, but with very little understanding of what a *relationship* is supposed to be like. From our childhood years, we start developing perceptions on what relationships are like, based upon our experiences and observations of the relationships of which we have firsthand knowledge, e.g. our parents, friends, relations, neighbours. As we develop in each dimension, we gain a greater insight into the differences of individuals, the uniqueness of the human being. If we don't engage in social interaction, we can't expect to have a very broad perspective on personalities or relationships. It's not too difficult to recognise a physical attraction, and an emotional attraction can also be fairly obvious. But the spiritual and mental dimensions are not so easy to recognise when they start coming together.

But I'm not just talking about marriage relationships here, because your relationship with your employer or with your employees is also important. How we communicate with people is a major determining factor of it being a successful or disastrous relationship. In the corporate sector, we have various hierarchical management structures. These have been put in place in order to keep the finger on the pulse of the organisation, and to maintain its efficient and effective management. But is the message and vision of the chief executive communicated right down the line as far as the janitor who cleans the floors? Is everything communicated through the high-tech "system", or posted on the noticeboard (that nobody ever reads anyway), or just mentioned at a monthly correlation meeting?

The term "high trust culture" is very prevalent among the training objectives in most corporations, but that high trust only becomes the culture of the organisation when it exists on a personal basis between the individuals working in the organisation. The chief executive should have more than a cursory communication with his board of directors and senior management teams. The heads of the various departments should communicate on a one-to-one basis with their respective managers, and the managers in turn should develop the habit of having one-to-one interviews with their staff. I'm not suggesting for one moment that the whole day should be taken up with long interviews, but I am suggesting that the most effective means of communicating a message, building the confidence of the individual, developing trust, and creating a more effective framework for individual growth and development is through brief ten-minute interviews or "chats" with your upline and downline. When a member of your staff sees that you think highly enough of them to take just ten minutes away from your busy schedule to enquire after their well being, or to hear their concerns, the message received is loud and clear —

that you care! Adopting the TMI (ten-minute interview) principle can be the start of a whole new dimension in communication, and become the first step on the road to that elusive "high trust culture" — TMI for HTC!

We can become too preoccupied with giving instruction, imparting knowledge, telling people what they should be doing and why they should be doing it. But we can get lost in the process if we don't gauge the response through appropriate feedback.

> *Nobody cares how much you know,*
> *until they know how much you care.*

Is your organisation a caring organisation, and do your colleagues and associates in the workplace know that, besides being their boss, you also care about them?

One of the greatest problems that we face in today's society is the lack of communication between children and parents. Children don't remain the same for any great length of time, and you can derive tremendous joy from just observing the growth and development of the personality and character, especially in the dreaded teenage years! When you buy a nine-year-old child a pair of shoes, they will fit nice and comfortably on their feet, the child will be delighted, and you're contented with the purchase because the child is protected from the cold and the wet. However, within a year the child will require another pair of shoes, and perhaps these will be a different style, and maybe they will need to be stronger because the child has grown. But you know it doesn't end there, because this procedure will continue at least once or twice a year as the child continues to grow. That's just the child's physical dimension being manifested, but the child is also growing and developing mentally, emotionally, socially, psychologically and spiritually. The same care should be taken in caring for the growth in these dimensions. You don't treat a nine-year-old the same way as you would treat a three-year-old, or a fifteen-year-old the same as a nineteen-year-old. In families and in corporations, we have to create a positive framework for growth and development, which means we must provide opportunities that can be grasped and used in this endeavour.

> *Everybody needs to be needed*
> *Everybody wants to be wanted*
> *Everybody loves to be loved.*

A family member needs to be needed, wants to be wanted, loves to be loved, and needs to know that the home is a safe haven from the storms and upsets that can happen in the outside world. Do they know this intuitively, or should you tell them? A member of a working organisation has much the same needs. But unless they develop the feeling that they *belong* in that organisation, that individual will eventually leave that organisation. Which means that somebody somewhere in that organisation has to demonstrate, by the way they treat that individual, that they *do* belong. Look at the number of homeless young people on the streets of the cities of the world. The majority of them left their homes because they did not have that comforting sense of belonging, the feeling of security within the home, the feeling of being wanted, needed, being part of the family and being loved.

Let me finish this section on relationships by reverting to the companion relationship, the marriage relationship. Two people come together in a relationship because at some stage they were struck by cupid's arrow and they fell in love. The union can be emotional, physical, mental or spiritual. But when all four dimensions are involved, the relationship is off to a flying start. We can have different types of personalities, the dominant, the submissive, the aggressive, the passive and the assertive. Often we have to make great efforts to encourage change in certain aspects of our companion's personality and character. But sometimes we have to learn to accept the "otherness" of others. The most important element in a successful relationship is the commitment that the two people have to each other. Not the commitment they have to their parents, their friends, their jobs, their leisure activities, their neighbours or even their children. When two people enter a serious relationship, and have the right level of emotional maturity, the awareness of the reality of their undertaking, the vision of what their relationship can be like, the discipline and self-mastery required for unselfish loving, the willingness to change whatever needs to be changed in order to make that vision come to pass, and the commitment to making it happen, then that relationship will blossom like the rose, and bring forth the greatest joy imaginable.

The road to happiness is so narrow that two cannot walk it
together unless they become as one.

Do you recognise The Five *Essential* Plateaus of Progress in this process? This will always involve change in various dimensions, change of attitudes, behaviours, habits and perspectives, because the new relationship is in itself a new dimension into which the two people are entering.

Letting go of the past can be most difficult for many people and, coupled with external influences, represent the biggest stumbling blocks to a happy, successful relationship. The wife who cannot live without her mother, the husband who cannot live without his friends, the habits of a single life that will not be sacrificed, are all things that can affect a relationship. But we must not allow them to interfere or taint this new relationship! The focus should be on each other and on the relationship; the loyalty is to each other, not to parents or friends. The principle of synergy should develop when two people form a relationship. That relationship becomes greater than the two individuals who form it. Of course, there is a huge element of sacrifice involved, but this is a great learning curve, an enormous step up to another Plateau, a new Plateau, a fresh perspective, a new start, the beginning of an eternal relationship! Don't neglect it; build it, nurture it, feed it, protect it, treasure it and enjoy it. Do you cherish your companion?

Vulnerability is part and parcel of an intimate and honest relationship. Of course you become extremely vulnerable, because all of your strengths and weaknesses are exposed to your partner. But isn't this what love is all about?

Love is not blind, it sees more.
But because it sees more, it is willing to accept less.

It's having the maturity and self-control never to use the other person's weaknesses against them. As part of the relationship, it is each person's duty to try to build those weaknesses into strengths.

Four Keys to Successful Relationships:

1. *Mutual respect* — you listen to the other person's opinions, you respect their beliefs and righteous aspirations. You have respect for their feelings, and you don't try to pressurise them into awkward or embarrassing situations.

2. *Fidelity* — being loyal and faithful to your companion, and to hold all the intimacies of the relationship as sacred and confidential, even the thoughts, feelings and actions within the re-

lationship. This applies to every dimension of the relationship, especially emotional fidelity.

3. *Communication* — overcoming the childish urge to bottle up frustrations and hurts, and reaching out to listen and to share your thoughts and feelings with your companion. Listening is a major part of communication.

4. *Commitment* — your companion is your priority, and everything you do in life is for the building of your relationship together, to become of one heart and of one mind, as you strive to make your dreams and visions a reality.

Mutual respect, fidelity, communication and commitment are the four essential ingredients for a successful relationship, and all of these are embodied in the single principle of love. Don't confuse love with the world of erotica and self-gratification, because they are the opposites of what love is all about. Love is *not* selfish, possessive, negative, coercive, domineering, deceitful or self-indulgent. Love *is* positive, persuasive, selfless, giving, enduring, persevering, caring and sharing.

I often quote John McCarthy, who spent almost five years imprisoned in Beirut, when asked if he had any regrets about his life prior to his incarceration. One of the two regrets he had was this:

> *"I regret that I didn't leave every relationship better for me having been part of it. I refer not only to my relationship with my companion, but all of my relationships with work colleagues, interviewees and everyone with whom I came in contact."*

Some Self-Check Questions

- Do you communicate effectively in all your relationships?

- Are you open to the other person's point of view?

- How do you rate your relationships with your work associates?

- Is your domestic relationship happy?

- Are you faithful, respectful and committed to your relationship?

- What are you doing to make every relationship more worthwhile?

PERSEVERANCE AND ENDURANCE

*The ability to persevere and bring an idea to fruition, whilst
enduring the temporary inconveniences and problems, is what
builds character, strengthens resolve, and makes you a better
person in the process.*

I remember as a child seeing a rather striking slogan on a packet of wallpaper paste, "Well begun is half done". This meant that if the job is started correctly, then the rest of the job will be so much easier. There is a lot of merit in that little slogan, but another slogan that could follow it should be, "Half finished is *not* finished", because there's nothing as infuriating as seeing someone leave a job unfinished. Don't give up until it's over, keep right on to the end of the road, but for goodness sake don't leave the job unfinished. When a job is left unfinished, it means that there has been no commitment, because it's the commitment that keeps the individual persevering to get the job done.

The inspiration, purpose, motivation and will to achieve are all positive driving forces. But the restraining forces can come in the form of fatigue, disillusionment, disappointment, frustration and in fact anything that whispers to us, "Give up, let it go, someone else will finish it, it's not that important anyway, you've done enough, it wasn't your job in the first place, it won't work anyway. . . ." Exercise the POD principle that we mentioned in an earlier chapter. It is only by endurance that we can build character, strengthen resolve, increase ability, and develop the stamina needed to make continual progress.

> *"That which we persist in doing becomes easier for us to do;*
> *not that the nature of the thing has changed,*
> *but that our capacity to do is increased."*
> — Heber J. Grant

No matter how well an athlete is physically trained for an event, it is the mental, emotional and spiritual commitment that carries him or her through to win. The old-fashioned notion that "brute force and ignorance" can accomplish anything is absolute nonsense. In attacking projects and chores that prove to be quite difficult, we must develop a type of "mental override" to rise above the physical and emotional inconvenience and discomfort, to see further than the moment, to reach for the vision, to lift ourselves above the physical plane, and persevere with the commitment that we have built up through the development of the spiritual dimension.

The principles of perseverance and endurance apply to the level of commitment given to seeing something through to the end, or to a successful conclusion. These principles are integral parts of the principle of commitment. Without perseverance and endurance, we would give up at the first obstacle.

Winners never quit. Quitters never win.

Some Self-Check Questions

> * Have you developed the quality of endurance in your life?
>
> * Do you find it difficult to endure difficult situations?
>
> * Have you ever enjoyed the satisfaction of persevering with a project against the odds?
>
> * How do you propose to develop the principles of perseverance and endurance in your life?

INTERDEPENDENCE

From the vantage point of interdependence we must view the world with an abundance mentality, and realise that selfish possessiveness is not conducive to joy, happiness and contentment. It is only when we share our talents, ideas and accomplishments with others that we experience and enjoy the wholesome rewards of the principle of interdependence.

Social interaction at its highest level is manifested in the implementation of interdependence. This also means having the courage to acknowledge personal shortcomings as well as talents and skills, and recognising the significance of pooled resources. It is the ability to share with others, and to partake graciously of the generosity of others, in recognising the value of acting and communicating in the spirit of co-operation and synergy.

It may have been a big step to move from a state of dependence to a state of independence, but this final step on the Plateau of Commitment to the state of interdependence brings you to an en-

tirely new dimension in relation to the development of trust in relationships. The principle of synergy can never really operate effectively in an organisation where the individuals have become so
independent that they feel they are indispensable and without any
obligation to co-operate with any other department or section in
the organisation. This builds little cocoons or mini-empires being
lorded over by intransigent, uncooperative, self-appointed rulers
who are so full of their own importance and prestige that they
eventually become a threat to the very survival of the organisation.
Awareness, vision, discipline, change, synergy, communication,
adaptability, balance, open-mindedness and every other character-
building principle has no possibility of being exercised in such an
unrighteously administered section of an organisation.

In an effort to determine the catalyst that sparks off the principle of interdependence, Lee Stanley, a US ex-marine, took three
hardened criminal youths and three terminally ill youths to an is-
land for a period of time in an exercise aimed at sharing spiritual
dimensions. The three hardened criminals were referred to as the
"throwaway kids", who had absolutely no hope, ambition or vision in life. But the three terminally ill kids, with only a short time
to live, had tremendous hope, ambition and vision. These sick
children had such a zest for life, such positive attitudes, such determination to make every minute count in their last months on
this earth. Lee Stanley was hoping that some of this enthusiasm
would rub off on the criminal youths. It was fascinating to see the
changes that came over some of these guys as the experiment progressed. They began to see more to life than just their own selfish
thoughts. And they began to realise that there were values in life
other than money and material possessions. The value of human
life suddenly became a precious and stark reality, and the concept

of friendship and trust were experiences totally new to these "throwaway kids". But the principle of interdependency became more evident as each day progressed, because these individuals had to work, rest, and play in close proximity every day. They had to cook for themselves, clean for themselves, hunt and fish for themselves, and before long they all recognised the value of sharing, not only in the physical dimension, but emotionally, socially, mentally and spiritually.

Good quality relationships are based upon a foundation of trust; good organisations are based upon a foundation of good relationships within the organisation and the trust can only be developed through exercising the principle of interdependence. Becoming interdependent means breaking out of yet another comfort zone, the comfort zone of independence. When two people get married, they have to leave the comfort zone of independence and become interdependent. It's this inability to break free of this comfort zone that creates the excess baggage in relationships. Is it fear, lack of trust, lack of confidence, selfishness, possessiveness, or the inability to communicate effectively that prevents people from embracing this noble principle of interdependence?

The principle of synergy is encompassed in the principle of interdependence. The human body, where every organ has separate functions, but cannot function separately, is another prime example of interdependence. The four dimensions of the human being, where the spiritual, mental, physical and emotional are all interdependent, is yet another example. Look at the world, communities, countries — we're all interdependent! The understanding and development of the principle of interdependence in our lives will bear abundant fruit.

Some Self-Check Questions

- Is the principle of interdependence evident in your organisation?

- Do you contribute to the spirit of interdependence in your own job and in the home?

- Do you willingly share your talents and information with others?

- How are you striving to develop the principle of interdependence in your life?

CHARACTER

"Strength of character is the ability to carry out a decision,
long after the emotion of making that decision has passed."
— Hyrum Smith

We have discussed many principles in this book. But the manner in which we utilise and practice all of these principles in our lives will determine our character. When we meet people, we almost instantly try to ascertain their personality and character through our own perspicacity. We really want to know what type of person we're dealing with, and whether or not we should develop the relationship. If we observe the habits and behaviour of the individual we should be able to gain some insight into their character, but the language and opinions expressed by the person will further enhance our knowledge of their character. However, it is really only under extreme pressure that the person's true character will be accurately manifested. Moments of crisis can be very revealing.

A person of good strong character is obviously an authentic person, but the character has been developed over the years by thoughts, actions and habits. If they have been engaging in weak and negative thoughts, they will develop weak and negative character. Conversely, if their thoughts have been strong, positive and honest, they will develop strong character.

When we read about the magnificent humanitarian acts of human endeavour that were and are carried out by ordinary men and women during times of war, we realise that these people had absolutely tremendous strength of character. But it was the "automatic conditioned response" that was at work in these instances, and that response was developed through repetitive use of the timeless principles we have been discussing throughout this book. The very idea of demeaning, or dehumanising, another human being is totally at variance with the moral code of one who lives by these principles. It is also impossible for anyone to deprive this calibre of individual of their human dignity, because their character is too strong to allow themselves to sink to such a level of degradation. They live on a higher plane, conform to a better code of practice, and are subject to a higher law. The strength of character comes from the commitment to live by these principles, to constantly strive to actualise potential, to be "in control", to develop self-mastery, and to become "inner directed" and driven by our values, vision and personal mission statements. All of this starts with the simple things we say and do and how we treat other people.

Have you reviewed your Personal Mission Statement draft? In the light of everything you have read in this book, have you updated and modified it to correspond to your vision, values and commitment? Remember that it will become a powerful driving force in your life, if it reflects the true desires of your heart, and if it inspires you to be a better and more productive person. I know that I pondered long and hard about the mission statement for my company, Paragon Communications, and the current mission statement reads as follows:

Paragon Communications Mission Statement

As an organisation involved in the continual learning process, and dedicated to producing effective training programmes, it is our endeavour to become the whetstone on which individuals and organisations may sharpen their awareness and skills, increase their knowledge and understanding of the significance of their contribution to this "global village" through effective and worthwhile communication; to encourage the adoption of a belief system, based upon timeless principles and guiding practices, that encompasses adaptability and shared vision, and the respect for the dignity and worth of the individual; and to live not by the laws of social acceptance, but to be inspired, motivated and driven by a higher law, to function at a higher, more ennobling and empowering level, and thus raise the level of our society to have the courage to break out of comfort zones and advance through the plateaus of progress in the pursuit of excellence.

Don't Drop the Baton

A chain is only as strong as its weakest link. We're all part of this human race, and we should all be travelling in the one direction. Each one's contribution is important, and each one's participation ensures that the race goes on. Imagine that life is like a relay race. The principle of a relay race is that the athletes channel all of their energies into a quick spurt of speed, and then pass the baton on to the next person on the team to continue running the race.

What happens if either runner drops the baton? It could result in that team losing the race. It's essential that they practise the passing of the baton in order to ensure a smooth pass on the day of the race. It's also important to practise running their assigned distance, so that they can concentrate all of their energy and effort into their section of the race.

Now consider your life to be your portion of the race, and the baton contains all the knowledge, understanding, expertise and qualities that you have developed throughout your life. When it comes time for you to run your part of the race, you have one chance to give it all you've got. Every ounce of energy and effort must be forced into that section allocated to you as you participate in this glorious race. And when you have given of your all, then you must pass on everything you know to the next person. You have to share your knowledge and experience.

Don't become a spectator in this magnificent race of a lifetime. Be in the race. Take hold of the baton. Train hard for the race. Become accustomed to passing the baton often and smoothly. Make sure that the baton contains sufficient knowledge for the next person. But carry the baton, participate in the race, give of your best, and don't drop the baton!

The Five Plateaus of Progress constitutes a life-skills programme, but it is of necessity an action programme. The principles of action are to define your role, your resources, and your objectives, and then define the action which is most appropriate.

The principles contained in every chapter of this book should help you in your personal development and growth. The aim of the book is to help you develop great strength of character through the practical application of the principles, and to share with others the things you have learned. Life is not a competition, but a journey on which we have the opportunity to meet with many other travellers. The purpose is not to compete with your fellow human beings, but to be the best person you can possibly be. To do the best job you are capable of doing. To be the best spouse you can possibly be. To be the best manager or employee you can possibly be. To help make your organisation the best organisation possible, through your example and contribution. To be the best possible influence on your family and your associates. To recognise your self-worth, develop your strength of character, and become the person you are capable of becoming.

> *"As daylight can be seen through little holes, so little things*
> *will illustrate a person's character."*
> — Anonymous

Some Self-Check Questions

- Have you drafted a final version of your personal mission statement?

- Do you recognise strengths of character in your friends and associates?

- How has the practical application of principles helped you to develop your own strength of character?

- Are you aware of your strengths and weaknesses?

- How are you developing strength of character?

ASSIGNMENTS FOR PLATEAU FIVE

1. With your knowledge and understanding of the principles and guiding practices covered in this book, write a final draft of your Personal Mission Statement.

2. To encourage and promote the principles of balance, adaptability and communication, outline how you propose to improve all of these areas in your relationships with your upline and downline work associates, and in your domestic life.

3. Identify any areas of stress in your life, the principles and practices you would use to eliminate these stressors, and how you propose to contain the level of pressure as a positive driving force.

4. Take a careful look at your work and domestic relationships, and by changing your behaviour and implementing correct principles, ensure that every relationship will be better for you being part of it.

5. Identify and take the steps in leadership development which are necessary to raise your level of emotional maturity and strengthen your character.

6

Plateaus of Progress

*"We must never cease from exploring, and at the end of all our
exploration is to find that we are in the same place,
but to know it for the first time."*
— T.S. Eliot

The words of T.S. Eliot apply precisely to *The Five Plateaus of
Progress*. If they sound a little bit like the chicken and the egg
situation, you're absolutely right, because it is one eternal round.
As soon as you have gone through the process of practising the
principles by completing the assignments on each Plateau, you
will immediately realise that in various dimensions, there are still
aspects of your life that are still on Plateau One, but you are now
aware of them. The word "aware" reminds me of a member of my
team in an organisation many years ago, who always responded to
any criticism with the statement, "Oh yes, I'm well aware of that",
but unfortunately he never *did* anything about it! As I mentioned
at the beginning of this book, don't allow your reading of this
book to become merely an academic exercise, because that would
defeat the purpose of the book. Now that you know the principles
and their applications, put them into practice.

"He who learns the rules of wisdom without conforming
to them in his life is like the man who laboured
in his fields, but did not sow."
— Saadi

Don't stay on Plateau One, but make the effort to *do something* about the heightened awareness that you have gained, implement the principles, and rise to the next Plateau. The whole concept of "The Five Plateaus of Progress" is based upon continuous progression by first becoming acutely aware of your situation. The awareness is both subjective and objective. You need to be aware of how you think, act and behave towards others, and how they think, act and behave towards you!

I spoke to a young woman one time who came to me with her domestic problem, which involved physical abuse from her husband. She related the story of how her marriage had progressed from its inception and, as I listened to her story, I had to ask her if she had been aware of the abnormal behaviour of her husband towards her. But she was quite unaware of what was happening until the physical violence started, and now she felt that there was no way out. There *was* a way out, and she got out! Her awareness is now at such a level that she will never allow herself to get caught up in any type of abnormal relationship. She has captured a vision of what her life can be like and has developed the discipline in her life to say "no" to the sometimes tempting but unrealistic offers. She has changed her lifestyle and her habits, and she is now committed to building a new career and a new life for herself.

Can you see how the application of "The Five Plateaus of Progress" transformed her life? I'm very concerned about our level of tolerance of unacceptable behaviour. There is a perception in the world that if anything is tolerated for long enough, it will gain public acceptance by society. And when it is accepted for long enough, it can become law. After all, isn't everybody doing it, so what's so wrong with it? Haven't we been doing it for years?

Tolerance > Acceptance > Law

Bad behaviour in companies, families and communities brings the same results. If people are allowed to get away with it, if nobody says stop! then by the principle of passive condoning, you're accepting it. So it must be alright, nobody said anything to me the last time I did it, etc.

"Most people intuitively recognise that if the law endorses everything it tolerates, we will eventually tolerate everything and endorse nothing, except tolerance."
— Bruce C. Hafen

Let's not confuse tolerance with endurance and perseverance. There are many situations in society that have been endorsed by the legal system, simply because it has been tolerated for a lengthy period of time. I have been particularly aware of the growing number of people who are convinced that the legalisation of certain illegal drugs would be a solution to the problem. One of the main reasons given is that "Everybody's doing it!" But does that make it right? There should be no onus on us to endorse everything that we tolerate. To tolerate is one thing, but to endorse is an entirely different matter. That gives credence to the issue, gives it respectability and sends out a signal that it's acceptable.

Concepts are nice to study, investigate and absorb, but they can never be fully understood unless they're tested. The same applies to principles. "The Five Plateaus of Progress" is an *action* programme, a testimony of which will never be gained unless first endured. Don't fall into the trap of applying only some aspects of this programme to isolated incidents in your life, and don't be satisfied with an academic knowledge instead of a thorough understanding. Don't ever think it's too late to change, that things have gone too far, or that your past has been too disastrous. You plan your future, you create your own reality by your *performance*. Don't allow excess baggage to slow you down or hold you back. Every mistake of the past can be turned into a positive learning experience. Live in the present, create your identity, find your inner self, become inner directed, and make things happen. Be able to do it! The things we do, and how we lead our lives in the present, are what create our future. But we must plan our future. The future is going to happen, whether we're ready or not, so let's make it a better future by planning for it.

The concept of "The Five Plateaus of Progress" can be applied equally to the sports, business, domestic and career arenas. I recently had occasion to talk with a prominent athlete about his goals and aspirations. We went through his training schedule, his lifestyle, his competitions, etc., and then applied the concept of "The Five Plateaus of Progress". Plateau One was an eye-opener for him, because he never realised that half of the things that he was doing were contradictory to his aspirations. Plateau Two firmly established exactly where he wanted to be in the next few years, and what he wanted to achieve. Plateau Three put the principle of discipline into his whole life, not just his training schedule, and helped him to realise that there was more than just the physical dimension to be considered. Plateau Four created some major changes in his attitudes, lifestyle and training schedules. Plateau Five gave him a clear perspective of life, and set him on the road to achieve his goals, no matter what.

Your journey of life should continue along many different plateaus, but be careful not to allow yourself to remain too long on any plateau, and always ensure that your progress is forward and upward to the next plateau of progress.

Some Self-Check Questions

* Have you fully grasped the concept of The Five Plateaus of Progress, and how to apply it in your life?

* Have you done all of the assignments at the end of the previous five chapters?

* Do you recognise what Plateau you are on in the various aspects of your life?

* Are you doing anything to progress to higher Plateaus in any areas of your life?

LIFT-OFF

Once the training, nurturing, planning, learning and practising is complete, and you have the technology and the ability, the next step is to put it all to the final test. This means concentrating all your efforts into propelling yourself into the fast lane. This is lift-off time!

Every time I watch a spacecraft being launched, I never cease to wonder at the immense power that it must take to propel that craft at such a speed to break free from the earth's atmosphere. Once the ship gets out of the pull of the earth's gravity, the rest of the journey is relatively easy, because there are no restraining forces trying to pull it back. However, it needs so much power to break the pull of the restraining force of the earth, it just has to smash that restraining force in order to enable the driving force to take its course and bring it to the moon, or wherever its destination may be. I believe more than 80 per cent of its fuel is used in that initial lift-off period, and the remainder of the fuel has to carry it to the moon and back!

Consider the first "Five Plateaus of Progress" as your lift-off stage, and now you continue to make progress from Plateau to Plateau in a never-ending progression. Remember that "success is never final", and the more you know, the more you realise how little you know and how much there is to know. When we come across experts in any field, we invariably find that they have spent many years in strict dedication to their particular profession or area of expertise, very often to the absolute exclusion of everything else. So many of these people are called "oddballs" because of their idiosyncratic behaviour. But it's no wonder they're eccentric. They've neglected their emotional and social growth by having no interpersonal relationships, no communication and no other sources of stimulation except their work.

The hardest part of making progress is taking the first step, and the first steps to real progress are along these first "Five Plateaus of Progress". They set the standards, introduce the procedures, create the framework for continuous growth and development. You can be intellectually stimulated by the concepts and principles discussed in this book, and you may or may not agree with everything that has been said. But unless you become *involved* in testing these concepts you will never really know their true value and you will never reach the level of achievement or enjoy the self-fulfilment experienced by progressing from one Plateau to the next.

JEKYLL AND HYDE EXISTENCE

The man who says and does everything in his life merely to impress or measure up to the opinions of other people will live his life miserably, never able to express his honest opinion, display his real identity, or manifest his true character. To create an image or façade that is as adaptable as the weather is to cultivate a Jekyll and Hyde personality, and an identity crisis of immense proportions.

I believe that many of our most heinous crimes could be prevented if more people were prepared to expose the perpetrators of these atrocities. The old cliché "He's a street angel, but house devil", applies to the cowardly individuals who live what I call the "Jekyll and Hyde" existence. They put on a front for the public eye. Take, for example, the man who batters his wife or abuses his children, and yet his friends and colleagues consider him to be an absolute gentleman, the life and soul of the office party, extremely obliging, and an excellent businessman. This is a fairly extreme scenario, but many of us go through stages of a similar type of existence from time to time by trying to be two different types of people.

Are you really the businessman, or the part-time musician, or the football coach, or the loving and caring husband, or the financially embarrassed golfer, or are you all things to all men? If there is some small amount of insincerity in your behaviour that stops you from being authentic, you must identify what it is and why it is there. The "Jekyll and Hyde" existence will never bring inner peace and harmony. Whatever hidden fears or apprehensions you have about yourself should be faced, identified and eliminated. The process begins back at Plateau One, Awareness.

The Spirit is Willing but the Flesh is Weak

"Watch and pray that ye enter not into temptation:
the spirit indeed is willing, but the flesh is weak."
— Matthew 26:41

How many times have you heard the expression, "But I really want to be slim, I just can't resist food"? The whole area of prioritising, choices, decision-making and breaking out of comfort zones highlights the importance of introducing discipline into your lifestyle. Discipline of thought, mental discipline, emotional discipline, social discipline, behavioural discipline and the introduction of routines to your daily life.

The purely *academic* knowledge of "The Five Plateaus of Progress" will never contribute to your growth and development, and you will sink lower into the abyss of weakened will power. This book will emphasise your plight, but it will also show you the brightness of the light at the end of the tunnel. However, unless you apply the principles, you will remain just an armchair philosopher. Have you ever listened to the pub philosophers in the lounges and bars at the close of the evening's drinking session? They will solve every problem that exists in the world, restructure the government administration, give professional counsel on each other's domestic problems — how to treat "the wife" when you get home. The pub philosopher then leaves the convivial atmosphere of the public house as the most amicable, intelligent, philosophical and socially amiable human being imaginable. However, the cold grey light of dawn casts a rather deflating complexion upon their delusionary self-image when they realise that in the real world you have to walk your talk, and all the talk in the world will not help to get them out of bed, or get rid of that penetrating hangover. The difference between success and failure is simply in doing it! Most of the great success in the world has been achieved by people who have developed the self-discipline of denying themselves the luxury of negative thoughts and procrastination, and who just get on with the job and get it done.

APPRECIATION

". . . that best portion of a good man's life,
His little, nameless, unremembered acts
Of kindness and of love."
— William Wordsworth, "Lines Composed a Few Miles Above Tintern Abbey"

We have discussed many principles and their practices, and in the course of exercising the various principles, you should find yourself developing different qualities. As each quality is developed, new principles start being applied, and the rate of improvement starts to accelerate, each Plateau grows shorter, and instead of just accepting challenges, you start to search for more challenging opportunities for stimulation, growth and development.

However, in relation to the principles of reciprocity, synergy, interdependence and communication, there is one principle that encourages rapid growth, raises self-esteem and opens the doors of communication. This principle is appreciation. Does your spouse or partner know how much you appreciate him or her? Do you appreciate the things other people do for you and do you show your appreciation? Do you appreciate the efforts being made by your boss or by your staff to make your life a little bit more comfortable and self-fulfilling? Do you appreciate the efforts of little children as they try to demonstrate their love and appreciation for you?

I love the television advertisement for a particular breakfast cereal, where the father and mother are in bed and the two little children arrive into the bedroom with a breakfast tray. The toast is obviously burned to a cinder, the tea or coffee is cold, the orange juice looks most unappetising, but the two bowls of cereal are ready for eating. But the parents obviously don't eat cereal in the mornings. However, in order to show that they appreciate the efforts of their children, they start to indulge in their lovely big bowls of cereal, and to their surprise they actually like them! The principle is appreciation and is shown by all four in this little television commercial. The children are showing appreciation for their parents by making the effort to make the breakfast. The parents show their appreciation by eating the breakfast, even though they would probably have preferred a nice cup of hot, strong coffee.

Sometimes we take people for granted, and in our rush to make progress or get things done, we forget to express our appreciation to those around us. A simple "thank you" can suffice for starters, but as you see how that can brighten the lives of the recipients, you will increase your vocabulary to express a more adequate comment of appreciation. In building yourself, you must build others, and not just *use* others or abuse their generosity. If everybody in an organisation decided to approach the day with a firm commitment to make a positive comment of appreciation to everyone with whom they came in contact in that organisation during that day, can you imagine how conducive to high performance and productivity the atmosphere would be in the organisation on that day?

FORGIVENESS

"There is a glorious miracle awaiting every soul who is
prepared to change. Repentance and forgiveness make a
brilliant day of the darkest night. When souls are reborn,
when lives are changed — then comes the great miracle
to beautify, warm and lift."
— Spencer W. Kimball, *The Miracle of Forgiveness*

Whatever happened to the "benefit of the doubt"? Under the topic of perceptions, we discussed how we see things, and also how we have to examine our perceptions from time to time. The person who has a closed mind will always have a narrow perception of events and people, and they become extremely narrow-minded people who are unable to see the other side of the story. Have you ever noticed how pride seems to be one of the greatest causes of long-term family feuds, business break-ups, divorces, court actions, strikes and many other contentious issues? When two individuals have different viewpoints, it's time to search for some common ground, locate a common denominator, and exercise the principle of empathy. However, arguments will occur, harsh words may be spoken, rash action may follow, and before long, legal wrangling exacerbates the situation, adds fuel to the fire, more expense to the pockets, and then we find two individuals who neither speak to one another, or even associate with one another. The spirit of contention builds individual pride, and in the aftermath of the argument, there lies a seething mass of hatred, revenge, hurt and sadness.

The principle of forgiveness can do more than ameliorate the situation; it can actually restore the sense of well-being and lift the dreadful burden of negative thoughts. Spencer W. Kimball, in his beautiful book called *The Miracle of Forgiveness*, explains that the miracle doesn't happen until you actually forgive the other person. There is no greater strength than gentleness, and the principle of forgiveness can build and strengthen the one who forgives, and also the one who is forgiven.

> *"To err is human, to forgive, divine."*

People often think that in order to forgive, they are also being asked to forget, but this is not always the case. There are some incidents and situations in your life that you will never forget, but that should not stop you exercising the principle of forgiveness. Nothing happens until you actually forgive the person in your heart, and then the burden of hate, prejudice, bigotry, resentment or whatever negative influence you had been suffering under is lifted from your shoulders, and you feel free to continue living.

> *"The essence of the miracle of forgiveness is that it brings peace*
> *to the previously anxious, restless, frustrated, perhaps*
> *tormented soul. In a world of turmoil and contention,*
> *this is indeed a priceless gift."*
> — Spencer W. Kimball

I live in a country that has been torn by civil/religious strife for such a long time. I'm talking about the divide between Northern Ireland and the Republic of Ireland. The religious wars have raged in the North for as long as I can remember. The Loyalists and Unionists against the Republicans and Nationalists. And even though there are occasional periods of peace during the ceasefires, the problem has not been solved, and the undercurrent of violence still goes on. Unfortunately, the hearts have not changed. There first has to be a change of heart.

Among all of the great politicians and orators who gave their opinions and offered solutions to the problems in Northern Ireland, none impressed me as much as the late Senator Gordon Wilson, a man who indeed "walked his talk". His daughter was killed in one of the many horrific bomb blasts in Northern Ireland, and instead of expressing his anger or hatred towards the perpetrators of such awful violence, he forgave them. Such an example of pure Christianity I have never seen. By his subsequent work in the Irish Senate, he commanded the greatest respect and admiration as he put forward his opinions on how best we can solve this continuing problem of violence, hatred, bigotry, prejudice and intolerance.

If there is no forgiveness, there is no progress, because we allow the negative feelings of hate or prejudice to hinder our progress. It will stop you from reaching out, from exposing your true feelings, from becoming fully involved, from being able to feel part of anything worthwhile, because you will be harbouring this abundance of negativity within your heart. Before you start trying to improve or progress, you first need to reconcile yourself with those who need your forgiveness, and then you can make real progress. Otherwise you're carrying negative excess baggage.

LOVE

"So whatever interlude of light,
real or pretended love
you see coming through the distance,
be ready and be open.
The cost of one warm moment
is considerable,
but worth the poverty
that always staying private means."
— Rod McKuen

Love is a four-letter word with immense impact. The great message from the Bible is for all mankind to "love one another". It's such a simple word, so easily said, but so quickly misunderstood. It is probably one of the most abused words in the English language. So often we read and hear about free love, love-ins, etc. These are very often misconceptions and misuse of the word love. Love must never be confused or associated with lust, because they are on opposite ends of the scale. Lust is selfish, one-sided, carnal, seeking gratification, indulgence without responsibility. Love, on the other hand, is giving, sacrificing, pleasing others, and comes with responsibility and accountability.

If we base our actions simply on the emotional feeling that thinks it is love, it will be very short-lived. Real love is far deeper than the emotional level. Love is not only a feeling, it is a verb, it is an action word, and it grows through recognition in the other dimensions of our make-up.

The love between mother or father and child is one of the purest forms of love and a great example of how selfless love really can be. The love of a parent for his or her child is not only on the physical level. This kind of love is deeply rooted in their spiritual dimension, firmly fixed in their mental dimension, and vibrantly expressed through their emotional and physical dimensions.

It's the lack of love that creates situations in families, communities, countries, that eventually develop into war. Prejudice, intolerance, intransigence, bigotry, are all examples of the lack of love for your fellow human beings. By trying to see through the various façades that people put up to camouflage their insecurities and weaknesses, we can get to the heart of the person. If we don't learn how to touch hearts in this life, how will we ever learn to teach? The mind will not be taught until the heart has been touched. It's only when our children see that we love them, that they will open their hearts to us. How can you have a "heart-to-heart" talk with one of your children unless you have touched that child's heart through love?

All the injustice, corruption, intolerance and moral degradation in this world would fade into oblivion if generous helpings of love were forthcoming from those involved. The power of love is immeasurable. Love commands the greatest power of all, because you will want to do things for the person you love, and who loves you in return. Love is generous, giving, reciprocal, unselfish, unwavering, caring and deep.

MY SOURCE OF STRENGTH

"If any of you lack wisdom, let him ask of God, that giveth to
all men liberally, and upbraideth not; and it shall be given."
— James 1:5

By way of conclusion, I feel it incumbent upon me to bear my own testimony of the concept of "The Five Plateaus of Progress", and also to endorse the principles by which I think we should live. In the late 1970s I had become quite disillusioned with organised religion. I also developed a very cynical attitude to training courses when I observed the behaviours of some of the individuals who conducted them. I could never equate a man with a large overhanging belly, smelling strongly of cigarettes and using inappropriate language, with the higher principles of salesmanship and personal development. I talked with a client recently who was most irate with an organisation which had conducted a course, for himself and about ten other chief executives, on the principle of time management. Punctuality is obviously an important ingredient of time management, but the course lasted for one week, and for the duration it never once started or finished on time.

I believe we are born into this beautiful world inherently good, and we are endowed with many talents and abilities for our own use and for the use of all mankind. If we cannot be of help to our fellowmen, or if we selfishly try to bury our talents, I believe that we will never reach a state of self-fulfilment, and our joy in life will be diminished considerably. When two people have a great love for one another and have developed the ability to express that love in a powerful and positive manner, the joy experienced is indescribable. It has to be experienced in order to be understood.

During my lifetime, I have had the pleasure and privilege of coming into contact with many wonderful people who live by the principles that I have described in this book. These people have common goals and aspirations, and it has been from their behaviour that I have gained my greatest knowledge and understanding of the humanity of mankind. It is by being engaged in the people-building business that they have had the opportunity to build me, and to encourage me to actualise my own potential. It's so easy to demolish a building, but so difficult to design and build one. The same principle applies to people, because a few words can destroy a person's self-esteem, and then it becomes a major building job to reinstate it.

My guiding force in life has been within my spiritual dimension, but not in a vague notion of some supernatural being "out there" overseeing the universe. I have been astounded at the number of people who write books on self-help, popular psychology and leadership development, but, although they encourage the stimulation of the spiritual dimension, they do not have any clear concept of their own spiritual identity.

The source of all goodness in life, and of everything that I have, know, understand and experience, is my Father in heaven. As a member of the human family of mankind I am one of His spirit children. He is my source of comfort, inspiration, encouragement and protection, and it is in the knowledge of His divine love for me, and my self-worth that I can persevere and endure in faith. He has manifested the greatest love for me by sending His only begotten son, Jesus Christ, to be the Saviour of the world. It is by following the example of Jesus Christ that I know I will some day return to live with Him once more in His celestial home. This mortal existence is but a probationary state, a testing ground in which to use and develop our talents, to rise to the expectations that He has of us, to complete our mission on this earth, and to return home with honour. In relation to teaching by example, and living exemplary lives, I came across a beautiful statement that highlights the importance of following the Saviour's example in trying to share His great message with other human beings.

To live your life in such a way that those who know you,
but don't know Him, will want to know Him,
because they know you.

It is through striving for perfection and following the admonition of the greatest teacher of all time, Jesus Christ, that I met my eternal companion, my wife Marina. Between us, we have six children — hers, mine and ours — and together we endeavour to rear our children to live by these correct principles, to respect one another, and to live by a higher law. However, one day our children will leave home to build their own lives with their respective spouses, and we will be left alone. Whether we are alone or in a crowded auditorium, whether our children are all around us or are living in different countries, is irrelevant. We have a singularity of purpose, the same aspirations and goals, and our focus is upon our relationship. The love is there and it grows stronger each day. But it still takes time, effort, sacrifice and empathy to build and strengthen our relationship. The rewards in this life are so beautiful that they defy description, and the ultimate joy in the eternities is the very purpose of our existence.

There is a beautiful line in a song called "Crazy Dreams" by Paul Brady, which speaks volumes about the powerful effect of love on an individual: "He needs a woman's love to make him stronger." We are gregarious by nature, but nothing can come close to the feeling of being loved by someone whom you love. Speaking from experience, I know that the influence my wife has upon my life is probably the most powerful influence for good in my life. Her love, and the many ways in which she expresses and demonstrates that love, inspires me to be a better person, a better husband, a better father, a better all-round human being. By her example and positive reinforcement, encouragement, support, understanding and patience, she inspires me to rise to the occasion, to stretch myself beyond my natural ability, break out of comfort zones, reach out, expand my horizons and become the person I am capable of becoming. She always stands firm to her own principles, will not be compromised and uses gentleness to achieve results. Richly endowed with an abundance mentality, she shares her time and efforts to make life more enjoyable for her children and her husband, and builds a happy home. She makes the atmosphere conducive to growth and development. With sacrifice, putting others first, their feelings, their wishes and their happiness, she demonstrates the unselfishness of true love. If the best way to love my children is to love their mother, that's easy. No bitching. No back-biting. No malice whatsoever. I believe that she is one of the pure of heart. I strive to be more like her every day.

I have a long way to go on my road to perfection, but as long as I constantly strive to live by these principles, and take the necessary steps to climb to the next Plateau of Progress, I will feel good about myself, and I will increase my capacity to help others. A mistake is never serious unless it's repeated. I make many mistakes in my life, but I constantly exercise the Law of Growth by *adjusting* and trying again.

> *"Only those who do nothing never make mistakes."*
> — Mikhail Gorbachev

I hope that reading this book and applying the principles in your life will help you to become a better, more effective and more content person. And that your influence on others will be of a positive nature.

Details of courses, seminars and workshops presented by Gerry Madigan on "The Five Plateaus of Progress" may be obtained from Oak Tree Press, Merrion Building, Lower Merrion Street, Dublin 2, Ireland.

Bibliography

Anonymous (1971), *Go Ask Alice*, Mandarin.

Chamberlain, Jonathan M. (1984), *Eliminate Your SDBs*, BYU Press.

Covey, Stephen R. (1992), *The Seven Habits of Highly Effective People*, Simon and Schuster.

Cranfield, Jack, Mark Victor Hansen and Kimberley Kirberger (1999), *Chicken Soup for the Soul*, Random House.

Friedman, Brian, James Hatch and David M. Walker (1998), *Delivering on the Promise*, The Free Press.

Handy, Charles (1997), *The Hungry Spirit*, Arrow Books.

Heider, John (1986), *The Tao of Leadership*, Gower.

Jeffers, Susan (1993), *Feel the Fear and Do It Anyway!* Random House.

Kimball, Spencer W. (1969), *The Miracle of Forgiveness*, Bookcraft.

Lee, Blaine (1998), *The Power Principle*, Fireside/Simon and Schuster.

Madigan, Julian (1996), *The Agony of Ecstasy*, Poolbeg Press.

Peck, M. Scott (1997), *The Road Less Travelled*, Simon and Schuster.

Pfeffer, Jeffrey (1999), *The Human Equation*, Harvard Business School Press.

Porter, Michael (1990), *The Competitive Advantage of Nations*, Macmillan.

Senge, Peter (1993), *The Fifth Discipline*, Arrow.

Index